SEAN O'CASEY

Modern Critical Views

These and other titles in preparation

Modern Critical Views

SEAN O'CASEY

Edited and with an introduction by

Harold Bloom
Sterling Professor of the Humanities
Yale University

CHELSEA HOUSE PUBLISHERS ◇ 1987
New York ◇ New Haven ◇ Philadelphia

© 1987 by Chelsea House Publishers,
a division of Chelsea House Educational Communications, Inc.,
  95 Madison Avenue, New York, NY 10016
  345 Whitney Avenue, New Haven, CT 06511
  5014 West Chester Pike, Edgemont, PA 19028

Introduction © 1987 by Harold Bloom

Printed and bound in the United States of America

∞ The paper used in this publication meets the minimum
requirements of the American National Standard for
Permanence of Paper for Printed Library Materials, Z39.48-1984.

Library of Congress Cataloging-in-Publication Data
Sean O'Casey.
    (Modern critical views)
    Bibliography: p.
    Includes index.
    Contents: The endless fantasy of Irish talk / Raymond
Williams — From ritual to romance in Within the gates and
Cock–a–doodle Dandy / Ronald G. Rollins — Master of
knockabout / David Krause — [etc.]
    1. O'Casey, Sean, 1880–1964—Criticism and
interpretation. [1. O'Casey, Sean, 1880–1964—Criticism
and interpretation.   2. English literature—Irish authors
—History and criticism] I. Bloom, Harold. II. Series.
PR6029.C33Z848   1987   822'.912   86–29953
ISBN 0-87754-647-9 (alk. paper)

Contents

Editor's Note

This book gathers together a representative selection of the best criticism that has been devoted to the dramas and other writings of Sean O'Casey. The critical essays are reprinted here in the chronological order of their original publication. I am grateful to Jennifer Wagner for her erudition and judgment in helping me to edit this volume.

My introduction offers readings of *Juno and the Paycock* and *The Plough and the Stars*. The eminent Marxist critic Raymond Williams begins the chronological sequence with an ambivalent overview of the three Dublin plays and *The Silver Tassie*, which he judges as a memorable collision between rhetoric and social reality, one that ensued not in social vision but in the "endless fantasy of Irish talk . . . singing, gesturing, suffering."

Within the Gates and *Cock-a-Doodle Dandy* are studied by Ronald G. Rollins as instances of O'Casey's mythopoeic imagination. David Krause, O'Casey's most comprehensive scholar, contributes an overall reassessment of the dramatist as a master of antic comedy, while Ronald Ayling reads *The Plough and the Stars* as an early instance of Brechtian "alienation." In an examination of how music and dance help shape O'Casey's later plays, Katharine Worth calls for new productions that will help us see these plays as they should be performed.

Bernice Schrank analyzes the limits of language in *The Shadow of a Gunman*, while Robert G. Lowery reopens the vexed question of O'Casey's relation to "socialist realism." David Krause then returns with a consideration of the bewildering fictive volumes that constitute O'Casey's autobiography. *The Silver Tassie*, rejected by Yeats and the Abbey, is eloquently defended by Carol Kleiman, while Heinz Kosok concludes this book with a retrospective account of O'Casey's undoubted masterpiece, *Juno and the Paycock*.

Introduction

I

Sean O'Casey, by circumstances not by birth an authentic working-class writer, was a crucial figure in that Irish Protestant tradition of playwrights who constitute very nearly all of the British drama that matters after Shakespeare: Congreve, Goldsmith, Sheridan, Wilde, Shaw, Synge, Yeats, O'Casey, Beckett. As the secretary of the Irish Citizen Army, the paramilitary wing of Jim Larkin's Irish Transport and General Workers Union, O'Casey helped prepare the way for the Easter Rising of 1916, but fortunately for literature he did not fight in it, because he had quarreled with James Connolly, who had succeeded Larkin as the leader of the Irish Labor movement. Connolly was executed for leading the Rising, together with the poets Pearse and MacDonagh, and the military man MacBride, who had married Yeats's Beatrice, the Nationalist agitator Maud Gonne. O'Casey survived to write one good play, *The Shadow of a Gunman*, and two great plays, *Juno and the Paycock* and *The Plough and the Stars*.

A nationalist riot against *The Plough and the Stars* at the Abbey Theatre in Dublin, on February 11, 1926, led by the formidable Mrs. Sheehy-Skeffington, widow of one of the hero-martyrs of the Easter Rising, helped create a climate of hostility that impelled O'Casey to take up permanent residence in England. This exile proved to be as unfortunate for O'Casey's art as his not joining the Rising was fortunate and became another sad instance of Emerson's iron law of Compensation: "Nothing is got for nothing." The plays that O'Casey wrote in London and Devon were all a waste of his genius; literature remembers him for his three grand Dublin plays, in which the shadow of revolutionary violence falls across the Hogarthian exuberance of the working-class tenements. All three plays were called tragedies by O'Casey, and critics call them tragicomedies, but their genre is pragmatically indescribable. They are, to use Ben Jonson's great phrase, rammed with life;

1

they have Shakespearean verve, though alas nothing like Shakespearean powers of representation or of language.

The Easter Rebellion of 1916 is the context of *The Plough and the Stars*,
while the Anglo-Irish War of 1919–21 between the Nationalists and the
British is the setting of *The Shadow of a Gunman*. *Juno and the Paycock*, O'Casey's
masterwork, takes the very different background of the Irish Civil War of
1922–23. O'Casey, essentially a Communist, believed only in class war and
therefore regarded the Easter Rising, the Anglo-Irish War, and the Irish
Civil War as betrayals of the Dublin working class, or at best irrelevant to
its interests. It is crucial to reading or attending O'Casey's Dublin plays that
we start with the realization of the dramatist's disaffection from all the Irish
patriotic myths and glorifications of national troubles.

Donal Danoren, the poet who is the rueful hero of *The Shadow of a
Gunman*, identifies himself with Shelley, and even more with Shelley's Prometheus, tortured by Jupiter. O'Casey, more truly a Shelleyan than a Marxist, always identified the Irish working class with the figure of Prometheus.
The satiric intensities of the Dublin plays mask, but only barely, O'Casey's
angry love for the Dublin poor. It is the curious triumph of O'Casey that
his two most important plays convert his compassion and identification into
an aesthetic quality. St. John Ervine, writing on *The Plough and the Stars* in
1927, made the best comment I have seen upon this:

> I have more than once described Mr. O'Casey as an Irish Chek-
> hov, and I abide by that description, but I might more aptly
> describe him as a sentimental Hogarth, a Hogarth without any
> savagery in him. Mr. O'Casey, who must have found himself in
> congenial company the other night when he sat by the side of
> Mr. Augustus John, paints his pictures with the same veracity
> that Hogarth painted his, but he has not Hogarth's insane de-
> tachment from his subjects. If anything is manifest in [the plays]
> it is the immense pity and love which Mr. O'Casey feels for the
> people in the tenements. They are offered to us without any
> middle-class palliation or contempt—a fact which no doubt ac-
> counts for the hysterical wrath of the refined ladies who kicked
> up a hullabaloo in the Abbey—and are neither condemned nor
> exalted. There they are, as they are and for what they are, crea-
> tures full of vanity and windy emotions, child-like, superstitious,
> sentimental, kindly, greedy, full of ferocity and fear, capable of
> courage, play-acting, and a sour sort of romance; and with it all,
> pitiable. They have their strutting vanity, and their mouths are

full of wrecked words, lost in Ireland when the Elizabethan tradition foundered in the appalling mess of industrialism in England; but they have, too, a comic dignity and glory which raises them above their sordid circumstances and relates them to the age of romance and the swaggering grace of men who still possess rights in their own minds. That is why these people, as they are offered to us by Mr. O'Casey, steal into our affections, even while we are informing each other that they are hopeless and can never be regenerate.

"A sentimental Hogarth" ought to be an impossibility; I would prefer "a Shelleyan Hogarth," which is even more uncanny. O'Casey's power as a dramatist in his two strong plays is that he does fuse incompatibles, perhaps not Shelley and Hogarth, but certainly a strain of militant idealism and a current of comic realism, so that a noble exuberance, original and heartening, momentarily comes to birth.

II

The Victorian authors who most influenced O'Casey were Ruskin and Dickens. Ruskin, who made so many thinking men and women into socialists, certainly contributed more than Marx or Lenin to O'Casey's Communism. Dickens shares with Shakespeare and the Protestant Bible the role of the crucial influence upon *Juno and the Paycock*, which merits the honor of being called a Dickensian play. "Captain" Jack Boyle has a superficial resemblance to the great Falstaff, but to bring Boyle and Falstaff into juxtaposition is to destroy Boyle, who is no monarch of wit. Poor Boyle needs defense, even against his creator, O'Casey, who somewhat maligned his creature in an afterthought of 1955:

> It is a tragedy of vanity, and of subservience to vanity. There is a touch of Boyle in all of us. We strut along thinking that our shadows shine. There's a touch of Joxer in a lot of us: saying yes where we ought to say no. And I hope there is some Mrs. Boyle in all of us. To be brave even at the eleventh hour.

If Boyle were vanity alone, a peacock strutting before his Juno, then even his flamboyance could not sustain the play. But he is sublimely comic, not mastering reality with wit, as Falstaff can, but ignoring reality as a grand charlatan must. He goes back through Dickens to the Ben Jonson of *The Alchemist*, partly because he is on the border between self-deception and a phantasmagoria that is a kind of near-madness. In an odd sense, the O'Casey of the Dublin plays was an Elizabethan throwback, an impression strengthened by the surviving traces of Elizabethan diction and rhetoric in the extravagant speech of Boyle, Joxer, and others. A lovely sequence in act 1 of *Juno and the Paycock* weaves together the chant of a coal vendor with Boyle's bluster and Joxer's supporting refrain:

> *The voice of a coal-block vendor is heard chanting in the street.*
> VOICE OF COAL VENDOR: Blocks . . . coal-blocks! Blocks . . .
>   coal-blocks!
> JOXER: God be with the young days when you were steppin'
>   the deck of a manly ship, with the win' blowin' a
>   hurricane through the masts, an' the only sound you'd
>   hear was, "Port your helm!" an' the only answer, "Port it
>   is, sir!"
> BOYLE: Them was days, Joxer, them was days. Nothin' was too
>   hot or too heavy for me then. Sailin' from the Gulf o'
>   Mexico to the Antanartic Ocean. I seen things, I seen
>   things, Joxer, that no mortal man should speak about that
>   knows his Catechism. Ofen, an' ofen, when I was fixed to
>   the wheel with a marlin-spike, an' the win's blowin' fierce
>   an' the waves lashin' an' lashin', till you'd think every
>   minute was goin' to be your last, an' it blowed, an'
>   blowed—blew is the right word, Joxer, but blowed is
>   what the sailors use. . . .
> JOXER: Aw, it's a darlin' word, a daarlin' word.
> BOYLE: An', as it blowed an' blowed, I ofen looked up at the
>   sky an' assed meself the question—what is the stars, what
>   is the stars?
> VOICE OF COAL VENDOR: Any blocks, coal-blocks; blocks, coal-
>   blocks!
> JOXER: Ah, that's the question, that's the question—what is the
>   stars?
> BOYLE: An' then, I'd have another look, an' I'd ass meself—
>   what is the moon?
> JOXER: Ah, that's the question—what is the moon, what is the
>   moon?
> *Rapid steps are heard coming towards the door.* Boyle *makes desperate
>   efforts to hide everything;* Joxer *rushes to the window in a
>   frantic effort to get out;* Boyle *begins to innocently lilt "Oh, me*

*darlin' Jennie, I will be thrue to thee," when the door is opened,
and the black face of the* Coal Vendor *appears.*

THE COAL VENDOR: D'yez want any blocks?

BOYLE (*with a roar*): No, we don't want any blocks!

JOXER (*coming back with a sigh of relief*): That's afther puttin' the
heart across me—I could ha' sworn it was Juno. I'd
betther be goin', Captain; you couldn't tell the minute
Juno'd hop in on us.

BOYLE: Let her hop in; we may as well have it out first as at
last. I've made up me mind—I'm not goin' to do only
what she damn well likes.

JOXER: Them sentiments does you credit, Captain; I don't like
to say anything as between man an' wife, but I say as a
butty, as a butty, Captain, that you've stuck it too long,
an' that it's about time you showed a little spunk.

How can a man die betther than facin' fearful odds,
For th' ashes of his fathers an' the temples of his gods?

BOYLE: She has her rights—there's no one denyin' it, but
haven't I me rights too?

JOXER: Of course you have—the sacred rights o' man!

BOYLE: Today, Joxer, there's goin' to be issued a proclamation
be me, establishin' an independent Republic, an' Juno'll
have to take an oath of allegiance.

JOXER: Be firm, be firm, Captain; the first few minutes'll be the
worst: if you gently touch a nettle it'll sting you for your
pains; grasp it like a lad of mettle, an' as soft as silk
remains!

VOICE OF JUNO OUTSIDE: Can't stop, Mrs. Madigan—I haven't a
minute!

JOXER (*flying out of the window*): Holy God, here she is!

BOYLE (*packing the things away with a rush in the press*): I knew
that fella ud stop till she was in on top of us!

Joxer parodies Hotspur on the nettle of danger and the flower of safety,
but the humor here is necessarily more Jonsonian than Shakespearean. The
voice of the coal vendor breaks like reality across the delicious absurdities
of Boyle and Joxer, and there is a fine contrast between the sublimely silly
"what is the moon?" and the sudden apparition of the not very moon-like
coal-black face of the vendor.

The final scene of the play, though still exquisitely comic, has a rancid intensity that is one of O'Casey's salient qualities. We watch Boyle and Joxer stagger in drunk and we are vastly amused, but we do not forget that Boyle's son has been dragged off to be executed by the Nationalists, and that Boyle's pregnant daughter, twice-jilted, has departed with the indomitable Juno, her mother. Boyle has been cast out by Juno, who will never return, but will devote herself to her daughter and grandchild. The last we hear from Juno, just before Boyle and Joxer stagger in, is a fierce prayer directed against the Irish Civil War:

> Sacred Heart o' Jesus, take away our hearts o' stone, and give us hearts o' flesh! Take away this murdherin' hate, an' give us Thine own eternal love!

Against that reverberation, the antics of Boyle and Joxer are partly hollowed out and yet remain a representation that gives us great pleasure:

> *There is a pause; then a sound of shuffling steps on the stairs outside. The door opens and* Boyle *and* Joxer, *both of them very drunk, enter.*
>
> BOYLE: I'm able to go no farther. . . . Two polis, ey . . . what were they doin' here, I wondher? . . . Up to no good, anyhow . . . an' Juno an' that lovely daughter o' mine with them. (*Taking a sixpence from his pocket and looking at it*) Wan single, solitary tanner left out of all I borreyed. . . . (*He lets it fall.*) The last o' the Mohicans. . . . The blinds is down, Joxer, the blinds is down!
>
> JOXER (*walking unsteadily across the room, and anchoring at the bed*): Put all . . . your throubles . . . in your oul' kit-bag . . . an' smile . . . smile . . . smile!
>
> BOYLE: The counthry'll have to steady itself . . . it's goin' . . . to hell . . . Where'r all . . . the chairs . . . gone to . . . steady itself, Joxer . . . Chairs'll . . . have to . . . steady themselves . . . No matther . . . what any one may . . . say . . . Irelan' sober . . . is Irelan' . . . free.
>
> JOXER (*stretching himself on the bed*): Chains . . . an' . . . slaveree . . . that's a darlin' motto . . . a daaarlin' . . . motto!
>
> BOYLE: If th' worst comes . . . to th' worse . . . I can join a . . . flyin' . . . column. . . . I done . . . me bit . . . in Easther Week . . . had no business . . . to . . . be . . . there . . . but Captain Boyle's Captain Boyle!

JOXER: Breathes there a man with soul . . . so . . . de . . . ad
    . . . this . . . me . . . o . . . wn, me nat . . . ive l . . . an'!
BOYLE (*subsiding into a sitting posture on the floor*): Commandant
    Kelly died . . . in them . . . arms . . . Joxer. . . . Tell me
    Volunteer Butties . . . says he . . . that . . . I died for . . .
    Irelan'!
JOXER: D'jever rade Willie . . . Reilly . . . an' his own . . .
    Colleen . . . Bawn? It's a darlin' story, a daarlin' story!
BOYLE: I'm telling you . . . Joxer . . . th' whole worl's . . . in a
    terr . . . ible state o' . . . chassis!

CURTAIN

I cannot imagine a more splendid conclusion to *Juno and the Paycock* than
the double truth: "Irelan' sober . . . is Irelan' . . . free," and "th' whole worl's
. . . in a terr . . . ible state o' . . . chassis!" We remember O'Casey, at his
best, as we remember Dickens (who also revered Ben Jonson). To be the
modern dramatist who returns us to the worlds of *The Alchemist* and of the
Pickwick Papers is no mean distinction. O'Casey became the friend and admirer of Eugene O'Neill, who returned the admiration and sincerely cried
out that he wished he could write like O'Casey. There is a sublime, even a
tragic grandeur in *The Iceman Cometh* and *A Long Day's Journey into Night* that
the exuberant O'Casey lacked to some degree. But one does indeed wish
that O'Neill could have written with the humor and "beautiful, laughing
speech" (Yeats on Blake) of O'Casey. I think sometimes that—despite the
splendor of Synge—the Irish playwright we lack in our time would have
combined O'Neill and O'Casey in a single body, as it were. And in any
case, with the common playgoer and the common reader, I find myself
happily in agreement; *Juno and the Paycock* is one of the permanent dramas
of our time. William Hazlitt, best of drama critics, would have adored it,
for it has what he demanded of art: gusto.

III

Though it lacks the ebullience of *Juno and the Paycock*, *The Plough and
the Stars* is an equally satisfying drama. Yeats, furious and eloquent as he
confronted the rioters at the Abbey, recalled a similar confrontation fifteen
years before when riots broke out against Synge's *Playboy of the Western World:*

You have disgraced yourselves again. Is this to be an ever recurring celebration of the arrival of Irish genius? Synge first and

then O'Casey. The news of the happening of the last few minutes will go from country to country. Dublin has rocked the cradle of genius. From such a scene in this theatre went forth the fame of Synge. Equally the fame of O'Casey is born here tonight. This is his apotheosis.

There is a story that O'Casey left the Abbey at this point in order to get home to look up the word "apotheosis." He had achieved an apotheosis in any case, and hardly because of Mrs. Sheehy-Skeffington and her fellow rioters. *The Plough and the Stars* has no central figures as memorable as Juno, Boyle, and Joxer, yet O'Casey's strength at characterization is powerful, manifested by the colorful subsidiary persons: The Covey, Fluther Good, Mrs. Gogan, the splendid Bessie Burgess, and the anonymous orator, the Figure in the Window, who is clearly Padraic Pearse, poet and revolutionary, the soul of the Easter Rising. Despite these vivid portrayals, I would locate the power of *The Plough and the Stars* elsewhere, in its savage representation of how an historical event like the Easter Rising, later mythologized, actually intersects with individual human lives.

Raymond Williams, the most severe of O'Casey's critics, has emphasized how inadequately *The Plough and the Stars* handles the political and social realities of the Easter Rising. I do not think that any critic can win over O'Casey on that matter, because O'Casey's point, in life and in his drama, is that he had no use for the Rising, which he saw as one more betrayal of the Dublin working class. *The Plough and the Stars* indeed treats the Easter Rebellion as an absurd and inhumane theatrical event, a monument to male vanity and to Padraic Pearse's sadomasochistic frenzy for Irish self-immolation. Hurt as O'Casey was by the Abbey Theatre riot, one feels that it was inevitable, so thoroughly are the martyrs discredited by O'Casey's tragic farce.

O'Casey, modifying the text of actual speeches by Pearse, gives us an orator who cries out that "bloodshed is a cleansing and sanctifying thing," and then delivers this peroration:

> Comrade soldiers of the Irish Volunteers and of the Citizen Army, we rejoice in this terrible war. The old heart of the earth needed to be warmed with the red wine of the battlefields. . . . Such august homage was never offered to God as this: the homage of millions of lives given gladly for love of country. And we must be ready to pour out the same red wine in the same glorious sacrifice, for without shedding of blood there is no redemption!

Too shrewd to ridicule Pearse's rhetoric, O'Casey juxtaposes it with his

vigorous pub scenes, which have a clear relation to the Falstaffian tavern
scenes of the *Henry IV* plays. James Agate, reviewing the play's first London
production in 1926, overstated the relation yet certainly caught O'Casey's
allusive intention:

> Mr. O'Casey has done what Balzac and Dickens did—he has
> created an entirely new gallery of living men and women. . . .
> You may be appalled, but you do not blame; these people are
> alive, and you refrain from judging them. . . . [The play] moves
> to its tragic close through scenes of high humour and rich, racy
> fooling, about which there is something of Elizabethan gusto.
> Young Covey roars his gospel of economic regeneration with the
> emphasis of Pistol; there is a Falstaffian ring about Fluther, mer-
> curial excitability taking the place of the lethargic sweep; old
> Flynn is Shallow all over again; and Rose is pure Doll.

That is to give O'Casey the best of it, rather too generously, but one
cannot begrudge the comparison, since what other modern dramatist except
Brecht could merit it, and Brecht has the vigor without the authentic high
spirits of O'Casey. As in *Juno and the Paycock*, O'Casey has his eye on Falstaff
and his companions, but actually gives us a touch of Ben Jonson's fierce
comedy and humors rather than Shakespeare's. At his best, as in the final
moment of *The Plough and the Stars*, O'Casey offers us an authentic originality.
Poor Bessie Burgess, tough and capable, has been shot dead by British troops,
under the delusion that she was a sniper. Bessie, a Protestant and a supporter
of the British Crown, feebly sings a hymn, and then dies. With marvelous
audacity, O'Casey gives us this as his final vision:

> *She ceases singing, and lies stretched out, still and very rigid. A pause.*
> *Then* Mrs. Gogan *runs hastily in.*
> MRS. GOGAN (*quivering with fright*): Blessed be God, what's afther
> happenin'? (To Nora) What's wrong, child, what's wrong?
> (*She sees* Bessie, *runs to her and bends over the body*) Bessie,
> Bessie! (*She shakes the body*) Mrs. Burgess, Mrs. Burgess!
> (*She feels* Bessie's *forehead*) My God, she's as cold as death.
> They're afther murdherin' th' poor inoffensive woman!
> Sergeant Tinley *and* Corporal Stoddart *enter agitatedly,*
> *their rifles at the ready.*
> SERGEANT TINLEY (*excitedly*): This is the 'ouse. That's the
> window!
> NORA (*pressing back against the wall*): Hide it, hide it; cover it
> up, cover it up!

SERGEANT TINLEY (*going over to the body*): 'Ere, what's this? Who's this? (*Looking at* Bessie) Oh Gawd, we've plugged one of the women of the 'ouse.

CORPORAL STODDART: Whoy the 'ell did she gow to the window? Is she dead?

SERGEANT TINLEY: Oh, dead as bedamned. Well, we couldn't afford to toike any chawnces.

NORA (*screaming*): Hide it, hide it; don't let me see it! Take me away, take me away, Mrs. Gogan!

Mrs. Gogan *runs into room, Left, and runs out again with a sheet which she spreads over the body of Bessie.*

MRS. GOGAN (*as she spreads the sheet*): Oh, God help her, th' poor woman, she's stiffenin' out as hard as she can! Her face has written on it th' shock o' sudden agony, an' her hands is whitenin' into th' smooth shininess of wax.

NORA (*whimperingly*): Take me away, take me away; don't leave me here to be lookin' an' lookin' at it!

MRS. GOGAN (*going over to* Nora *and putting her arm around her*): Come on with me, dear, an' you can doss in poor Mollser's bed, till we gather some neighbours to come an' give th' last friendly touches to Bessie in th' lonely layin' of her out. [Mrs. Gogan *and* Nora *go slowly out.*]

CORPORAL STODDART (*who has been looking around, to* Sergeant Tinley): Tea here, Sergeant. Wot abaht a cup of scald?

SERGEANT TINLEY: Pour it aht, Stoddart, pour it aht. I could scoff hanything just now.

Corporal Stoddart *pours out two cups of tea, and the two soldiers begin to drink. In the distance is heard a bitter burst of rifle and machine-gun fire, interpersed with the boom, boom of artillery. The glare in the sky seen through the window flares into a fuller and a deeper red.*

SERGEANT TINLEY: There gows the general attack on the Powst Office.

VOICES IN A DISTANT STREET: Ambu . . . lance, Ambu . . . lance! Red Cro . . . ss, Red Cro . . . ss!

The voices of soldiers at a barricade outside the house are heard singing:

They were summoned from the 'illside,
They were called in from the glen,
And the country found 'em ready

At the stirring call for men.
Let not tears add to their 'ardship,
As the soldiers pass along,
And although our 'eart is breaking,
Make it sing this cheery song.

SERGEANT TINLEY *and* CORPORAL STODDART (*joining in the chorus, as they sip the tea*):

Keep the 'owme fires burning,
While your 'earts are yearning;
Though your lads are far away
They dream of 'owme;
There's a silver loining
Through the dark cloud shoining,
Turn the dark cloud inside out,
Till the boys come 'owme!

We receive the shock and mourning of the women, and then we close on the Tommies singing as they drink their tea, with Bessie shrouded under the sheet nearby and the window illuminated by the red glare of a burning Dublin as the British machine guns and artillery open up on Pearse, Connolly, and their diehards barricaded in the General Post Office. O'Casey has no politics in his ultimate vision, and no feeling against the Tommies. Pearse has made the tenements of Dublin into a bonfire, and O'Casey is not exactly grateful to the murderous idealist, but we have to infer that reaction throughout the play. Raymond Williams must have understood, implicitly, that O'Casey, who died a good Communist and perpetual admirer of Stalin, nevertheless was, like G. B. Shaw, a Ruskinian rather than a Marxist. The final burden of *The Plough and the Stars* is that the proper answer to the blood-intoxicated Pearse is Ruskin's great apothegm from *Unto This Last:* "The only wealth is life." Fluther and his companions are O'Casey's sense of Irish life: drunken, ranting, vain, but vital, vital to the end.

RAYMOND WILLIAMS

The Endless Fantasy of Irish Talk

Irish history had broken into revolution, a war of liberation and civil war by the time O'Casey began to write for the Abbey Theatre. His first acted play, *The Shadow of a Gunman* (1923) is at once a response to this experience of violence and, in its way, a bitter postscript to Synge's *Playboy of the Western World*. It is set in the crowded overflowing life of a Dublin tenement house which is O'Casey's major early setting. The Irish drama, in this sense, has come to town. The turbulent history through which Ireland had been living breaks into these tenements. As a direct action it is on the streets, and the people crowded in the houses react to it, in essential ways, as if it were an action beyond and outside them. This viewpoint determines most of O'Casey's early drama.

The Shadow of a Gunman is in this sense exact. It is the shadow that falls across a quite other life, but also it is the *Playboy*'s action of a false hero: the frightened sentimental poet Davoren who is built up, by gossip and surmise, into a gunman's reputation:

And what danger can there be in being the shadow of a gunman?

It is the contrast between the bitter action of the history and a feckless, deceiving and self-deceiving talk that O'Casey uses as his dramatic point. Men are killed elsewhere, but within the tenement:

No wonder this unfortunate country is as it is, for you can't depend upon the word of a single individual in it.

From *Drama from Ibsen to Brecht*. © 1952, 1968 by Raymond Williams. Oxford University Press, 1968.

The only victim within the play is the girl Minnie:

> DAVOREN: . . . I'm sure she is a good girl, and I believe she is a
>   brave girl.
> SEUMAS: A Helen of Troy come to live in a tenement! You
>   think a lot about her simply because she thinks a lot about
>   you, an' she thinks a lot about you because she looks upon
>   you as a hero—a kind o' Paris . . . she'd give the worl'
>   and all to be gaddin' about with a gunman.

It is Minnie who is killed, after a raid on the house: found hiding arms
because she believes in Davoren. The bitterness is carried right through, in
that Davoren, after her death, can react only in the stereotyped "poetry"
which has been his pretence and his reality:

> Ah me, alas! Pain, pain, pain ever, for ever!

With real killing in the streets, the poverty and the pretence cross to make
new inadvertent victims.

This kind of irony, in O'Casey, is very difficult to follow through. The
central language of *Shadow of a Gunman* is bare and taut; it is there, in reality,
in the crowded life, as a tension with the endless romanticizing, boasting,
sentimentality; or, again characteristically, with the simple misuse of language by the uneducated, which O'Casey always emphasizes, as here in
Gallogher's letter:

> ventures to say that he thinks he has made out a Primmy Fashy
> case.

It is done from the inside, this tenement life, but with an eye on the audience,
on external and "educated" reactions. O'Casey moves from this kind of
caricature to a simpler excited naturalism—the endless overflowing talk:

> They didn't leave a thing in the kitchen that they didn't flitter
> about the floor.

It is a dramatist speaking at once from inside and outside this rush of life;
in *The Shadow of a Gunman* with genuine uncertainty, and using the tension
of the farcical and the terrible.

Juno and the Paycock, which followed in 1924, is in the same structure
of feeling. The life is seen as farce, with death cutting across it. This can
be rationalized, as in O'Casey's late description of *Shadow of a Gunman* as
expressing "the bewilderment and horror at one section of the community
trying to murder and kill the other." But this is never, really, what the plays
show. What is there is a feckless rush, endlessly evading and posturing, while

through it one or two figures—mainly women—take the eventual burden of reality. In *Juno and the Paycock* the dominant action is the talk of Boyle and Joxer: idle talk, with a continual play at importance: the false colours of poverty, which has gone beyond being faced and which is now the endless, stumbling engaging, spin of fantasy. The formal plot is rooted in this, as it might have been in Synge: the false expectation of a legacy, which will alter this world. But what comes, in the real action, is the killing from outside: first Tancred, the Republican fighter, and then Johnny, the son of the house, who betrayed him. The bereaved mothers in each case, and in the same words, call:

> Take away our hearts o' stone, an' give us hearts o' flesh! Take
> away this murdherin' hate, an' give us Thine own eternal love!

It is a deep, convincing, unconnected cry. It is what the mothers feel, in the terrible disturbance of the fighting. But what the play shows is not the "hearts of stone"; it is, counterpointing and overriding these moments of intense suffering, the endless, bibulous, blathering talk.

This is, of course, an authentic structure, but it is not that which is usually presented. It is always difficult to speak from outside so intense and self-conscious a culture, but in the end we are bound to notice, as a continuing and determining fact, how little respect, except in the grand gestures, the Irish drama had for the Irish people. It was different when the people were remote and traditional, as in *Riders to the Sea*. But already what comes through the surface warmth of *Playboy of the Western World* is a deeply resigned contempt—a contempt which then allows amusement—for these deprived, fantasy-ridden talkers. Synge got near this real theme, and O'Casey is continuously dramatically aware of it. But it is a very difficult emotion to control: an uneasy separation and exile, from within the heart of the talk. And because this is so, this people's dramatist writing for what was said to be a people's theatre at the crisis of this people's history is in a deep sense mocking it at the very moment when it moves him. The feelings of the fighters, in that real history, are not dramatically engaged at all; all we see and hear is the flag, the gesture, the rhetoric. The need and the oppression are silent, or at best oblique in some consequent action. What is active and vociferous is a confusion: the victims trapped in their tenements and abusing or flattering each other. What can be said by the mother, authentically, is

> Take away this murdhering hate

—a reaction to the fact of a dead son, in whatever cause. But what is primarily and finally said is Boyle's

The whole worl's in a terrible state of chassis

—the authentic confusion translated into a refrain and a verbal error; the error and inadequacy of this people. It is strange, powerful, cross-grained: a tension worked out, in full view, in this unusual kind of play: the facts of farce and the facts of killing.

II

The crisis of O'Casey's drama is the working-out of this complicated emotion. What is at issue, always, is the relation between the language of men in intense experience and the inflated, engaging language of men avoiding experience. It is a very deep disturbance, which I suppose comes out of that confused history. But what seems to me to happen, as O'Casey goes on, is the hardening of a mannerism which overrides this crucial and difficult distinction. *Juno and the Paycock* is powerful and unforgettable because the distinction is dramatized, in the loose but authentic form which alone, within naturalism, could express it. *The Plough and the Stars* (1926) has resemblances to this, and in fact moves nearer the action that would finally have to be faced if this endless paradox—the reality of suffering and the pathetic winking confusion—was to be directly explored. But there is a change in the language, a development from the earlier plays but now exceptionally self-conscious, as if always with an eye on the audience:

> It would take something more than a thing like you to flutther a feather o' Fluther.
> Is a man fermentin' with fear to stick th' showin' off to him of a thing that looks like a shinin' shroud?

Phrases like this have been repeatedly quoted as an "Elizabethan" richness; but they are, in their origin and development, and where successful in their direct dramatic use, the consistent evidence of poverty: of a starved, showing-off imagination. I remember reacting very bitterly against them, and against the repeated tricks of colour—the naming of colours—which O'Casey carried to the point of parody. But the real point is more complex. Through all the early plays, it is the fact of evasion, and the verbal inflation that covers it, that O'Casey at once creates and criticizes: Boyle and Joxer, or again Fluther, are in the same movement engaging and despicable; talking to hold the attention from the fact that they have nothing to say. Yet then the manner spills over, into a different dramatic speech. It flares, successfully, into the shouted abuse of the overcrowded people, as here in *The Plough and the Stars:*

BESSIE: Bessie Burgess doesn't put up to know much, never
  havin' a swaggerin' mind, thanks be to God, but goin' on
  packin' up knowledge accordin' to her conscience: precept
  upon precept, line upon line; here a little, an' there a
  little. But thanks be to Christ, she knows when she was
  got, where she was got, an' how she was got; while there's
  some she knows, decoratin' their finger with a well-
  polished wedding-ring, would be hard put to it if they
  were assed to show their weddin' lines!
MRS. GOGAN: Y' oul' rip of a blasted liar.

This almost formal rhetoric, in the daily quarrels, connects with the more
difficult use: the almost habitual showing-off. But it is critically different
from what looks like the same manner applied to intense feeling, as in Nora
in *The Plough and the Stars*:

> While your little red-lipp'd Nora can go on sittin' here, makin' a
> companion of th' loneliness of th' night. . . .

> It's hard to force away th' tears of happiness at th' end of an awful
> agony.

The paradoxical force of the language, endlessly presenting and self-conscious, at once to others and to the audience, drives through the play, but
not as richness: as the sound, really, of a long confusion and disintegration.
A characteristic and significant action is repeated: while the men are dying,
in the Easter Rising, the people of the tenements are looting, and lying about
themselves. It is an unbearable contrast, and it is the main emotion O'Casey
had to show: of nerves ragged by talking which cannot connect with the
direct and terrible action. The use of random colour, of flags, of slogans, of
rhetoric and comic inflation, of the sentimental song, of reminiscences of
theatre (as in Nora repeating the mad Ophelia) is a rush of disintegration,
of catching at temporary effects, which is quite unique: in a way, already,
the separated consciousness, writing from within a life it cannot accept in
its real terms yet finds endlessly engaging and preoccupying: the structure
of feeling of the self-exile, still within a collective action, which can be neither
avoided nor taken wholly seriously; neither indifferent nor direct.

III

Those three Abbey plays—*Shadow of a Gunman*, *Juno and the Paycock*,
The Plough and the Stars—are a substantial but increasingly precarious achieve-

ment. The emotion is so difficult, so deeply paradoxical, that no simple development was possible. As it happened, O'Casey went away: all his remaining plays were written in exile, and there was a turning-point in his life when the Abbey Theatre, stupidly and unjustly, rejected *The Silver Tassie*. We have already seen the paradox, when the connection with Irish life and theatre was direct. That essential tension might have worked out differently, in a continuing contact. As it was, O'Casey went on elaborating his unusual forms: in a way released, in a way deprived.

The Silver Tassie (1928) is a serious experiment in a new form: an extension of naturalism to what is presented as an expressionist crisis. The first and last acts are again the crowded, overflowing talk of the Abbey plays; excited and colourful in its superficial actions—the winning of the cup, the victory dance, the songs—but with a cold using of people, a persistent indifference to each other, that repeats, more bitterly, the paradoxical emotions of the earlier plays. The more the cry of colour and of triumph goes up, the more deprived and shut-off are the honest people. To praise the colour and excitement in abstraction is then not only critically foolish; it insults this genuine and persistent sense of loss and poverty. But the difficulty is inherent: O'Casey shows an emptiness, a terrible passivity,through the continual jerking of what presents itself as excitement. It is as if, as often in the earlier plays, he is at times himself carried away by the surface vitality; though what he always comes back to, when he shows the people, is an empty incapacity, an indifference and a cruelty.

The two middle acts of *The Silver Tassie* are a newly direct presentation—in their form critically conscious—of the determining suffering. It is the repetition, in bitter parody, of the recourse to song: the exposed soldiers finding a desperate voice, and beside them the alienated, clipped orders—the false clarity of the war. The second act is still one of the most remarkable written in English in this century, but it has the same uncertainty, the root uncertainty, of the earlier work. The critical showing, of what the war does to these men, is brilliantly achieved:

> Stumbling, swiftly cursing, plodding,
> Lumbering, loitering, stumbling, grousing,
> Through mud and rain and filth and danger
> Flesh and blood seek slow the front line.

But they are not only exposed victims. Their final chant is to the glory of the gun: they compound their suffering. And they cannot break through, at the crisis of exposure, to reason:

But wy'r we 'ere, wy'r we 'ere,—that's wot I wants to know.
Why 's 'e 'ere, why's 'e 'ere—that's wot 'e wants to know.
We're here because we're here, because we're here, because
    we're here.

It is the persistent feeling: the exposed and deprived who cannot understand what is happening to them; who can talk, within limits, in their own idiom, but then fall for an alien rhetoric. It is a very deep kind of despair, and when the soldiers have become numbers, in the casualty ward, what we see again, in the reactions of others, is an indifference and cruelty. O'Casey had here his hero: the footballer who is paralysed by a wound, who watches his girl despise him and go dancing with his friend. It is the image he always returns to: of a trapped consciousness, suffering the noisy vitality of what is supposed to be a liberation. The songs point the feeling, but also, in a sense, compound it:

Let him come, let him sigh, let him go,
For he is a life on the ebb,
We a full life on the flow.

It is that ebb, that long ebb, that O'Casey writes, but through that what sounds, in inattention, like life on the flow.

IV

The Silver Tassie is memorable and important. The uncertainty and the paradox find their way into parts of the form, but the general power is still there. In this later work, O'Casey experimented continually, out of touch with the theatre. What got him another kind of reputation was a play like *The Star Turns Red* (1940): a formally rhetorical Communism, which overlies the difficult and incompatible social experience, the shouting frustration and loss. He dramatizes a class of attitudes, with the flags and slogans now offered in their own right. Only a careless external glance would accept them. *Red Roses for Me* (1943) is a replay of the Abbey work, with the mannerism of colour—the external colour of names and sashes—intense. But the most interesting later work is where the interest always was: in the true nature of that endless fantasy of Irish talk. There is an unusually straight dramatization of the theme—the frustration of ordinary life under the sparks of a now organized showing-off—in the post-liberation Ireland of *The Bishop's Bonfire* (1955), a directly successful play. There is also the experiment—away on his own—with an area between pantomime and folk-play, as in *Cock-a-Doodle Dandy* (1949). It is a different Irish experience that he now has in view: he has identified the enemies of the people as the Church and business and order; what crows against this is the life and play—the liberation through fancy—which he had seen, in his earlier work, shot through by the killing— at once irrepressible and their own worst enemies. It was easier, perhaps, when he could identify a cause; but it was a distance—a felt dramatic distance—from that original confusion and intensity. It is to the Abbey plays that we still go back, but watchfully, moved and involved and yet without sentiment: seeing what happened, what so strangely happened, as the rhetoric and the reality collided, memorably, and then lurched away singing, gesturing, suffering.

RONALD G. ROLLINS

From Ritual to Romance in Within the Gates and Cock-a-Doodle Dandy

> *The writer can use traditional myths with varying degrees of consciousness (with Joyce and Mann perhaps most fully conscious in our time), and he often does so with no premeditated intention, working from symbolic equivalents in his own unconscious. . . . Just as there are varying degrees of consciousness, so there are varying degrees of fruitfulness in these uses of traditional patterns, ranging from dishonest fakery at one extreme to some of the subtlest ironic and imaginative organizations in our poetry at the other.*
> —STANLEY EDGAR HYMAN, "The Ritual View of Myth and the Mythic"

Sean O'Casey simultaneously mimics and modifies some distinguishing dimensions of myth, both Christian and pre-Christian, in his *Within the Gates* (1934), a modern morality set amidst the vanishing greenness of a crowded London park, and in his *Cock-a-Doodle Dandy* (1949), an Aristophanic allegory situated in a drought-seared, fence-enclosed Irish garden. Indeed, O'Casey's mythopoeic imagination achieves a marriage of myths in these two dramas as Christian clerics collide with fertility figures, maypole dancing challenges formal Christian worship, and ancient fertility symbols like the silver shaft and the cock's crimson crest contrast with the pious parishioners' cross and rosary beads. O'Casey's basic intent, however, seems to be a desire to use myth both structurally and satirically: (1) to employ myth as a means of organizing his dramas into ritual sequences, and (2) to employ myth as a satiric stratagem which accentuates the difference between the function of

From *Modern Drama* 17, no. 1 (March 1974). © 1974 by the University of Toronto, Graduate Centre for the Study of Drama.

mythico-ritualistic elements in the lives of ancient and modern man. Emphasizing the degenerative adaptation of antique mythical patterns—patterns designed to restore potency to people and provinces—O'Casey apparently laments modern man's reluctance to enter joyously into the rites of revivification which could redeem and revitalize both self and society—the sick soul and the modern wasteland.

The sequence of events in both plays is similar. *Within the Gates* records the progressive disintegration of a young London prostitute named Jannice who has been abandoned by her father, the Bishop; terrified by nuns, with their obsessive concern with sin and the landscape of hell; reviled and shoved about by her drunken mother, the Old Woman; and exploited and then discarded by a motley of scheming males concerned primarily with sexual gratification and social security. Unsuccessful in her attempts to find enduring love and laughter, Jannice finally dies dancing and the Dreamer, her friend and wandering minstrel, laments her passing from the park which is congested with cynics, religious extremists, and the shuffling Down-and-Outs. *Cock-a-Doodle Dandy* likewise chronicles the career of a vital, young woman named Loreleen who also wants a courageous, compassionate companion in love with life. Instead, Loreleen is exploited and manhandled by Sailor Mahan and other lusty males, denigrated and stoned by the Irish villagers, and then reviled and sent into exile by Father Domineer, a one-dimensional clerical villain who influences virtually all aspects of life in Nyadnanave, Irish nest of knaves. The other attractive and vital village women and Robin Adair, another wandering minstrel, follow Loreleen into exile, leaving the cowardly and disconsolate villagers to fondle their rosary beads—their clerical chains.

It is in the constantly evolving natural settings in both plays that we first discover the birth-growth-decay pattern so prominent in various vegetation and fertility rituals designed to mirror the fundamental rhythm of nature. Cyclical in design, O'Casey's dramas are clearly arranged in a ritualistic fashion so as to serve as symbolic representations of the birth and death of one year and one day. The four scenes in *Within the Gates*, for example, move us from the splendor of spring to the starkness of winter. Scene 1 unfolds in the park on a clear spring morning as birds search for food and build nests, fowl swim in the water or preen themselves on the banks, and yellow daffodils search for the sun. A chorus of young boys and girls, representing trees and flowers, enters to sing "Our Mother the Earth is a Maiden Again." A sexual union is suggested as the Earth Maiden seeks out her bridegroom, the Sun, in the "lovely confusion" of birds, blossoms, and buds. Scene 2 occurs during a summer noon yet the colors are now chiefly golden glows tinged with gentle reds. The daffodils have been replaced by hollyhocks which cluster beneath the shrubbery. Red and yellow leaves flutter to the ground and the sunflowers are "gaunt" in scene 3, set on an autumn evening. It is a cold winter's night in scene 4 and the bare branches of the trees form strange patterns against the black canopy of the sky. Only the light from three stars penetrates the chilly darkness.

A similar yet drastically abbreviated cyclical pattern is visible in *Cock-a-Doodle Dandy* as we move from morning brilliance to evening darkness. Scene 1 takes place in the garden in front of bog owner Michael Marthraun's house on a glorious summer morning as tough grass, buttercups, daisies, and sunflowers struggle to retain their vivid vitality in the midst of a long drought that has tinted the vegetation with a deep yellow hue. It is noon of the same day in scene 2 and although a strong breeze causes the Irish Tricolor to stand out from its flagpole, the "sunshine isn't quite so bright and determined." Scene 3 occurs appropriately at dusk of the same day now much colder. The vivid reds, greens, and yellows of the earlier scenes have now been replaced by sombre hues. As the sun sets, the flag pole and house stand black against the sky; the sunflowers have also turned a "solemn black" and the evening star is but faintly visible.

The discernible changes in the landscape are correlated with corresponding changes, both physical and psychological, which the two young women, Jannice and Loreleen, undergo as they interact with others, especially the two clergymen. In scene 1 of *Within the Gates* Jannice, despite her concern for her fainting spells resulting from a defective heart, is identified as a courageous and sensitive person whose main desire is "for a bright time of it." She affirms: "If I have to die, I'll die game; I'll die dancing!" In scene 2 Jannice is still hopeful and tenacious as she seeks the Bishop's support in arranging a marriage with Ned, the Gardener, and she assures the Dreamer that she has not forgotten his "sweet song" with its carpe diem thesis. Jannice is both faltering and frantic during the cold greyness of the autumn evening in scene 3. Often pale and short of breath, she is increasingly fearful of the fiery torment which she thinks she must endure because of her many transgressions. In the final bleak winter scene, Jannice, breathing erratically with a fixed look of fear on her face, must be supported by the Dreamer in the dancing which she attempts. Drained of energy, she finally collapses and dies as the Bishop assists her in making the sign of the cross.

Yet O'Casey's young woman may not have danced and died in vain. Shortly after her demise the purple-black sky begins to change as it is pierced with golden shafts of light, "as if the sun was rising, and a new day about to begin." Moreover, the Old Woman predicts: "A few more moments of

time, and Spring'll be dancing among us again . . . the birds'll be busy at
building small worlds of their own . . . the girls will go rambling round,
each big with the thought of life in the lions of young men." The seasonal
sequence prepares to repeat itself.

Loreleen's career follows an analogous course in *Cock-a-Doodle Dandy*.
Amidst the dazzle of the summer morning in scene 1, Loreleen is jaunty and
confident, blowing kisses and chiding the villagers for their rejection of
revelry in favor of religion. In scene 2 Loreleen—illuminated with golden
shafts of light—dances, drinks toasts to the dancing cock, symbol of the *élan
vital* in man and nature, and defies the priest who fears the lovely but
shameless young women who tempt men to sin with their indecent dress.
With the coming of the chilly dusk of scene 3, however, Loreleen loses her
composure and her face reflects "intense fright." Her clothes torn and dis-
arranged, her face bruised and bloody, she pleads with Father Domineer to
show mercy; he refuses. As Loreleen departs from the gloomy garden of
deepening darkness, the Messenger pleads for the gracious women to come
forth in "golden garments" or "reckless raiment" so that the hopeful may
"dance along through Ireland gay." Unlike Jannice, Loreleen may continue
her quest and the Messenger's last lyric hints that May Day rites will continue
to occur despite the unrelenting and harsh efforts of clerics like Father
Domineer to suppress or eradicate them: "Or lads follow lassies out nutting
in May / For ever and ever and ever!"

As two women of beauty, passion, and vigorous affirmation, Jannice
and Loreleen emerge as fertility figures whose function is to restore or release
energies in both the withering wastelands and their infirm inhabitants—the
dead souls. Moreover, the names of both contain mythopoeic overtones. The
name Jannice links O'Casey's dancing protagonist with Janus, the Roman
god of doorways and the special patron of all new undertakings. As god of
beginnings, Janus's blessing was sought at the beginning of each day, month,
and year, and at all births, the beginning of life. Jannice is, therefore,
O'Casey's guardian of the park gates, and is the fair maid alluded to in the
May Day rites in the early moments of scene 1 as the chorus of young boys
and girls sing "Our Mother the Earth is a Maiden Again."

Like her Roman namesake, Jannice is also a woman with two faces or
two distinct aspects to her person. At intervals she thinks of prayer, penance,
and self-denial; at other times she favors wine, song, dancing, and sexual
self-indulgence. Anxious to emphasize this dichotomy in his heroine,
O'Casey thereby links Jannice with Diana, another Roman goddess with
two faces. Diana was, as most myth students know, the guardian of flocks
and fields, the chaste goddess of the hunt. Hence hers was largely a migratory

life of abstinence. Yet Sir James Frazer points out in *The Golden Bough* that Diana evolved from earlier, more primitive fertility figures in ancient vegetation ceremonies. Thus Diana, "as goddess of nature in general, and of fertility in particular," also came to be regarded as "a personification of the teeming life of nature, both animal and vegetable." Hence Diana was associated with both chastity and sensuality.

Although Diana was frequently depicted with a bow, quiver, and javelin, she was also sometimes identified with a crescent. It is not accidental, therefore, that O'Casey repeatedly stresses the fact that his Jannice has a black crescent on her head and a scarlet one on her hip. Jannice's mother, for example, mentions this detail twice in scene 4, reminding us again of the psychic ambivalence of the heroine. Additionally, the Dreamer reinforces this woman-nature, fertility goddess motif in scene 2 when he compares Jannice's legs to the fresh, golden branches of a willow, and her breasts to gay, white apple blossoms. Again in scene 2 he states that Jannice's hand resembles a lovely, blue-veined, pink-tipped lily.

As a fertility figure, Jannice is pursued by many of the males in the park, but it is Ned the Gardener who celebrates her physical beauty in song. Moreover, it is the Gardener's singing that inspires the group of couples to sing of an earlier garden when Adam first saw Eve's "beauty shining through a mist of golden hair." Additionally, it is the Gardener who carries the black maypole, ancient phallic symbol, that is to be used in the folk dancing designed to make England "merry again." Moreover, it is the Man with the Stick who lectures the Gardener about the maypole as "symbol" in scene 1, informing him that "It represents life, new life about to be born; fertility; th' urge wot was in the young lass [Jannice] you hunted away." It is appropriate, therefore, for the chorus of young girls and boys dancing around the maypole to sing the folk song "Haste to the Wedding" because Jannice repeatedly insists that she must have a husband, child, and home to be fulfilled. Ironically, the Gardener does not really want to make things grow; he shuns marriage and so must carry a black maypole, symbolic of his denial of life's creative urges.

Loreleen's name likewise evokes myth. Like the Lorelei of German legend, she is given the alluring traits of a temptress who would lure men to their ruin. In scene 3 Father Domineer associates her with the snake and the Garden of Eden. Both Father Domineer and bog owner Marthraun agree that it is the "soft stimulatin' touch" of woman's flesh and the graceful, provocative movements of "good-lookin' women" like Loreleen which place men in peril. Yet Loreleen would tempt men to live not die—would tempt men and women to reject domestic drudgery and Christian duty for dalliance

and dance. As defender-performer of the Dionysian dance, Loreleen is likened to a "flower" that has been blown by a winsome wind into a "dread, dhried-up desert." Because she is responsive to the fundamental rhythms of life, especially sexual and instinctive, she is consistently identified with the color green. When she arrives from London in scene 1 she wears a dark green dress and a "saucy" hat of brighter green; when she departs in scene 3, refusing to be suffocated under Father Domineer's black clerical cape, she wears a green cloak over her shoulders, an external sign of her inner vitality. Moreover, Loreleen, like Jannice, is associated with the color scarlet—a color which hints at both passion and piety—voluptuous woman and fallen woman—in both plays. If Jannice has a scarlet crescent on her hip, Loreleen has a scarlet crescent on her hat, an ornament which resembles a cock's crimson crest, and it is the crowing cock, with his vivid colors and agile movements, who is obviously an incarnation of the eros of life that animates both men and nature in *Cock-a-Doodle Dandy*.

If the two questers resemble fertility figures, the two clerics remind us of the sick fisher king whose illness brings a blight—a plague—to the land. The Bishop in *Within the Gates*, a man of sixty, has lost much of his vitality, and O'Casey indicates that his powers are "beginning to fail." Comfortable, complacent, and hypocritical, he refuses to involve himself in the sordid stress and strife of daily life; he peddles pious platitudes in the religious debates; ignores the murder, rape, suicide, and divorce headlines in the daily press; pats babies of respectable parents on the head; refuses alms to the poor; and recoils from many of the pleas of Jannice, his daughter sired when he was a young theology student. With his concern for ritual and social decorum, his aloofness, and his general ineptness, the Bishop has helped create the despairing cynicism, atheism, and amoral opportunism—the spiritual plague—which affects the lives of the Down-and-Outs, the men with hats, the chair attendants, the nursemaids, and others in the park-wasteland. His encounters with Jannice, however, help him discover his deficiencies, and he manifests new energy, humility, and compassionate purpose in his actions at the play's close. Jannice has assisted at his rebirth, which bodes well for future park visitors.

Such is not the case with Father Domineer in *Cock-a-Doodle Dandy*. An inflexible father who would frighten people into obedience, Domineer defends tradition against individual talent while raging at the carnal desires of men. A bigot and a bully, he has a restricted and restrictive religious code distinguished by an abnormal, Jansenistic fear of the flesh. He surrounds himself with unthinking sycophants who assist him in his activities which include physical abuse, exorcisms, ceremonial marches, and caustic, non-

Christian tirades. Loreleen cannot enlighten and liberate this cleric, and so the spiritual desolation must remain to stifle the conforming souls of Nyadnanave. The clerical chains remain to choke or confine those who lack the courage to rebel and depart like the young woman in green.

If the two clergymen remind us of the fisher king and his drought or pestilence-plagued land of pre-Christian myth, the two young men who perform choral functions in the two dramas—the Dreamer in *Within the Gates* and the Messenger in *Cock-a-Doodle Dandy*—resemble the wandering minstrels of earlier historical interludes. With his soft, broad-rimmed hat and vivid orange scarf, the Dreamer lives off the land, wandering from place to place to peddle his poetry. He gives money to Jannice from the advance which he has received on a book that is to be published, and he patiently strives to diminish Jannice's fear of hellish punishment. After Jannice's death he asserts that God will find room for one "scarlet Blossom" among his "thousand white lillies," and he hopes that future children will "sing and laugh and play where these have moaned in misery." The Messenger wears a silver-grey coat adorned with a pair of scarlet wings, green beret and sandals, carries a silver staff, and leads the strutting cock around with a green ribbon. Hence he resembles the messenger—attendant to the gods of Greek and Roman myth. Yet his name Robin Adair links him with the Robin Hood romances. With his accordion and gentle airs, this Ariel-like figure finally departs with maid Marion, affirming that passionate young men and women will always obey the impulse to circumvent clerics to engage in the ancient and exhilarating fertility rites of spring.

It is apparent, therefore, that O'Casey both contrasts and commingles ancient ritual and modern, ironic romance in these two ceremonial, song-seasoned dramas, utilizing a congeries of provocative mythical constructs to impose design upon his material and to accentuate his satiric indictment of modern man's spiritual decline. O'Casey admitted that in writing *Within the Gates* he had attempted to "bring back to drama the music and song and dance of the Elizabethan play and the austere ritual of Greek drama, caught up and blended with life around us." Later he adds: "Within the Gates. Probably could be, maybe is, a 'Morality Play,' tho' I didn't write it from that viewpoint. I had myth in mind."

As for *Cock-a-Doodle Dandy* O'Casey apparently wanted observers to view Loreleen's career as a duplication, with variations, of ancient scapegoat ceremonials. According to Frazer, the scapegoat pattern involved a three-part process: first, a sin-saturated community (like Nyadnanave) isolated one talented, handsome, or possessed individual as its leader or representative; this community then paid extravagant homage to this hero-scapegoat for a time; finally the community exiled or killed its hero. The sins and guilt feelings of the community, concentrated in the victim-hero, were expiated by his departure or death, and so the community, with men like Marthraun walking its streets, is free to live in relative peace until the cyclical pattern demands another "crucifixion" for community cleansing. Loreleen's career embraces all the major features outlined by Frazer in a manner that is, to be sure, more than coincidental.

Certainly the ritual—the patterned pageantry of the past—is transparently present in both of these plays, but the romance is not. True, lovely maidens, wearing gay garments and rehearsing high hopes, dance spiritedly but all too briefly through a green, pastoral world, but the handsome, knightly male, with his heightened ethical awareness and love of comradeship and challenge, is largely absent, replaced by sycophants, false seers, and gombeen men. Merriment and marriage have given way to migration and martyrdom. And it is the mythical patterns which become the objective correlatives in these ritual-romance dramas, facilitating the audiences' cognition of O'Casey's bias for an age with a greater fondness for and commitment to faith and frolic than our own.

DAVID KRAUSE

Master of Knockabout

Although there are no doubt many ways to reassess the genius of O'Casey, I believe he remains above all a master of knockabout or antic comedy, in his tragicomedies, his symbolic moralities, his comic fantasies, his one-act farces, his extravagant autobiography. If he often releases his knock of comic aggression in a world of tragic suffering, the provocation of broad laughter is calculated to mitigate the ache of the tragedy, in precisely the way that gallows humor mocks the indignity of suffering and death. Eric Bentley, perhaps our wisest critic of drama, has stated that

> Gallows humor is an accommodation to the gallows, to a world
> that is full of gallows. . . . The expression "grin and bear it" says
> all. It is the grinning that enables us to bear it. Gallows humor
> again: such humor is not an outlet for aggression to no purpose.
> The purpose is survival: the easing of the burden of existence to
> the point that it may be borne.
>
> *(The Life of the Drama)*

Bentley here is commenting on the nature of aggressive humour in modern tragicomedy, particularly in the plays of Samuel Beckett, but it should be apparent that his remarks also illustrate the compensatory function of knockabout comedy in the works of O'Casey, and indeed in Irish comedy in general, whether in the fiction of William Carleton and James Joyce, the

From *Sean O'Casey: The Man and His Work: An Enlarged Edition.* © 1960, 1975 by David Krause. Macmillan, 1975.

poetry of Brian Merriman and the *Vision of MacConglinne*, or the drama of
J. M. Synge and Brendan Behan.

The comic aggression of O'Casey's knockabout, then, is an ironic ac-
commodation to what Captain Jack Boyle calls a "world of chassis." The
antic characters confront the chaos with an hilarious alternative to despair,
a series of comic explosions, visual and verbal, that mock the process of
disintegration which threatens to annihilate their world. This comic counterattack is in fact the chief source of the "energy of his theatre," as Beckett
described it in a little-known review of an early O'Casey work, *Windfalls*. It
is this same source of knockabout energy and resilience which accounts for
the comic survival of the Blooms in Joyce's *Ulysses*, and Christy Mahon, the
Douls, the tramps and tinkers in Synge's plays. And in this context it might
be appropriate to modify Yeats's tragic vision in the following manner: "The
centre cannot hold; mere *comic* anarchy is loosed upon the world"; which is
an ironic modification that Yeats himself saw fit to dramatise as his comic
vision in his mock-heroic *Player Queen*.

Beckett, in his approach to what he accurately described as "the principle
of disintegration" in O'Casey's early works, concentrates on *Juno and the
Paycock* and two one-act farces, *A Pound on Demand* and *The End of the Beginning;* but O'Casey was to go on extending his mastery of knockabout throughout his career, even into his eightieth year when he was writing such playful
works of mere comic anarchy as *The Drums of Father Ned*, *Behind the Green
Curtains*, *Figuro in the Night*, and *The Moon Shines on Kylenamoe*. Meanwhile
Beckett, in defining "the principle of disintegration" in O'Casey's works in
1934, was also anticipating the future path of his own career as a dramatist,
since he was to create a somewhat similar world of comic disorder twenty
years later, in *Waiting for Godot*, *Endgame*, *Krapp's Last Tape*, and *Happy Days*.
The prophetic parallels between the methods of comic disintegration in the
works of O'Casey and Beckett are magnified when we discover the knock of
recognition in these comments by Beckett:

> Mr. O'Casey is a master of knockabout in this very serious and
> honourable sense—that he discerns the principle of disintegration
> in even the most complacent solidities, and activates it to their
> explosion. This is the energy of his theatre, the triumph of the
> principle of knockabout in situation, in all its elements and on
> all its planes, from the furniture to the higher centres. If "Juno
> and the Paycock," as seems likely, is his best work so far, it is
> because it communicates most fully this dramatic dehiscence,
> mind and world come asunder in irreparable dissociation—"chas-

sis" (the credit of having readapted Aguecheek and Belch in Joxer
and the Captain being incidental to the larger credit of having
dramatised the slump in the human solid). This impulse of material to escape and be consummate in its own knockabout is
admirably expressed in the two "sketches" that conclude this
volume, and especially in "The End of the Beginning," where
the entire set comes to pieces and the chief character, in a final
spasm of dislocation, leaves the scene by the chimney.

("The Essential and the Incidental")

O'Casey, like Beckett after him, relies upon these comic spasms of
disintegration—dissociations and dislocations in which "mind and world
come asunder"—in order to expose the disruptive forces in society, "even in
the most complacent solidites." It is a most ingenious method of fighting
folly with folly: tragic chaos is exploded by comic chaos, and "the slump in
the human solid" is consummated in its own knockabout. This is the cathartic
function of farce or antic comedy in the plays of O'Casey and Beckett: the
disorder of society creates its hilarious antidote in comic disorder, and as a
result profane laughter shakes the sacred foundations, "from the furniture
to the higher centres," until Cathleen Ni Houlihan becomes as illusory and
discredited as Mister Godot.

This method of achieving a catharsis through profanation, or a psychic
release from repression, may well be indigenous to low comedy, for as Wylie
Sypher has shrewdly observed, "The comic rites are necessarily impious,
for comedy is sacrilege as well as release." Commenting on the specific nature
of this comic release or catharsis in relation to comic irreverence, Sypher
adds further evidence in support of Beckett's principle of disintegration in
these illuminating remarks on tragedy and comedy:

Tragedy has been called "mithridatic" because the tragic action,
inoculating us with large doses of pity and fear, inures the self
to the perils we all face. Comedy is no less mithridatic in its
effects on the self, and has its own catharsis. Freud said that
nonsense is a toxic agent acting like some "poison" now and again
required by the economy of the soul. Under the spell of this
intoxication we reclaim for an instant our "old liberties," and after
discharging our inhibited impulses in folly we regain the sanity
that is worn away by the everyday gestures. We have a com-
pulsion to be moral and decent, but we also resent the obligation
we have accepted. The irreverence of the carnival disburdens us
of our resentment and purges our ambivalence so that we can

return to our duties as honest men. Like tragedy, comedy is
homeopathic. It cures folly by folly.

(*"The Meanings of Comedy"*)

The mithridatic cure may be more psychic than actual, the return to
duty and honesty may be less credible or desirable, when the laughter has
subsided, but in their varieties of risible subversion O'Casey and Beckett
dramatise this irreverent carnival of disorder and catharsis. While they are
both masters of knockabout, the reverberations set off by their farcical explosions operate on different wave lengths and call for somewhat different
responses. O'Casey's comedy is more insurrectionary and therefore more
aggressive in its sweeping disorder; Beckett's comedy is more nihilistic and
therefore more portentous in its teasing irresolution. O'Casey's comic syntax
is loose or open, more voluble and self-indulgent in its rhetoric; Beckett's
comic syntax is taut or hard, more stoical and astringent in its rhetoric.
Words are more often weapons of assault for O'Casey's characters, whose
comic garrulity eases the burden of existence by animating a state of outrage
in the game of survival; words are more often scrupulously measured rituals
of restraint for Beckett's characters, whose comic incantations ease the burden
of existence by animating a state of paralysis in the game of survival.
O'Casey's plays become progressively more urgent and joyful in their free-
wheeling attacks on the hardening orthodoxies of society; and some of the
later works, *Purple Dust* and *Cock-a-Doodle Dandy*, *The Bishop's Bonfire* and *The
Drums of Father Ned*, call for a comic apocalypse. Beckett's plays become
progressively more fatalistic as their ever-shrinking orbits of graveyard
knockabout undermine the metaphysical structures of the universe itself; and
if they call for anything at all it might only be an oblique form of comic
subversion that may ultimately dissolve the whole system along with its
comic scapegoats, which is implicit in the ominous tone of *Waiting for Godot*
and *Endgame*, and explicit in *Krapp's Last Tape* and *Happy Days*.

Nevertheless, for all these differences in the language and tone of their
comic subversion, O'Casey and Beckett have structured the action of their
plays along similar patterns of plot reversal. Their plays actually invert the
traditional order of main plot and subplot, so that in this new ironic structure
the subplot and its comic supernumeraries become the central focus, while
the normally heroic main-plot action is now consigned to a secondary position
and often occurs offstage. And since the main action of *Gunman* and *Juno*
and *Plough*, *Godot* and *Endgame* and *Krapp*, is dominated by antic comedians,
the patriotic and cosmic figures and forces of potentially tragic proportions,
now hidden in the wings, at the barricades, in the heavens, or in the tapes,

are mocked structurally as well as thematically. James Agate must have been aware of these ironic implications when, in his review of the London premiere of O'Casey's second play, he wrote:

> *Juno and the Paycock* is as much a tragedy as *Macbeth*, but it is a tragedy taking place in the porter's family. Mr. O'Casey's extraordinary knowledge of English taste—that he wrote his play for the Abbey Theatre, Dublin, is not going to be allowed to disturb my argument—is shown by the fact that the tragic element in it occupies at the most some twenty minutes, and that for the remaining two hours and a half the piece is given up to gorgeous and incredible fooling.

Agate's shrewd estimate of the disproportionate time allotted to the comedy in contrast to the tragedy is characteristic of the plays of O'Casey and Beckett and reveals the structural strategy of their tragicomedies.

Furthermore, Agate is certainly accurate in his argument that the gratifyingly impure taste of English and Irish audiences demands an excess of "gorgeous and incredible fooling" in the theatre, even in the midst of tragedy. It is a phenomenon that once more reminds us of man's psychic necessity to grin in order to bear the pain of existence. In a related argument, William Empson has commented on the stubborn survival of the tragicomic double plot in English drama:

> The old quarrel about tragicomedy, which deals with part of the question, shows that the drama in England has always at its best had a certain looseness of structure; one might almost say that the English drama did not outlive the double plot.
>
> (*Some Versions of Pastoral*)

Empson also describes this loose double plot structure as part of the " 'tragic king—comic people' convention," so characteristically illustrated in Shakespeare's plays, notably *Henry IV, Part 1*. Modern Irish drama certainly did not outlive the loose structure of the double plot; in fact, in the plays of O'Casey and Beckett and Behan, for example, it sustained the double plot by inverting it, by relocating the "comic people" in the main plot and the "tragic king" or his surrogates in the subplot. Harold Pinter accomplished precisely this relocation in many of his plays, particularly *The Dumb Waiter* and *The Birthday Party;* and Tom Stoppard did it brilliantly with his tragicomic reversal of the *Hamlet* structure in *Rosencrantz and Guildenstern Are Dead*. There are of course further examples of this structural inversion in the plays of Genet and Ionesco.

In his remarks on the tentative nature of the setting and the characters in *Waiting for Godot*, Hugh Kenner seems to be raising a similar point about structural inversion when he tells us that Gogo and Didi appear to be supernumeraries filling in time while we wait for the main action to begin:

> The tree is plainly a sham, and the two tramps are simply filling up time until a proper dramatic entertainment can get under way. They are helping the management fulfill, in a minimal way, its contract with the ticket holders. The resources of vaudeville are at their somewhat incompetent disposal: bashed hats, dropped pants, tight boots, the kick, the pratfall, the improper story. It will suffice if they can stave off a mass exodus until Godot comes, in whom we are all so interested.
>
> (*Samuel Beckett, A Critical Study*)

This ironic denial of our expectations goes to the heart of the structural joke: the tramps have displaced Godot and all his profundities, just as Boyle and Joxer have displaced Cathleen Ni Houlihan and her offstage patriots. And Kenner's reference to "the resources of vaudeville" should remind us that O'Casey and Beckett share an unqualified affinity for the profane delights of the music-hall tradition, the consummate theatre of knockabout, with its decrepit comedians and anarchic routines, its slapstick disintegration of the furniture and all the respectable foundations of society. Sometimes the guardians of society recognize the function of music-hall comedy as a safety valve for repression, as Empson's anecdote illustrates: "I believe the Soviet Government in its early days paid two clowns, Bim and Bom, to say as jokes the things everybody else would have been shot for saying." But in the unintimidated world of art, comic subversion is not for sale. The dramatist must be free to create his own Bims and Boms, Boyles and Joxers, Gogos and Didis, even at the risk of liquidation or exile.

Captain Boyle and Joxer Daly owe as much to Gallagher and Sheen, Laurel and Hardy, as they do to Mak and Gill, Sir Toby Belch and Andrew Aguecheek, Falstaff and Bardolph, Pistol and Nym; and with reasonable modifications the same lineage applies to Gogo and Didi. This line of comic descent, from medieval drama to Shakespeare to O'Casey, has been reinforced by J. L. Styan. Writing about Empson's notion of the loose structure that traditionally accompanies the double plot, Styan believes that this looseness "reproduces the sensations of life with its complexities and contradictions":

> We get the feeling that, in Empson's words, "the play deals with life as a whole." From the spontaneous eruption of tomfoolery

within the sacred framework of the medieval mystery plays to the contrivances of O'Casey to show his subject from opposed points of view in, say, *The Plough and the Stars*, we are reminded again that the point of reference is life; but if this is true, the looseness is merely apparent and not real.

After the magnificent Shakespearian rhetoric of Henry's "Once more unto the breach . . . ," which ends, we remember, with an injunction to "follow your spirit," what better way of having us keep our wits and hear a ring of truth than by dragging on Nym, Bardolph and Pistol immediately?

BARDOLPH: On, on, on, on, on, to the breach, to the breach.

NYM: Pray thee Corporal stay, the knocks are too hot.

(*The Dark Comedy: The Development of Modern Comic Tragedy*)

The terrible knocks of life and possible death are indeed too hot. And therefore these clowns must counter with some profane and heated knocks of their own which celebrate their comic survival. This process occurs in most of the O'Casey plays with the counter-knocks of Seumas Shields, Boyle and Joxer, Fluther Good, Bessie Burgess, Ginnie Gogan, The Covey, Peter Flynn, Rosie Redmond; and in the later plays with all the shrewd Irish peasants in *Purple Dust, Red Roses for Me, Cock-a-Doodle Dandy, The Bishop's Bonfire, The Drums of Father Ned*, and all the one-act plays.

This counter-knock of comedy can also be explained as a psychological strategy of defense, if we consider some of R. D. Laing's studies of schizophrenia from a comic point of view. Laing reports "that *without exception* the experience and behavior that gets labeled schizophrenic is *a special strategy that a person invents in order to live in an unlivable situation.*" Comedy, then, can be an alternative to madness. The mask of the clown becomes his special strategy which the terrors of life have forced him to invent in order to go on living in an unlivable world. When the knocks become too hot, he creates his knockabout.

Consider some affirmative aspects of this surival strategy in O'Casey and Beckett. At the end of *Juno and the Paycock*, when the drunk and bewildered Boyle and Joxer stagger into an empty room to find their world in "a state o' chassis," they could well be rehearsing for or anticipating the appearance of Gogo and Didi, or even Hamm and Clov, Nagg and Nell. "The blinds is down, Joxer, the blinds is down!" It is the end of a slapstick survival game that never ends. Knockabout comedians never die, they only play games, they wait or fall down, suffering and laughing for all of us. In *Waiting for Godot* Didi pleads, "Come on, Gogo, return the ball," and in his incompetent way Gogo always does. In *Endgame* Clov asks, "What's to keep me here?" "The dialogue," Hamm replies, returning the ball. In *Juno* Boyle says, "I ofen looked up at the sky an' assed meself the question—what is the stars, what is the stars?" And Joxer returns the ball: "Ah, that's the question— what is the stars?" They all grin and bear it because, as Didi says, "We're inexhaustible." In the midst of an argument Clov says, "There's one thing I'll never understand. Why I always obey you. Can you explain that to me?" and Hamm replies, "Perhaps it's compassion. A kind of great compassion." After an argument Boyle says, "Now an' agen we have our differ, but we're there together all the time." And Joxer returns the refrain: "Me for you, an' you for me, like the two Musketeers." Thanks to their comic duels and duets, they're all there in the chaos together; they're all inexhaustible; they're all bound together by the great compassion of low comedy. They can't affirm the world, but they can affirm each other.

A knock of affirmation emerges clearly from O'Casey's later plays, but even in the tragicomic dislocation of his earlier works he never doubts the saving grace of mundane humanity in his grotesque clowns, and continually celebrates their comic vitality. Only insofar as the sheer energy of low comedy is itself a form of stubborn survival is there anything that resembles an open affirmation or celebration in the plays of Beckett. But the inexhaustible art of knockabout comedy may itself be an affirmation for Beckett. On this fine point, however, it is again necessary to invoke the wisdom of Eric Bentley, who rightly insists that "artistic activity is itself a transcendence of despair, and for unusually despairing artists that is no doubt chiefly what art is: a therapy, a faith." And Beckett, he would have us believe, "got rid of the despair, if only for the time being, by expressing it."

O'Casey's comedy is his therapy, his faith. He was in full control of his artistic power whenever he relied upon his abundant resources of knockabout comedy to transcend a despair that grew out of man's failure to eliminate or control the chaos of modern life. His work is more likely to be uneven or excessively hortatory, didactic, when he departs from his comic or tragicomic muse, for his non-comic characters often if not always fail to achieve a life of their own, an authentic life apart from O'Casey's own voice. Philosophy and comedy can be strange bedfellows in the theatre, and even Shaw had his difficulties in trying to yoke them. But it is in the nature of Beckett's stoical genius that he can be philosophic and comic at the same time; it is in the nature of O'Casey's effusive genius that he can be least comic when he is most philosophic. At his best, however, like Synge, O'Casey is a comic and tragicomic poet in the theatre.

The poetry of laughter is the antidote to despair. If the sources of Beckett's despair are cosmic in origin, associated with the capricious and inaccessible mind of Godot, the sources of O'Casey's despair are social in origin, associated with the tyrannizing hierarchies of society; it involves the difference between a comic quarrel with God and a comic quarrel with the household gods. Although O'Casey liked to call himself an atheist, he really had no quarrel with God—"He may be but a shout in th' street," he echoed Joyce. His quarrel was with man, with God's self-appointed guardians of church and state and their self-sanctified institutions of repression. In his appropriately titled essay, "The Power of Laughter: Weapon against Evil," he identified some of those household gods who were among the chief targets of his profane and liberating knockabout:

> Laughter tends to mock the pompous and the pretentious; all man's boastful gadding about, all his pretty pomps, his hoary customs, his wornout creeds, changing the glitter of them into the dullest hue of lead. The bigger the subject, the sharper the laugh. No one can escape it: not the grave judge in his robe and threatening wig; the parson and his saw; the general full of his sword and his medals; the palled prelate, tripping about, a bless-ing in one hand, a curse in the other; the politician carrying his magic wand of Wendy windy words; they all fear laughter, for the quiet laugh or the loud one upends them, strips them of pretense, and leaves them naked to enemy and friend.

Of course O'Casey preferred the loud upending laugh for these impos-tors or *alazons*, but the overall strategy of his knockabout technique is not fully apparent until we see how he exploited the clowns who were responsible for the pratfalls, his rascally *eirons*. Henri Bergson's theory of comedy, limited to a brilliant study of the *alazons*, or humour-characters, whose rigidity or automatism exposes their folly, does not take into account the role of the *eirons*, or laughing characters, whose flexibility or instinctive wit unmasks the *alazons*. We must therefore reach beyond Bergson and turn to that il-luminating work, Francis Macdonald Cornford's *Origin of Attic Comedy*, where the traditional game of comedy is described as a duel between those incomparable adversaries, the *eirons* and *alazons*, the ironical or cunning self-deprecators and the inflated impostors or pretenders. But even more im-portant, Cornford insists that the *eirons* often assail the *alazons* "with a mixture of 'Irony' and 'Buffoonery,' " and it is precisely this mixture of wisdom and folly which defines the double nature of O'Casey's knockabout comedians. It is a dual function that allows us to laugh with as well as at these ridiculous and resilient characters. Borrowing from Aristotle, Cornford accounts for this comic mixture in the following manner:

Aristotle seems to have classified the characters in Comedy under three heads: the Buffoon (*bomolochos*), the Ironical type (*eiron*), and the Impostor (*alazon*). . . . The Buffoon and the Ironical type are more closely allied in Aristotle's view than a modern reader might expect. They stand together in opposition to the Impostor in all his forms. It will be remembered that in the *Ethics* the Ironical man and the Impostor or swaggerer confront one another in the two vicious extremes which flank the virtuous mean of Truthfulness. While the Impostor claims to possess higher qualities than he has, the Ironical man is given to making himself out worse than he is. This is a generalized description, meant to cover all types of self-depreciation, many forms of which are not comic. In Comedy the special kind of Irony practised by the Impostor's opponent is feigned stupidity. The word *eiron* itself in the fifth century appears to mean "cunning" or (more exactly), "sly." Especially it meant the man who masks his batteries of deceit behind a show of ordinary good nature; or indulges a secret pride and conceit of wisdom, while he affects ignorance and self-depreciation, but lets you see all the while that he could enlighten you if he chose, and so makes a mock of you. It was for putting on these airs that Socrates was accused of "irony" by his enemies. The *eiron* who victimises the Impostors masks his cleverness under a show of clownish dullness. He is a fox in the sheep's clothing of a buffoon.

The archetypal comic character in O'Casey's plays, then, is invariably something of a fox masquerading in the sheep's clothing of a buffoon. His comic weapons are therefore that mixture of irony and buffoonery that Cornford describes because he must pretend to be a greater fool than he is in order to disarm his more pretentious and dangerous opponents. His disguise of "feigned stupidity" may be conscious or unconscious—more instinctive in Captain Boyle, more calculated in Joxer Daly—but he is a buffoon with the cunning of an *eiron* "who masks his batteries of conceit" behind a stratagem of "ignorance and self-depreciation." In the context of the Roman comedy of Plautus, this would be the equivalent of saying that O'Casey's clowns combine the folly and cunning of the braggart warrior *and* the clever slave, which is a parallel to Cornford's way of describing the comic complexity of wise fools: the irony and buffoonery of Sir Toby and Falstaff, Seumas Shields in *The Shadow of a Gunman* and Fluther Good in *The Plough and the Stars*, as well as Boyle and Joxer. At various times O'Casey's *eirons* succumb to what might be called the Gadshill-folly, for they are all comically discredited for their cowardice and mendacity; and yet they are also capable of a complementary attitude that could be called the Shrewsbury-wisdom, for they all know that a corpse on the battlefield, or in the war-torn slums of Dublin, is a poor excuse for honour. They are comically and ironically damned and saved; and in their knockabout salvation they profane whatever is excessively rigid or sacred in society. And holy Ireland is a country of many sacred nets, outside of which lies comic freedom.

Knockabout comedy can therefore be a game of salvation as well as a carnival of pratfalls. In her standard study of the Fool, Enid Welsford recognizes the general wisdom in the clown's masquerade of folly, but she tends to deny him his essential irony; she dilutes his power and treats him as an innocuous entertainer when she writes, "The Fool does not lead a revolt against the Law, he lures us into a region of the spirit where, as Lamb would put it, the writ does not run. . . . There is nothing essentially immoral or blasphemous or rebellious about clownage." It might equally be argued that there is nothing essentially moral or pious or respectable about clownage. House-broken or amenable clowns may be found in Ruritania but not in Ireland; not in the England of Falstaff or Tony Lumpkin, either, or the America of Huck Finn or Buster Keaton. So the whimsical sentiments of Miss Welsford with her quaint appeal to Lamb's airy-fairy-land cannot help us here. For the ultimate wisdom of disguised folly, for the flexible *eiron*'s comic revolt against the world of rigid *alazons*, we must turn to Cornford not Welsford.

Cornford can also guide us to a confrontation with the non-comic or ethical side of O'Casey's works. In his references to Aristotle and Socrates, Cornford identifies another kind of ironic wisdom, the serious wisdom of the ethical man who occupies the middle ground or golden mean between the Ironical clown and the pretentious Impostor—"the virtuous mean of Truthfulness." In some of his later plays O'Casey creates a non-comic or truthful hero who defends that "virtuous mean"—it may even be a "virtuous extreme" if the middle ground has become an excuse for the status quo—a character who suffers or dies for an ideal value. This attitude would apply to his two outstanding martyrs, Harry Heegan in *The Silver Tassie* and Ayamonn Breydon in *Red Roses for Me*, the most obvious examples of his serious or ethical *eirons*. It would be unfair to insist that O'Casey had to continue writing in his best tragicomic or comic manner, for it is clear that he felt the artistic and emotional need to experiment with serious themes and symbolic techniques. Nevertheless, it would be inaccurate to insist that he did not pay a price for these ambitious risks. The portentous rhetoric of Heegan and Breydon is often too "literary" and contrived, and as characters they suffer from an excess of romantic idealism or Truthfulness. Their symbolic voices are too prophetic, too pure, too didactic. Perhaps they are too noble in their sacrificial conception, which unfortunately means that they are immune from the saving graces of irony and buffoonery. Vivian Mercier properly raised this issue when he wrote:

> O'Casey's decline as a comic dramatist dates from the period when he ceases to have a divided mind about most of his characters. Compare, for instance, two *personae* of O'Casey himself: the poltroon poet Donal Davoren in *The Shadow of a Gunman* and the All-Irish boy Ayamonn in *Red Roses for Me*, a much later play.
>
> (*The Irish Comic Tradition*)

But in light of his curious illustrations, Mercier's otherwise sound judgement must be qualified and corrected. He is right in claiming that O'Casey was at the height of his comic power when he approached his characters with "a divided mind," a very perceptive description of the double-view that accounts for the resilience and richness of his comic *eirons*. He is less than accurate, however, in his comparison of characters. Breydon is undoubtedly an autobiographical figure, an ethical hero who, admirable as he may be, is so close to O'Casey himself that he lacks aesthetic objectivity as well as irony. But it is highly questionable whether Davoren is in any sense intended to be a self-portrait of the playwright, since he is damned for his dangerous illusions and detachment, his shadow-self which deceives the people around him, especially the innocent Minnie Powell, and precipitates the tragic denouement. If anyone is the play speaks for O'Casey it must be the peddler Seumas Shields, who does it indirectly through the *persona* of a wise clown, an ironist *and* braggart, a buffoon *and* coward. He is full of comic complexities. In revealing his own frailties he also exposes the greater folly of patriotic fanaticism and poetic illusions. Therefore, in his characteristic manner, O'Casey has "a divided mind" about Shields, his comic mock-hero, not Davoren, his straight man. And if one is to draw comparisons between some of the characters in these two plays—granting that Breydon is overburdened with the idealistic image of the "All-Irish boy"—why not make a connection between Shields and Brennan o' the Moor, Brennan the miserly *and* magnanimous clown, the bigot *and* balladeer, about whom the audience as well as O'Casey must have the "divided" feelings of folly and wisdom, the double-view that distinguishes all the comic *eirons*?

It is also questionable whether O'Casey "declined" as a comic dramatist in his later plays, since so many of them are mock-pastoral comedies with a profusion of knockabout clowns and music-hall antics, even though some pastoral straight men occasionally try to dominate the scene—such rampant comedies as *Purple Dust, Cock-a-Doodle Dandy, The Bishop's Bonfire, The Drums of Father Ned, Figuro in the Night, The Moon Shines on Kylenamoe*. And even in those darker plays in which he shifted the main focus from comedy to prophecy—*The Silver Tassie, Within the Gates, Red Roses for Me, The Star Turns Red, Oak Leaves and Lavender*—he subordinated but did not abandon those comic characters who continue to inspire "divided" feelings and persist in stealing any scene in which they appear; jesters like Sylvester Heegan and Simon Norton, Roory O'Balacaun and Mullcanny, Feelim O'Morrigun and Mrs. Watchit, to name a half-dozen among many. Nor should we overlook the fact that there are notable successes as well as failures in these plays, particularly such spectacular innovations of total theatre—symbolic stage-craft, ritualistic action, stylized imagery—as the surrealistic second-act war configuration in *Tassie*, the cinematic and cyclical versions of pastoral in *Gates*, and the miraculous third-act transformation in *Red Roses*. These are monumental achievements, especially when one considers that they are the dramatic metaphors of a half-blind exiled playwright working in the theatre of his mind. Perhaps Gordon Rogoff raised the ultimate issue when he commented that these plays, and all the later works, are beyond us until we find the right director and theatre group to do them justice:

> Published and frozen before reaching the stage the most intriguing of them—*Red Roses for Me, Purple Dust, Time to Go*, and most of all *Cock-a-Doodle Dandy*—never found *their* director. . . . What may well be missing is some gloriously dotty Irish Berlin Ensemble led by an equally improbable Bertolt Littlewood.

In further pursuit of the comic O'Casey, it might also be enlightening to concentrate briefly on the language of some of the minor but memorable clowns in the too often neglected one-act plays. These characters all indulge themselves in O'Casey's favorite game of comic survival in a world of knockabout disintegration, the mock-battle of the flyting, a game which they share with all the Boyles, Fluthers, and Prodicals. The tradition of the flyting, a contest of raillery and ridicule, goes back to the Greek satyr plays, the medieval Celtic bards, Chaucer and Shakespeare, the renaissance Scottish poets, and in our own time comes forward to the parallel game of "the Dozens" played by American blacks. It is a mock-battle of poetic invective in which words become the weapons of otherwise disarmed combatants, and the trading of comic insults is inflated to a rude and merry art of psychic liberation. It is a survival game that can also be explained by Freud's theory of the function of jokes as a safety valve for repression, what he calls the circumventing process of jokes: "They make possible the satisfaction of an instinct (whether lustful or hostile) in the face of an obstacle that stands in the way. They circumvent this obstacle and in that way draw pleasure from a source which the obstacle had made inaccessible." The obstacle in the flyting is another character, another clown or *alazon*, though one has the distinct feeling that in the plays of O'Casey it is the repressive and disintegrating world itself, with its sacred institutions of restraint, that is the ultimate *alazon*.

RONALD AYLING

Early Dramatic Experiments: "Alienation" and The Plough and the Stars

We had to convince average men and women, and to do this by an art that must blunder and experiment that it might find some new form.
  —"Two Lectures on the Irish Theatre by W. B. Yeats" (*1922*)

THE PHILOSOPHER: *The causes of a lot of tragedies lie outside the power of those who suffer them, so it seems.*

THE DRAMATURG: *So it seems?*

THE PHILOSOPHER: *Of course it only seems. Nothing human can possibly lie outside the powers of humanity, and such tragedies have human causes.*

THE DRAMATURG: *Even if that were true it wouldn't make any difference to the theatre. In the old days opponents used to confront one another on the stage. How's it to be done now? Somebody in Chicago can set a piece of machinery going that will destroy twelve people in Ireland, or maybe twelve thousand.*

THE PHILOSOPHER: *Then obviously that machinery must stretch as far as Ireland. The opponents can confront each other on the stage. There'll have to be a lot of technical changes, of course. A lot of human characteristics and passions that used to be important have ceased to matter. Others have taken their place. In any case, it's difficult to grasp very much without seeing beyond the individual to the major group conflicts.*
  —BERTOLT BRECHT, *The Messingkauf Dialogues* (1939–1942)

One has grown so used to criticisms of supposed structural incoherence and formlessness in the avowedly experimental dramas of the later period of O'Casey's career that it is perhaps salutary to recollect that the very same

From *Continuity and Innovation in Sean O'Casey's Drama: A Critical Monograph.* © 1976 by the Institut für Englische Sprache und Literatur, Universitat Salzburg.

kind of objections were made to his early "apprentice" work and even to his Abbey dramas. Though now widely accepted as classics in their own right, *The Shadow of a Gunman, Juno and the Paycock*, and (especially) *The Plough and the Stars* have all been taken to task for what was said to be their "very real lack" of structure and of form.

To illustrate the persistence of this attitude one might merely cite arguments by O'Casey from three distinct periods of his career. In each case the writer is defending a particular play from markedly similar attacks. In one letter he argued:

> What is called "formlessness" may be a form in itself, as for instance, in *John Bull's Other Island*, Chekhov's plays, and Shaw's *Heartbreak House*. Few places can be so formless as is Ireland at the present time. It is like a kaleidoscope, but giving . . . no settled or discernible pattern, however one may twist it slow or with speed. This the play tried to show, with the confusion animated by the activity of the Tostal in which there was hope and resolution.

In another counterattack (intended to be provocative and mixing personal animus with justifiable indignation at his treatment by members of the Abbey Theatre board of directors, of whom Professor Starkie was one) he wrote:

> Dr. Starkie says that "the fault of *The Silver Tassie* is that it is too vague and indefinite." He does not say where it is vague and where it is indefinite. He hints at the last two acts. There is not a docker, who is not a duffer (the percentage of duffers among dockers is low, and far less than the percentage of duffers among dons), who would fail to understand a single sentence or fail to feel a single emotion that is spoken or manifested in any one act of the play.

Finally, there is his reply to another adverse criticism by an Abbey Theatre director (Yeats, in fact, though the comments were unsigned) which accompanied the returned manuscript of one of his plays. In the report it was said (among other things):

> I find this discursive play very hard to judge for it is a type of play I do not understand. The drama of it is loose and vague. . . .
> It is a story without meaning—a story where nothing happens except that a wife runs away from a husband, to whom we had

not the least idea that she was married, and the Mansion House lights are turned out because of some wrong to a man who never appears in the story.

The dramatist answered as follows in a letter to Lennox Robinson:

> I was terribly disappointed at its final rejection, and felt at first as if, like Lucifer, I had fallen never to hope again. I have re-read the work and find it as interesting as ever, in no way deserving the contemptuous dismissal it has received from the reader you have quoted. Let me say that I do not agree with his criticism. . . . *What could be more loose and vague than life itself?* Are we to write plays on the framework of the first of Genesis; and God said let there be light and there was light; and he separated the light from the darkness and he called the light day, and the darkness he called night; and the morning and evening were the first Act. *It is the subtle vagueness in such writers as Shaw and Ibsen that—in my opinion—constitute their most potent charm* [my italics].

In the above extracts O'Casey was replying, respectively, to criticisms of *The Drums of Father Ned, The Silver Tassie,* and *The Crimson in the Tri-Colour* made in 1958, in 1928, and in 1922. The similarities are startling, though that does not mean that the three plays in question have a great deal in common other than the intention of challenging the ordered symmetry of the well-made play convention. In each case objections were made to vague and indefinite aspects in O'Casey's construction, and we encounter the very same criticisms with regard to *The Plough and the Stars* when that play made its initial appearance on stage and in print in 1926. It is obvious that the author deliberately refused to delineate certain features too sharply in these works, preferring to stress the flux, fluidity, and unpredictability of life as he saw it, though such features (which are perfectly attuned to Elizabethan and Jacobean staging) were distinctly unfashionable in an age still dominated by the practice of Pinero and the theories of William Archer. Although the degree of artistic success varies with each of O'Casey's plays, it should be said from the outset that each possesses a form of structure fashioned for the particular purposes of the work in question. The criticism that they "lack form" is absurd. Each has its own form, its own distinctive structure which may certainly be open to criticism but must be assessed in terms of what the dramatist is trying to do. Individual works may be too vague or too diffuse, in practice, but the standards of criticism must not be (as they have been too often) those of the well-made play.

II

Too little critical attention has been given to practical aspects of Sean O'Casey's stagecraft. Though this part of the monograph deals with only one facet of the subject, it nonetheless involves a detailed analysis of one of the most significant and effective dramatic devices used in *The Plough* and *The Silver Tassie:* this is the means whereby certain characters and their actions are "distanced," when it looks as though they might become too well liked by the audience, or if there is the likelihood of spectators identifying themselves uncritically with the feelings or values of the stage creations. The effect is obtained in various ways, as we shall see. For the sake of convenience, I use the word coined by Bertolt Brecht, "alienation," to describe the phenomenon. John Willet writes that Brecht's *Verfremdung* means "estrangement, alienation or disillusion in English; dépaysement, étrangement or distanciation in French: a wide choice of equivalents, none of which is exactly right," but if none of them precisely describes O'Casey's method, either, they still offer useful shorthand guides to what he is attempting.

From the late 1920s, Brecht became increasingly opposed to Naturalist character-creation and acting. He was hostile to heroes and heroines as such, preferring an objective stage presentation of men and women as social beings and as individuals. Similarly, at the time that *The Plough and the Stars* was first preformed in Dublin, O'Casey said in a debate on the play that he "was not trying, and never would try, to write about heroes." Brecht, moreover, distrusted empathy. He thought that the essential message of a writer was sometimes destroyed because people identified themselves with, or felt sorry for, morally undesirable characters, and that social criticism was blunted by individual compassion. Instead of emotional identification Brecht wanted intellectual distancing. Characters in plays were to be regarded solely as stage figures created for a particular purpose by a playwright and imitated for an audience's entertainment by actors who were not to appear as other than imitators. However heroic or admirable a stage personality might appear to be, the onlookers must never relax their vigilance and accept that character at his or her face value or identify his joy or suffering too completely with their own experience.

In his dramatic writings Brecht used many alienating devices to prevent empathy and to make spectators aware, throughout the play, that they were witnessing a stage performance. There was no attempt to use lighting for illusion or to simulate realistic stage settings, though essential stage properties (like Mother Courage's cart) were faithfully reproduced. The plot or narrative outline of the drama was often divulged in advance of the action by means of placards or film projection. Songs and spoken narration interrupted acted sequences, and broke any illusion temporarily created by the actors. These *Verfremdung* techniques were designed to combat uncritical emotional responses on the part of audiences and to encourage spectators to criticise and judge the dramatic action as it proceeded. Brecht was not, of course, completely hostile to emotion on the stage or to leading characters who dominate the action in a play—we find both in his work—but he believed that both the emotion and the characters should be strictly controlled and subservient to the theme or message of the play as a whole.

The objective presentation of dramatic events is to be found, in various forms, throughout the history of drama—the use of the chorus in Greek tragedy is an obvious example. Brecht's innovation was his deliberate use of a wide range of objective methods to serve his own didactic purposes. Some degree of estrangement of stage characters from the sympathy of audiences has been practised by playwrights in all ages, and writers far less didactic in intention than Brecht have found it necessary, unconsciously, to employ one or other of the devices that he used consciously. Because dramatic figures are represented on the stage by flesh-and-blood people, it is possible for them to take on what is almost an independent life of their own and, accordingly, for them to unbalance the dramatic as well as moral basis of the play in which they appear. There is always the danger, too, that the audience will fall in love with stage characters even against the wishes of the author.

Shakespeare's Falstaff and O'Casey's Captain Boyle are both characters who seem so much larger than life, and so full of humour and vitality that undesirable and anti-social traits in their characters, that would be attacked were they living people, have been overlooked and even excused on the stage. How else can one explain the fact that critics, from Maurice Morgann in the eighteenth century to A. C. Bradley and John Palmer in the twentieth, have spoken so indignantly of Hal's cold-blooded inhumanity when he behaves as any socially responsible man would do in his circumstances, and, on becoming monarch, banishes Falstaff from his company? (The fact that Bolingbroke's son cannot be wholly accepted on his own terms, either as prince or king, is neither here nor there insofar as his necessary rejection of the man who's immediately prepared to ride roughshod over the laws of the land upon the accession of his "patron" is concerned.) The newly crowned king's speech of expulsion, "I know thee not, old man: fall to thy prayers," merely makes explicit what was inevitable in the dramatic pattern of *Henry IV* from the beginning of the first part, and what the subtle alienation effects have implied throughout the whole play, especially in the second part. As examples of character alienation, for example, one might instance the in-

creased stress on the age, disease, and lechery of Falstaff and also the coars-
ening of his wit in *Part 2*. Moreover, unfavourable aspects of his character
which—in *Part 1*—had only been criticised verbally are *seen* in action in the
second part, and this is more damaging: in particular, his callous treatment
of the conscripted soldiers and his exploitation of Mistress Quickly and
Justice Shallow. In act 2 scene 4 of *Part 2* we witness Falstaff making love
to Doll Tearsheet and the grossness of the episode is pointed (in a Brechtian
manner) by the commentary of Hal and Poins. Thus we may find the *Ver-
fremdungseffekt* in traditional forms of drama, and when Brecht's terminology
is used to describe O'Casey's techniques it is not because he deliberately
followed the German playwright's theories—on the contrary, he was totally
unaware of Brecht's plays and theoretical writings when he wrote *The Plough*
and *The Tassie*—but because today we can see that his aims and approach in
these plays were in some ways similar to those of Brecht in his work.

O'Casey's methods were chosen for his own purposes. It is no accident
that any detailed analysis of plays like *The Shadow* and *Juno* must be largely
taken up with matters relating to characterisation. Yet, though this is an
important element in both plays, O'Casey still showed something akin to
Brechtian detachment in his character drawing. Even in his portrayal of
"Juno" and Mary Boyle there is considerable criticism of their failings as
well as genuine warmth and understanding; indeed, the sympathy is impressive precisely because it is so open-eyed. Throughout his works, including his most experimental writings, there are varying admixtures of
emotional involvement and critical detachment; and even in the works most
influenced by expressionist techniques there is a deliberate attempt to rec-
oncile two-dimensional stereotype figures with more rounded human
characters.

In various articles written in the 1950s and 1960s O'Casey opposed what
he believed to be an over-intellectual trend in modern drama and in contemporary theatre criticism. He criticised Brecht for (as he believed) appearing
to elevate intellectual criteria above all else in the creation of drama. The
following short quotations from two articles [reprinted in *Blasts and Benedictions*] about possible future trends in theatre give some idea of his attitude
in general:

> What the future of the theatre may be I cannot tell—it depends
> on so many things. I do not agree with those who would banish
> emotion from the theatre (Brecht seems to imply this), for, to
> me, emotion burns within the veins of life. We all feel it in sorrow,

in joy, in fear, in hate, at births, weddings, burials, and when
we achieve things.

> ("Art Is the Song of Life")

Some say, I believe, that the theatre of the future will be an
intellectual one. I don't think so; for intellects differ, the one from
the other; different intellects are superior in differing subjects,
and can the future dramatist's intellect be so supernatural that it
will understand all, and put an incontestable synthesis of them
all, glowing, upon the stage? . . . Imagination is a far greater
power in the drama than intellect of the highest.

> ("An Irishman's Plays")

At the same time, however, he took pains to stress the need for intellectual
discipline in the creative process itself and for mental stimulation as part of
the total dramatic experience:

The dramatist must make his imagination serve him; he must
control it; if he doesn't, it will make all the difference between
an interesting but disorderly play and a fine work of dramatic
art.

> ("Art Is the Song of Life")

It is the plays that influence the mind and the emotions . . . that
live a lasting life. And this is what every dramatist should aim
at, even though he may never achieve it.

> ("An Irishman's Plays")

When O'Casey wishes spectators to view the dramatic action and its
social implications with critical insight, he does not necessarily demand
detachment at the same time—as Brecht did, in theory if not always in
practice. Instead, as in the curtain scenes of *The Shadow* and *Juno*, he seeks
to arouse feelings of disgust and, sometimes, anger as well. Even the use of
stylization and ritual, as in the second act of *The Tassie*, does not preclude
emotion in favour of abstract or dispassionate criticism. The ironic and
sometimes moving effects created by familiar liturgical language and
rhythms, for one thing, invoke an archetypal response on the part of the
audience at a level other than the rational. O'Casey never scorned emotional
involvement by the audience; indeed, he actively encouraged it by using
(among other things) sentimental hymns, music-hall songs, and full-blooded

infusions of melodrama, elements which some critics have apparently found too obvious or superficial for serious dramatic purposes. In this respect we may recollect the long-lived critical distaste for much of Charles Ives's music because he, too, used many "pop" ingredients such as negro spirituals, brass band marches, and evangelical hymns, often in direct juxtaposition with or counterpointed to classical musical forms; yet Ives's bold experiments have recently received more sympathetic critical attention. In O'Casey's case, the intrusion of blatant farcical material at moments of tragic intensity is another method used to forestall any possibly complacent or stereotyped reaction on the part of the audience.

O'Casey's playwriting allows for a considerable degree of *rapport* between spectators and certain of his *dramatis personae*, yet the empathy thus engendered does not impede alienation. On the contrary, the distancing that he achieves for critical purposes is reinforced, and not undermined, by the creation of conventional empathy for particular individuals, from whom the audience's sympathies are subsequently estranged by shock tactics of one kind or another. The depth and quality of the spectator's emotional attachment to a particular stage creation necessarily conditions the impact of the eventual alienation. If the character is initially well liked the disillusionment will be the more unexpected and painful. For one thing, the *volte-face* is a blow to the spectator's self-esteem and belief in his or her own judgement. The shock may thus produce a more critical scrutiny of the audience's values and judgements, fresh recognition of the unpredictability of human nature, and of the uncertain conditions of life.

III

There may be doubt as to the degree of O'Casey's awareness of his intentions and techniques in writing *The Plough* and *The Tassie*—as there may be of any artist in the act of creation—but his letter to W. B. Yeats on the subject of *The Tassie* stressed the deliberate control of characterisation. One thinks of that passage where he spoke of the (obviously conscious) diminution of character in each of the plays that followed *Juno and the Paycock*:

> I'm afraid I can't make my mind mix with the sense of importance you give to "a dominating character." God forgive me, but it does sound as if you peeked and pined for a hero in the play. Now is a dominating character more important than a play, or a play more important than a dominating character? In *The Silver Tassie* you have a unique work that dominates all the characters

in the play. I remember talking to Lady Gregory about *The Plough*
before it was produced, and I remember her saying that *The Plough*
mightn't be so successful as *Juno*, because there wasn't in the play
a character so dominating and all-pervading as "Juno," yet *The
Plough* is a better work than *Juno*, and, in my opinion, . . . *The
Tassie*, because of, or in spite of, the lack of a dominating character,
is a greater work than *The Plough*.

I do not think there is any doubt that, after *Juno*, O'Casey consciously
toned down his characters in order to avoid creating personalities quite so
dominant as Seumas Shields or Jack Boyle. There were probably various
reasons for him to do this, one of the most important being that Dublin
audiences and critics had so much revelled in the personal idiosyncracies of
these figures that they had often ignored the social and moral criticism
implicit in the plays, criticism that was primarily directed at the irresponsible
fantasies and hypocritical values of such characters. Even in *Juno*, indeed,
there is an attempt in the last act to tone down the more attractive qualities
in Boyle and to expose quite unambiguously the selfish and vicious traits in
his nature. As with Falstaff, critics have been only too willing to take Jack
Boyle at his own estimate and to regard the character as first encountered
in the play to be the only reality. Actors in both roles, moreover, often play
up the genial humour and mitigate savage characteristics in them. Saros
Cowasjee writes in *Sean O'Casey: The Man behind the Plays* that "Captain Boyle
remains so irresistibly comic that we often forget to pity Juno and Mary."
This is certainly not true in the third act, though it may have been so earlier.
Even a critic as well-balanced as David Krause can say sentimentally:

> The Captain remains the "struttin' paycock" in his glorious de-
> terioration; even in his drunken raving he remains a magnificently
> grotesque anti-hero. Juno must reject him, yet we can forgive
> him, for he maintains his falstaffian spirit to the end.

He remains a "grotesque anti-hero," to be sure, but there is nothing glorious
or magnificent or falstaffian about him at the end. On the contrary, he is in
turn maudlin and vicious, self-pitying and vindictive. The really savage attack
on his pregnant daughter is meant to sicken us; the scene should be performed
with no redeeming features whatsoever. Moreover, earlier more attractive
qualities in his character appear in a debased form in the final act. His humour
lacks its former bite and exuberance, deadened as it is by the whining self-
pity that increasingly engrosses him; what's more, his earlier resourcefulness
appears to desert him and "friends" and neighbours like Joxer, Mrs. Madigan,
and Nugent—formerly dominated and exploited by him—take advantage of

its decline. The rich idiomatic language that characterised his speech in the first two acts disintegrates until it becomes broken phrases while the imaginative fantasy of "the deep sea sailor" of act 1 becomes drunken babble about the Easter Rising at the end of the play. As Boyle's personality wilts in the face of the misfortunes that strike the Boyle family, his wife's character progressively gains in stature: the contrast naturally emphasises Boyle's deterioration even more markedly. Though the technique of gradual self-exposure is subtly practised in *Juno and the Paycock*, the process is taken further in later dramas where the malignancy of the villains and the dangerous effects of antisocial behavior by the wastrels are presented in more overtly critical ways.

It is noticeable, too, that in the plays that immediately followed *Juno* no one character is allowed to disturb or disrupt the overall dramatic balance. In *The Plough* both Bessie Burgess and Fluther Good, and in *The Tassie* Harry Heegan, are potentially dominating characters, but they are carefully controlled and their personalities either subdued or subsumed within the larger dramatic patterns of the action whenever it looks as though their undue prominence might undermine the drama as a whole. In other words, characterisation is subordinate to theme, though individual and even idiosyncratic portraits are still memorable in *The Tassie* and *Within the Gates*, while *The Plough* presents a diverse group of dramatic figures. *Group* is the operative word, of course, in each of these works. Increasingly, we see in them the individual forced to conform to a set pattern of behaviour, or occupied in a group or mass activity which drastically reduces his or her individuality. Huge forces in contemporary society, in peace as in war, dwarf the individual; increasing mechanisation in social organisation and greater political conformity are other aspects of modern life reflected in O'Casey's drama. In each case, the process is realised theatrically by various devices of stylization. O'Casey's earlier method of characterisation was thus modified in response to a drastic enlargement of theme: the change accompanied an increasing emphasis on formal arrangement in settings and other theatrical devices aimed at presenting his vision of society in a more objective manner.

This conclusion may appear self-evident, yet, though several critics have recognised some such process at work, few have tried to come to terms with the playwright's intentions and practice in this respect. To my knowledge, only Vincent de Baun has attempted to describe this facet of the author's stagecraft, though he does not trace the technique in action in any detail, and his definition has been strongly criticised by Saros Cowasjee. De Baun's main contention (which is italicised in the following quotation) seems valid from any point of view, however, and may be abundantly illustrated from a close analysis of the text:

A study of the characters in the play suggests none is a truly dominating personality, except, perhaps, Bessie Burgess. . . . It certainly could not be said that any of the characters in *The Plough and the Stars* is "unreal." The points being made here are that *although each character is an individual, he is still made subservient to the author's purpose in the creation of a total effect*—i.e., the author's interpreted and shaped "facts"—so that *we must therefore view the play as a total work of art where no single character can legitimately draw our attention from the playwright's tragic purpose*. To be sure, O'Casey has not created a tragedy in the classical sense; he has simply created an ordinary group of people whom we see trapped by circumstance. But he has been careful not to distract our attention from the group by the presence of a single dominating individual. It is this "levelness" of characterization which indicates a part of his first leaning toward expressionism.

Unfortunately, in the article itself de Baun goes only halfway towards an understanding of the playwright's new methods. To me, one of the most impressive formal achievements in *The Plough* is to be found not so much in the subordination of characterisation to thematic design—though this is the final effect of the technique, of course—as in the superb control that is exercised in modulating the rise and fall, attraction and alienation of character in the course of the drama. Despite the deliberate diminution of character and the author's concern to see that no single figure is allowed to distract attention from the total effect, it is not true to say that there is no "truly dominating character" or that there is a uniformity of portrayal. De Baun's "levelness of characterisation" gives the impression that dramatic tension is drained from the play, leaving it colourless, restrained, even, perhaps, monotonous. Instead, individual figures come to the fore in the course of the narrative, appear to be about to monopolise the action, but are then firmly distanced before they can disrupt the balance of the whole. As we shall see, this method is particularly marked in the case of Fluther Good and Bessie Burgess. Far from creating uniformity, the technique makes for a fluctuating and unpredictable portrait-gallery which maintains the intrinsic pyschological interest and individual energy afforded by good naturalist "character drama," yet subjects the spectators to the shocks and surprises of unexpected developments in plot and in character, while keeping individual characterisation strictly subordinate to the overall dramatic design.

At certain moments in the action different people are outstanding. In the first act, for instance, Nora is in complete command of the short tea-scene; she dictates the speed and progress of the action and "bosses" all the men on stage. In the fourth act, Bessie is conspicuous for much of the time, and may be said to command most attention, though it is clear that the overall impression by this time in the drama is of the communal rather than the individual disaster. At other points in the action one or more figures— it might be two, or groups of pairs, as in the superb quarrel scenes in the second and third acts—temporarily take the initiative or dominate the scene and the other people on the stage. In every case, such ascendancy is short-lived. The important aspect, technically, is O'Casey's success in engaging the audience's interest in, and (where necessary) sympathy for individual characters at particular moments in the action, and his ability afterwards in changing or distancing these feelings, in response to the requirements of the theme. Conversely, his operation of what one might call the reverse-alienation technique is equally effective, in making us see—at unexpected moments of revelation—creative and positive human qualities in people who had earlier been dismissed as seemingly worthless or good-for-nothing characters. Our expectations are turned upside down and we are consequently forced to reconsider our values and judgements.

O'Casey is sceptical of the personal and political values of the Easter Week "insurgents" in *The Plough*. But it is not only the Platform Orator, Clitheroe, and those characters who participate actively in the political struggle who are distanced critically in the course of the action. We are deliberately restrained from complete empathy with *any* of the characters in the drama. Important characters are omitted for entire acts: Nora Clitheroe, for instance, does not appear at all in act 2, although the preceding act revolved about her and built up the story of her personal dilemma. Jack Clitheroe, who seemed to be the potential hero of the play in the first act, only appears for a few seconds in act 2 (and then without individuality and for only four lines of dialogue); he has one short though important scene in act 3, but is absent altogether from the last act. We are not allowed, moreover, to dwell overlong on any one of the personal tragedies, being moved rapidly from one situation to another in the last two acts: from Mollser to Nora; from her to Langon and back to Nora; we return to Mollser with news of her death, followed by Nora's madness, the report of Jack's death in action, the shooting of Bessie, and, finally, the torment of a whole city in flames.

IV

In *The Plough*, as in *The Silver Tassie*, it is the crushing and dehumanizing experience of war that, however temporarily, compels people into group attitudes and group responses, dominated by the conformity bred of fear or military discipline or both. In *Within the Gates* the economic depression of the 1930s is responsible for the involuntary mobilization of an army of the Down-and-Out, whose individuality has been completely destroyed in the struggle for physical survival. The mass subjugation of personality is realised most comprehensively in the second act of *The Tassie*, of course, where hitherto lively and free-wheeling characters like Harry and Teddy are absorbed into the automaton ranks of fatigued soldiers in the rest camp near the front line. The same process is seen in *The Plough*, though in a minor key. Jack Clitheroe, who was depicted as a distinct if weak individual in the first act of the play, has altogether lost any sign of a separate identity when he makes a brief appearance in act 2. He and the other two freedom-fighters, Brennan and Langon, have been deeply influenced by the mass emotions of the political meeting. They move and speak as though in a trance, conversing in antiphonal-like responses: "You have a mother, Langon"—"Ireland is greater than a mother"—"You have a wife, Clitheroe"—"Ireland is greater than a wife." In striking contrast to the unpredictable, boisterous, and passionately contentious characterisation realized in act 1 and in the pub scene throughout act 2, the language and actions of the three men are stylized and rigidly controlled—"they have been mesmerized by the fervency of the speeches," as a stage direction indicates. The complete unanimity of their aims and ideals also stands out in sharp and mechanical relief against the clamorous dissensions (on every subject) of all the other characters in the action. Like the British soldiers in *The Tassie*, the three men are represented, temporarily, as an unthinking part of a mass movement, subsumed in a corporate experience. Thus, in stylization and incantatory language alike, the short scene with the three "rebel" soldiers in the public house looks forward to the large-scale expressionism of the second act of *The Tassie*.

A further diminution of personality, as the result of adverse circumstances, is realised in the last act of *The Plough* without using stylization. Although the ebullient nature of Fluther is never wholly suppressed, nor the bickerings of the Covey and Uncle Peter altogether stopped, they are nonetheless much subdued by, first of all, the presence of the sick Nora sleeping in the next room, and, later, by the armed invasion of the Tommies, who herd the men together as prisoners and lead them away. By subduing the hitherto irrepressible nonconformity of the tenement menfolk in this way, O'Casey is enabled to convey the overall tragic situation without irrelevant distractions; or, to put it another way, the tragic situation itself creates a subdued scene of collective suffering. It is not without significance that the playwright, who had allowed leading characters the last words in each of his earlier plays (Davoren and Shields in *The Shadow* and Joxer and

Boyle in *Juno*), is careful to remove all the important characters from the concluding scenes of *The Plough* and *The Tassie*. The menfolk are forcibly removed in the former play, and the death of Bessie and the departure of Nora and Jinnie Gogan leave the curtain scene to two minor figures. In like manner, in *The Tassie*, Harry and Teddy leave the dance hall, accompanied by their relatives, just before the end of the play, and it is left to two relatively insignificant characters, Simon Norton and Mrs. Foran, to bring the drama to a similarly ironic close. O'Casey's change of technique may have been motivated by ignorant critical interpretations of the first two plays. Attracted by the wayward eccentricities of Shields and Boyle, the final effect of each work on Dublin audiences and reviewers was uncritical laughter rather than horror. Accordingly, the playwright may have resolved to make the tragic irony chillingly unmistakable in his subsequent curtain-scenes.

Alienation performs another important function in addition to broadening the social criticism and realising something in the nature of group drama; it is also able to show more than one side to a given situation, and more than an individual vision of reality. In *The Plough* and *The Tassie*, for instance, the effects of poverty and warfare are depicted in both a personal, subjective manner and an external, objective one, too. Such shifts of viewpoint are achieved by using expressionist and symbolic as well as naturalist techniques, of course, but character alienation contributes a significant part of the effect. In practice, it means that the dramatic figure concerned is placed in a full social context, so that the audience's relationship with the character is accordingly modified. This entails seeing that one's natural predisposition to favour (that is, to pity or even identify oneself with) a human being in adversity or distress is not exploited at the expense of other characters in the play. The audience's fluctuating attitude towards Harry Heegan in the course of *The Tassie* is a case in point; Nora Clitheroe's position in *The Plough* is somewhat similar. We are never wholly unsympathetic to either person, and, at times, we are very close to both Harry and Nora in their mental and physical anguish. Yet at certain significant moments the playwright deliberately prevents us from coming emotionally too near either figure so that we are forced to recognise the priority of other people's needs over theirs. Nora's appalling situation towards the end of act 4, for instance, is suddenly overshadowed by the death of Mrs. Burgess, which takes place in Nora's presence. The fact that the terrified Nora makes no move to help Bessie in her death agonies inevitably (if temporarily) affects the audience's response. Insane as she is, Nora can no longer be held morally responsible for her actions—or inactivity; but the spectators, deeply moved by Bessie's sufferings, which follow hard upon her devoted nursing of Nora, can hardly ignore Nora's presence at such a moment, nor be indifferent to the dying woman's denunciation of her, however unjust that attack may be. One's response must be compounded of conflicting feelings at this point, and—whichever emotion is dominant—it must be acknowledged that the interplay of human relationships and feelings is projected in a complex and challenging manner. Similarly, while never wholly estranging our sympathies from Harry Heegan, O'Casey makes us view him as self-absorbed and impossibly possessive—an understandable result of his physical incapacity, of course—at significant moments during the last two acts of *The Tassie*, when his selfishness threatens the future welfare or happiness of other people like Jessie, Barney, and even Susie. On such occasions, we are distanced from his personal dilemma in order to see it in some kind of perspective with regard to the total situation.

V

It is in his handling of Fluther Good and Bessie Burgess, however, that the playwright shows most clearly his consummate command of stagecraft in *The Plough*. It has been intimated already that they are both potentially dominant figures. At certain moments, each one is heroic in the conventional sense. In act 3 Fluther risks his life to find Nora at the barricades. Bessie faces death in the same act to bring a doctor to the sick woman. In act 4 we see Bessie's great care of and devotion to the mad woman, with whom she had fought earlier in the drama, and we hear of Fluther's courage in making arrangements for Mollser's funeral while heavy fighting continues in the neighbourhood. But at other crucial moments in the action, our sympathies are alienated from both characters. After his heroism early in the third act, for instance, Fluther joins in the looting of the shops; he returns dead drunk and is incapable of helping Nora when she most needs it. Bessie, who, until this moment in the play—and we are almost three quarters of the way through it—has been consistently estranged from the audience's sympathies by her coarse and unpleasant brawling, is the only one in the tenement who will bring a doctor to Nora.

This episode in act 3 is a powerful scene of fluctuating moods and moral judgements. When Fluther enters he is a conquering hero, for all the visual comedy of his appearance. We saw his heroism earlier in the act, and we enjoy his racy language and exuberance:

Bessie *looks at* Nora *lying on the street for a few moments, then, leaving the window, she comes out, runs over to* Nora, *lifts her up in her arms, and carries her swiftly into the house. A short pause, then down the street is heard a wild, drunken yell; it comes nearer, and* Fluther *enters, frenzied, wild-eyed, mad, roaring drunk. In his arms is an earthen half-gallon jar of whiskey; streaming from one of the pockets of his coat is the arm of a new tunic shirt; on his head is a woman's vivid blue hat with gold lacing, all of which he has looted.*

FLUTHER (*singing in a frenzy*): Fluther's a jolly good fella! . . . Fluther's a jolly good fella! Up th' rebels! . . . That nobody can deny! (*He beats on the door*) Get us a mug or a jug, or somethin', some o' yous one o' yous, will yous, before I lay one o' yous out! . . . (*Looking down the street*) Bang an' fire away for all Fluther cares . . . (*Banging at the door*) Come down an' open th' door, some o' yous, one o' yous, will yous, before I lay some o' yous out!

But we soon become aware of the essential selfishness of his attitude, and his irresponsibility when his subsequent yell, "Th' whole city can topple home to hell, for Fluther!," immediately precedes "a scream from Nora, followed by a moan." Oblivious to all about him, however, he continues to sing "furiously" and to kick at the hall-door:

His frantic movements cause him to spill some of the whiskey out of the jar.

FLUTHER: Blast you, Fluther, don't be spillin' the precious liquor! (*He kicks at the door*) Ay, give us a mug or a jug, or somethin', one o' yous, some o' yous, will yous, before I lay one o' yous out!

(*The door suddenly opens, and* Bessie, *coming out, grips him by the collar.*)

BESSIE (*indignantly*): You bowsey, come in ower o' that . . . I'll thrim your thricks o' dhrunken dancin' for you, an' none of us knowin' how soon we'll bump into a world we were never in before!

FLUTHER (*as she is pulling him in*): Ay, th' jar, th' jar, th' jar!

(*A short pause, then again is heard a scream of pain from* Nora. *The door opens and* Mrs. Gogan *and* Bessie *are seen standing at it.*)

BESSIE (*determinedly*): I'll risk it. . . . Give her a little of

Fluther's whiskey. . . . It's th' fright that's brought it on
so soon. . . . Go on back to her, you.

Mrs. Gogan *goes in, and* Bessie *softly closes the door. She is moving
forward, when the sound of some rifle shots, and the tok, tok, tok
of a distant machine-gun bring her to a sudden halt. She hesitates
for a moment, then she tightens her shawl round her, as if it were
a shield, then she firmly and swiftly goes out.*

BESSIE (*as she goes out*): O God, be Thou my help in time o'
trouble. An' shelter me safely in th' shadow of Thy
wings!

CURTAIN

Fluther has been diminished before our eyes, while Bessie's strength of
purpose and courage rise to the occasion magnificently, being thrown into
sharp relief by the comic helplessness of Fluther and the cowardly evasions
of Jinnie Gogan. Bessie is contemptuous of them both, yanks Fluther inside
the house and orders the woman indoors with scarcely concealed disregard:
"Go on back to her, you." She doesn't think of trying to find excuses, but
fixes her mind on what has to be done. Her prayer acts as a fine curtain to
the act, coming as it does as a striking reversal of her usual use of biblical
language, which has earlier served exclusively either for malevolent prophecy
(at the end of act 1) or abuse.

After this episode at the end of act 3 Fluther never regains dominance
(though it should be noted that he is not at all prominent in a large part of
the first act, either, and he is carefully kept out of much of the action in act
3 itself), despite his spirited verbal resistance to the English soldiers in the
final act. By the end of the play Fluther is only one of a group herded into
captivity, unable to alter or influence the course of events in any way. Though
livelier in spirit than the others, he has become part of the mass of helpless,
if not entirely passive human beings affected by the war situation, and he
is soon forgotten, when led offstage by the troops, because the action onstage
is immediately intensified with the entrance of Nora and the subsequent
killing of Bessie. Like the other tenement characters of act 4, Fluther is
overshadowed by the masterful personality of Bessie Burgess, toned down
though this is by O'Casey's deliberate stress on her fatigue throughout the
act, and the subdued speech and actions necessitated by the close presence
of the sleeping Nora. A striking example of Bessie's domination is demonstrated when the card game between Fluther, the Covey, and Peter Flynn
looks as though it is getting out of control The men quarrel noisily, but
Bessie's terse threat, "If I hear a whisper out o' one o' yous again, I'll . . .

gut yous," rapidly subdues them. Once Bessie has gained ascendancy, at
the end of the third act, she maintains it until her death; but her mastery is
achieved without sacrificing theme or diverting attention from the situation
of the tenement folk as a group.

Bessie is herself alienated from the audience's sympathy, though never
from its interest, for the major part of the play. There appears to be nothing
worthwhile about her character and actions in the first half of the drama.
She is merely a drunken virago with a gift for invective. Our first glimpse
of her—and first impressions are important—is when she bursts in upon
Nora and, obviously the worse for drink, makes an unprovoked attack upon
the younger woman:

> As Nora *is opening and shutting* [*the*] *door,* Mrs. Bessie Burgess
> *appears at it. She is a woman of forty, vigorously built. Her face
> is a dogged one, hardened by toil, and a little coarsened by drink.
> She looks scornfully and viciously at* Nora *for a few moments
> before she speaks.*
> BESSIE: Puttin' a new lock on her door . . . afraid her poor
>   neighbours ud break through an' steal.

She speaks louder and louder until she is screaming abuse at Nora:

> Nora *tries to shut* [*the*] *door, but* Bessie *violently shoves it in, and,
> gripping* Nora *by the shoulders, shakes her.*
> BESSIE: You little over-dressed throllope, you, for one pin, I'd
>   paste th' white face o' you!
> NORA (*frightened*): Fluther, Fluther!
> FLUTHER (*running over and breaking the hold of* Bessie *from* Nora):
>   Now, now, Bessie, Bessie, leave poor Mrs. Clitheroe
>   alone; she'd do no one any harm, an' minds no one's
>   business but her own.

The other inhabitants of the tenement know Bessie well and seem to
have little or no respect for her, though we later discover that this is an
erroneous impression. Fluther speaks to her in a calm and gentle manner in
the above scene, but this might not be because he likes or pities her, but
because he thinks she should be humoured when drunk. He says of her to
Mrs. Gogan, when trying to prevent a fight in the pub later:

> Whisht; she's always dangerous an' derogatory when she's well
> oiled. Th' safest way to hindher her from havin' any enjoyment
> out of her spite, is to dip our thoughts into th' fact of her bein'

a female person that has moved out of th' sight of ordinary sensible people.

Mrs. Burgess maintains her pugnacity throughout the first three quarters of the play, and though Nora is her opponent in the first act, Bessie is particularly antagonistic towards Mrs. Gogan in the following two acts. Indeed, the incessant hostility between the pair of slum women parallels the constant bickering of Peter and the Covey.

As the action gathers momentum, Bessie is further alienated from the spectator's sympathies: the "choke th' chicken" sequence in act 3 shows her at her most selfish if dynamic. Taunting the insurgents and their civilian supporters among the tenement people from her attic window from time to time throughout the act—her interjections are carefully selected by the playwright, so that she can act as a critical irritant, and (occasionally) counteract any possible sentimentality evoked by Nora's sufferings—the fruit-vendor is increasingly disliked by the audience as well as by the *dramatis personae* involved in the action. This increase in hostility is occasioned by the worsening position of the "rebels" and of the civilian population. As the war comes closer, Bessie's provocative actions become more intolerable. When all that is known of the fighting is based on gossip and rumours, many of doubtful validity, Bessie's chanting of "Rule, Britannia" has genuinely comic connotations. But her vindictive intervention as the anxious and hysterical Nora is brought in by Fluther evokes a strong reaction from him which almost certainly represents the audience's attitude also:

NORA: My Jack will be killed! . . . He is to be butchered as a sacrifice to th' dead!

BESSIE (*from upper window*): Yous are all nicely shanghaied now! Sorra mend th' lassies that have been kissin' an' cuddlin' their boys into th' sheddin' of blood! . . . Fillin' their minds with fairy tales that had no beginnin' but, please God'll have a bloody quick endin'! . . . Rule, Britannia, Britannia rules th' waves, Britons never, never, never shall be slaves!

FLUTHER (*with a roar up at the window*): Y'ignorant oul' throllop, you!

We are most strongly estranged from Bessie during the episode a little later, when Clitheroe and Brennan enter, helping the wounded Langon to retreat from the firing line. Her jibes at them show both her courage—for they are armed and have already threatened to fire upon a street crowd barring their way—and her insensitivity also, for the men are in trouble, facing heavy odds, while Langon is evidently badly injured. Her shouts and jeers—"Runnin' from th' Tommies . . . choke th' chicken! Runnin' from th' Tommies . . . choke th' chicken!"—act as an effectively jarring counterpoint to the poignant struggle taking place in the street below, with Clitheroe torn between comforting his wife and helping his dying comrade. Bessie's role here, in fact, contributes a further method of alienation, preventing the scene from becoming either too sentimental or heroic. Whatever Clitheroe's decision, wife or duty—and the one chosen is that which could have been depicted in melodramatically chauvinist terms—Bessie's critical commentary ("General Clitheroe'd rather be unlacin' his wife's bodice than standin' at a barricade") will allow romanticising of neither love nor patriotism. And Bessie herself seems least human *immediately* before she enters to pick up Nora—thrown to the ground by Clitheroe—and carry her indoors, to nurse her devotedly. We are flung straight from hating her, into admiring her.

Yet there have been indications earlier, in occasional deft touches, that Bessie is a more complex personality than appears at first sight. Even while slanging the Republicans, at the beginning of the act, a hint of her innate kindness is revealed to the audience, though not to her neighbours on stage. She emerges in the doorway of the tenement house (near which the sick Mollser sits sunning herself), hiding something beneath her shawl; few spectators will notice Bessie's furtive movement as the attention on stage at the moment is directed towards the exhausted Nora, who is being attended to by Mrs. Gogan:

> She is led in by Mrs. Gogan as Bessie comes out with a shawl around her shoulders. She passes by them with her head in the air. When they have gone in, she gives a mug of milk to Mollser silently.

Significantly, Bessie *says* nothing kind or gentle—though she must have made a special point of remembering Mollser, for Bessie's flat is at the top of the tall building—contenting herself with a scornful outburst directed at Fluther and the Covey as she passes by them on her way off stage:

> You an' your Leadhers an' their sham-battle soldiers has landed a body in a nice way, havin' to go an' ferret out a bit o' bread God knows where. . . . Why aren't yous in the G.P.O. if yous are men? It's paler yous are gettin'. . . . A lot o' vipers, that's what th' Irish people is! *She goes out.*

No doubt Mrs. Burgess would hate anyone seeing her give the milk to the poor consumptive child; she deliberately cultivates a rough and belligerent manner, and the girl is the child of her arch-enemy, Mrs. Gogan. But Mollser is undoubtedly neglected, and Bessie obviously has a soft spot for her; it is clear from Mrs. Gogan's revelations in act 4, after Mollser's death, that Bessie's act was not an isolated one. The bereaved mother says to her neighbour:

> Indeed, it's meself that has well chronicled, Mrs. Burgess, all your gentle hurryin's to me little Mollser, when she was alive, bringin' her somethin' to dhrink, or somethin' t'eat, an' never passin' her without liftin' up her heart with a delicate word o' kindness.

As we have seen, once Bessie becomes an acknowledged heroine in her own right at the end of act 3, the audience remains favourably disposed towards her for the duration of the play. There is the real danger that her forceful personality might overshadow the other figures in the final act, however, and care is taken to see that she does not disrupt its delicate tragicomic balance. She is worn out, physically, in act 4, as a result of her care for Nora, and is forced to sit and doze through a large part of the action onstage. Her speech and actions are consequently unusually restrained throughout. This is an effective and credible way of subduing her while retaining the audience's new-found sympathy. Her muted behaviour in act 4—in itself a striking reversal of her role in the first three acts—is skilfully accomplished by the playwright, and is perfectly attuned to the prevailing mood and atmosphere of the scene.

The street fruit-vendor's death brilliantly realises the two conflicting sides of her nature. Generosity and kindness are responsible for her receiving the fatal gunshot wound; she dies cursing Nora and singing a sentimental hymn. She is a fine woman, epitomising some of the major faults and virtues of her class. We neither admire nor despise her indiscriminately, for her heroic stature is enhanced, though never exaggerated, by seeing her character in perspective. In subtle particulars of stagecraft her role in the play is thus subordinated to the total thematic pattern: like *The Tassie*, *The Plough* is, as its author claimed, "a unique work that dominates all the characters in the play." The tragedy is that of the tenement society as a whole, not simply that of two or more individuals in that society, and the dramatist has taken care to emphasise the general suffering as well as the individual anguish. In this analysis we have examined alienation effects with reference only to characterisation. The present line of enquiry could profitably be extended to other aspects of the subject, especially to the ways in which O'Casey

achieves distancing in *The Silver Tassie* by the structural organisation of the
work itself. . . .

VI

While considering the complex nature of Bessie Burgess's various roles,
one further aspect of importance may be noted. This concerns her brief but
extraordinary appearance at the conclusion to act 1. Here, enacting a Cas-
sandra-like role, Bessie is distanced in a manner different from the alienation
realised elsewhere in the drama; she is made anonymous and even scarcely
human, perhaps, though never stepping outside the bounds of possibility
inherent in her character and occupation in the play. In this scene she enters
at a climactic moment in the narrative—the newly pregnant Nora deserted
on her birthday evening by her husband—and what might well have appeared
(for the time being) a trivial domestic incident is, by Bessie's wild and
seemingly "supernatural" intervention, projected as a potentially tragic situation with universal significance. De Baun writes of the incident as one of
the "positive indications of O'Casey's drift from naturalism" in *The Plough;*
his description is excellent, and, indeed, his argument deserves to be taken
further:

> Toward the end of act 1 . . . Bessie makes a drunken entrance.
> In the distance is the fading sound of marching feet, a brass band,
> and soldiers singing "It's a Long Way to Tipperary." Her intox-
> ication has inspired one of her occasional surges of religious fer-
> vor, and she is speaking in tag-lines from Scripture. Her speech
> is weirdly prophetic: "Yous'll not escape from th' arrow that flieth
> be night, or th' sickness that wasteth be day . . . An' ladyship
> an' all, as some o' them may be, they'll be scatthered abroad, like
> th' dust o' th' darkness!" This strange whirl of metaphors, spoken
> in half-light by a dishevelled harridan, is an unusual device in a
> naturalistic play.

It is indeed an unusual formal intrusion in a realistic play, but it would
not be out of place in O'Casey's later work. Bessie Burgess is performing
the function that, in O'Casey's later drama, would be undertaken by a
symbolic character created particularly for that purpose. Toward the end of
Purple Dust, for instance, a mysterious being enters the Tudor manor house
that is the setting of the play to announce the imminent danger that threatens
the house and its inhabitants. The occurrence has symbolic significance, of
course—the winds of change are about to destroy inherited privilege and

material power—and consequently O'Casey utilises an anonymous figure, whose only appearance is in this scene, to point the warning in suitably heightened terms. As in Bessie's speech, the biblical idiom is effectively used, though more formally integrated into the character's rhetoric than in the earlier drama, where the playwright is content to let the vague emotional overtones of the scriptural phrases suffice to create the effect, without shaping them into a distinctly new or personal utterance:

> *The room has darkened; the wind rises; the one light in the room*
> *flickers. The* Postmaster *and* Poges *watch it. Then the*
> Postmaster *turns to go, but halts when a* Figure *of a man is*
> *seen standing at the entrance leading to the hall. He is dressed*
> *from head to foot in gleaming black oilskins, hooded over his*
> *head, just giving a glimpse of a blue mask, all illuminated by the*
> *rays of flickering lightning, so that* The Figure *seems to look*
> *like the spirit of the turbulent waters of the rising river. The*
> Postmaster *goes back, startled, till he is beside* Poges, *and the*
> *two men stand and stare at the ominous* Figure. . . .
>
> BASIL: The river is rising!
> BARNEY: Risin' high!
> CLOYNE: An' will overwhelm us all!
> THE FIGURE (*in a deep voice*): The river has broken her banks and
> is rising high; high enough to come tumbling in on top of
> you. Cattle, sheep, and swine are moaning in the whirling
> flood. Trees of an ancient heritage, that looked down on
> all below them, are torn from the power of the place they
> were born in, and are tossing about in the foaming energy
> of the waters. Those who have lifted their eyes unto the
> hills are firm of foot, for in the hills is safety; but a
> trembling perch in the highest place on the highest house
> shall be the portion of those who dwell in the valleys
> below!
> *The lightning ceases for a moment; the entrance becomes dark and The*
> *Figure disappears.*
>
> (*Purple Dust*, act 3)

One of the household servants—Barney, for instance, who enters immediately after The Figure—could easily have conveyed the message, but O'Casey clearly wanted to project it on a different level from the preceding foolery. For all the farce in *Purple Dust*, the change envisaged is a spiritual one as much as anything else, as the biblical phrasing indicates. Those who

have "lifted their eyes" are the men of vision, of course, and the staging here
is accordingly attuned to a symbolic experience that can be interpreted in
realistic terms and yet (like similar dramatic incidents in, say, *The Tempest*
or *The Winter's Tale*) has at the same time potentially supernatural implications. Obviously, there can be a perfectly rational explanation for the appearance of a man in oilskins and hooded features in such circumstances: he
could be a local civil defence worker, for one thing, called out in an emergency
and warning others in the neighbourhood of the flood danger. Technically,
this scene in *Purple Dust* obviously has a good deal in common with that at
the end of act 1 in *The Plough*, in formal stagecraft as well as in dramatic
intention. It provides a further instance of how *The Plough* looks forward to
the dramatist's later experiments, where he handles with greater freedom
ideas and situations first explored in the early dramas written for the Abbey
Theatre. Development and innovation mark each stage of O'Casey's career
as a dramatist but the continuity throughout is equally remarkable.

KATHARINE WORTH

Music and Dance and the Shaping
of O'Casey's Later Plays

In *Within the Gates* O'Casey made an ambitious attempt to use dance in a more complex way, relating it both to the external world of Hyde Park and the Depression, and to the inner world of the characters' dreams and visions. The first time the Young Woman dances the emphasis is social: she is the "innocent prostitute" defying the public forces of defeatism which are the target of O'Casey's satire in the play. The defeatists range from the Atheist and the Bishop's Sister—in different ways both afraid of life—to the chorus of Down and Outs who represent the defeated unemployed. Saros Cowasjee has suggested that the germ of the play is contained in Toller's poem about the power of dance—"Only in dance do you break your fetters, / Only in dance do you shout with the stars." But O'Casey's intention is more complex, for the chief conflict of the play is a private one, fought between the Dreamer and the Bishop for the soul of the Young Woman. There is no obvious right and wrong here. O'Casey saw the Bishop as "good-natured, well-intentioned, religious and sincere" but nevertheless one whom life had passed by. He can help the Young Woman only at the moment of death, with encouraging talk of Christ and the immortal life of the soul. The Dreamer is the man for the *present;* a Nietzschean character, "symbol of a noble restlessness and discontent . . . of ruthlessness to get near to the things that matter." He too is lacking in full sympathy; all he can do for the Young Woman is urge her not to give in to the pressures of society but dance while she can and live from one crowded hour of glorious life to the next. The Young Woman's

From *The Irish Drama of Europe from Yeats to Beckett.* © 1978 by Katharine Worth. Athlone Press, 1978.

dancing is an embodiment of the Dreamer's creed, and O'Casey indicates the creed's inadequacy by making her first dance bitter and unhappy. She taunts the Bishop—"Faith in God, old purple buttons, faith in God! Be merry, man, for a minute . . ."—and dances to the tune of "Little Brown Jug," accompanied by the two crippled Chair Attendants. That servile and unctuous pair are deeply unsympathetic characters; their grotesque accompaniment—"Sling aht woe, 'ug joy instead, / For we will be a long time dead!"—undermines the value of the dance and emphasises its sense of feverish insecurity.

With the second dance the emphasis tilts towards private, inner experience. The Young Woman, dying of consumption, does as she has sworn she would, dance to the end: "I'll go the last few steps of the way rejoicing; I'll go, go game, and I'll die dancing!" It is still a gesture against demoralising social pessimism, but more important now, it represents an affirmation of spiritual vitality in the girl herself. Now she dances to the song of the Dreamer, as if a deeper vision were being projected in the dance—perhaps that part of his vision which she accepts, as she also accepts part of the Bishop's. We are to perceive some subtle movement of mind here, so O'Casey indicates in his stage direction: the music she dances to is faint "as if the tune was heard only in the minds of the Dreamer and the Young Woman."

This faint music of the interior is heard increasingly in the later plays. I will conclude with a few illustrations of how O'Casey adapts the Yeatsian total theatre technique to the transformations of reality which are his special interest—those changes that come about in solid "real" materials as the mind shapes them to its individual purposes and communicates them to other minds. The fantasies of the "multiple mind" (to use his own phrase) are something he excels in depicting, though in the latest plays he finds increasingly subtle means of modulating from the communal to the private vision.

Red Roses for Me (Olympia, Dublin, March 15, 1943) shows him taking over an old, popular form—in this case the spectacular transformation scene of pantomime and melodrama—and making it, in Yeats's phrase, "subtle and modern." In the third act the idealistic hero, Ayamonn, on the eve of the workers' strike which he is leading, is confronted with a group of the Dublin poor, women flower sellers and unemployed men, dispiritedly lounging on a bridge over the Liffey. The stage direction tells us that the place is known as the Bridge of Vision, and this is the clue to the experience O'Casey aims to involve us in. First he constructs an elaborately coloured picture as a stage image of the "multiple mind." Dull and dark colours predominate, brown parapets, black dresses, drab-coloured baskets and the black figure of Nelson on his red pillar. A touch of contrast comes into the picture when the Rector and the Inspector pass by, the one with a green scarf enlivening his professional black and the other brilliant in blue and silver uniform; the colours are taken up into the metamorphosis which Ayamonn's vision brings about. First the atmosphere is insidiously changed by music; the old man, Brennan, sings to his melodeon in a husky baritone, the mood becomes more emotional and Ayamonn is inspired to declare his prophetic message; "We will that all of us shall live a greater life." The glowing words cause the stage scene literally to glow. The materials remain the same but under the play of coloured light they show their hidden aspect; it is a group of living statues we see now in sumptuous colours, green, bronze and silver. "Something funny musta happened," says one of the loungers, "for, 'clare to God, I never noticed her shinin' that way before." We may laugh, but we are meant to be feeling something of the awe that spreads among the people as they see themselves in a new light, feel a new dignity: "Our city's in th' grip o' God."

It is only this one scene which moves away from the rational, realistic convention, and the break is not total, for the transformation can easily enough be accounted for; the sun has emerged from behind the clouds. But what we actually see when the change begins is something more mysterious than that. The stage is cast into darkness so that only certain objects stand out in startling perspective, and then, most strangely, Ayamonn's head appears "set in a streak of sunlight, looking like the severed head of Dunn-Bo speaking out of the darkness." The Yeatsian image of the severed head has been re-created in a context that is more external and worldly and yet manages to suggest the remoteness and strangeness of the interior, for an unearthly quality comes in when Ayamonn and the youngest flower seller dance a gavotte to music from an unknown source, a flute mysteriously played "by someone, somewhere." As they move round the stage to the pure flute notes, she in a golden pool of light, he in a violet-coloured shadow, the daylight world recedes and we do seem to be looking into a deep of the mind, where the transforming vision originated.

That ethereal music is not heard in *Purple Dust* (People's Theatre, Newcastle-on-Tyne, December 16, 1943), the play from which my next illustration comes. The sounds are more robust here, in tune with the general boisterousness of this satire on the two English businessmen who take over a Tudor mansion in the West of Ireland to indulge their pastoral fantasy. The play shows O'Casey's skill in adapting the technique derived from Yeats to a more extrovert and comically satirical drama: it also shows how visionary "moments" could still be achieved, even in so farcical a context.

Music and dance make a second language in *Purple Dust*: the conflict between the Englishmen and the Irish workmen who resent their attempts to settle in the ancient Irish house, is fought out very largely in musical terms. The note is struck at the start, when Stoke and Poges come dancing on with their Irish mistresses, all dressed in smocks decorated with stylised animals, carrying dainty rakes and hoes garlanded with ribbons and singing a ludicrous pastoral number: "Rural scenes are now our joy: / Farmer's boy, / Milkmaid coy, / Each like a newly-painted toy, / In the bosky countrie!" It is an absurdly self-conscious imitation of the unselfconscious absurdities of Christmas pantomime and of musical comedies like *The Arcadians* with their prettily dressed "rustic" choruses. That takes it a very long way from the prototype folk from which all these rituals ultimately derive: the point is not an academic one for it is the Englishmen's affected cultivation of old traditions that especially enrages the Irishmen. They fight back with genuine folk song and dance, as when, in contrast to the musical comedy "country dance," a true Irish reel is introduced; the leading spirit among the Irish workmen, O'Killigain, encourages Stoke's young Irish mistress to abandon herself in the dance to an air lilted by the workmen standing round; the reel becomes a wild ritual, ending with lines which might have come straight out of *The Cat and the Moon*. "Bow to your partner," says O'Killigain, and when she does so, "Bow, bow to the bards." The ritual is destroyed at that point, for he takes the opportunity to give her "a sharp skelp on the behind"; it is a no-nonsense start to a love affair that in the end takes her from her English lover. The Englishmen are defeated, one might say, by Irish airs. O'Killigain captures Avril's imagination with the lilting strains of songs like "Rory O'More" which represent, as they are presented in the play, the life of true feeling. Stoke and Poges cannot compete, since they find it so hard to distinguish the true from the imitation.

Scenic, musical and sound effects combine to express the absurdity of their pastoral dream. A fantastic soundscape develops, with rural noises coming in on cue with exaggerated insistence. The cock crows, the cuckoo responds and the sequence works up to a surrealistic symphony of birds shrilling, dogs barking, cattle lowing, sheep bleating, pigs grunting and hens cackling. "Damn that cock and cuckoo!" says Poges, giving the game away completely.

The tone is lighthearted, but serious notes sound increasingly in the last act when the house is threatened by flood waters from the rising river. Astonishingly late in so farcical a context, O'Casey then contrives a "moment" of supernatural intensity (whether it could work as he intended is very much a question for the stage designer, as so often in these late plays). A Figure suddenly appears, dressed from head to foot in black oilskins; he has come to warn them that the river has broken its banks, so there is a rational explanation for his presence, but O'Casey's stage direction makes it impossible to take him so prosaically. The scene was to be spectral, an effect he aimed at by darkening the stage and having one flickering light focused on the "gleaming" black oilskins and on the blue mask which is all there is for a face. The Figure, he says, should seem "like the spirit of the turbulent waters of the rising river." It is also as if some inkling of the truth of things had risen up at last in the mind of the more sensitive Englishman, for as the waters tumble into the room and the refrain of the departing Irish, "Far away O!" recedes, Poges is left in totally changed mood, brooding: "My comfort's gone, and my house of pride is straining towards a fall."

The strange apparition provides a Yeatsian moment, highlighted, un-usually for O'Casey, by the use of a full mask. Yeatsian echoes are stronger still in *Oak Leaves and Lavender*, a play which was in part at least a tribute to England at a time of peril in the Second World War; although it has its share of farce and exaggeration (some striking scenic distortions are called for), the sense of historical actuality is much stronger than in *Purple Dust*.

Yet it is in this more time-bound war play that O'Casey takes a further step into the timeless zone of the interior and comes closer than ever to Yeats in doing so. The topical, "real-life" action is entirely enclosed in a ghostly framework. Lighting, music and movement combine to convey a twilight effect closer to the dreamy monotones of the Yeatsian, or even the Maeter-linckian interior style than any one could have imagined O'Casey capable of in the days of *Juno and the Paycock*. In a misty light figures in powdered wigs and "mistily" grey eighteenth-century costumes dance to the faint strains of a minuet into the room where the whole scene is set. All their movements are slow and stiff as if in a dream where it is hard to move at all; the piano accompaniment too is slow and "somewhat staccato, as if the player found it hard to press down the notes": when the dancers speak, their voices are faint and uninflected. Everything is muted and attenuated except for the brilliant colouring and clear bell-like voice of the mysterious being who presides over the dance, the Young Son of Time. He seems a force outside the history in which the modern characters (and perhaps the dancers) are trapped.

A curious impression develops of many possible dimensions of existence. One of the dancers speaks of "the deep silences of where we always are," yet there they are in the room, moving, talking and somehow able to sense the terrible events approaching the modern characters who live there. A sound is heard from the street outside, the tender and musical cry of a girl selling lavender. Where does it originate? We can have no idea: it is not a cry of the "present" time and yet to the dancers of the time gone by it seems equally strange and unfamiliar; "from another world," one of them says. We are forced to wonder whether it comes from some region beyond the veil which we are permitted dimly to perceive at the beginning and end of the "real" action.

None of the flesh-and-blood stage characters perceives the dancers until the final scene when the house has become a factory and its owner, Dame Hatherleigh, has lost her son in the war. Then the bereaved mother, in the sensitivity of her grief, apprehends the presences around her. The stage returns to its misty grey, and the dancers are revealed, grouped in the pattern of the dance as though they had been there all the time. Only the Young Son of Time is missing: Dame Hatherleigh stands where he did, wearing the black and silver (though not the youthful green) of his costume; as if she had been drawn into a space he was keeping for her. In this time of death she seems to become more aware of life. A dancer dwells fearfully on "the wistful look of eternal life" and Dame Hatherleigh reflects aloud, as if answering her: "Only the rottenness and ruin must die. Great things we did and said; things graceful, and things that had a charm, live on to dance before the eyes of men admiring."

She is almost one of the grey figures now: her voice is "toneless" and she sense that "the dancers are very close," though she is still on this side of the threshold. At the end, when she sinks down by the clock as if taking leave of time, she calls, "Wait a moment for me, friends, for I am one of you, and will join you when I find my son." Her voice becomes "a little more wakeful" at this point, an ambiguous stage direction which suggests that the dance may not be a dream but a glimpse into some larger reality to which we are not normally awake. The stage scene affirms this view, for as she falls silent, it comes back to its ghostly life. The dancers move once more through the minuet, the music becoming fuller when they curtsey to one another, and the Lavender Seller's voice is heard musically extolling the sweetness of lavender from a dimension which can never be identified.

This is Yeatsian territory indeed, as O'Casey seems to be reminding us through an important detail of his dance. Like the unhappy pair in *The Dreaming of the Bones*, these dancers, though always together, can never touch each other. For those who know Yeats's play, the echo brings out the greater optimism in O'Casey's view of life in time. For though the dancers' faintness and stiffness suggest a running down (in historical terms, England losing contact with her past greatness), there is communion and continuity too; the graceful dance, with its "fair deeds" endures and can still be appreciated by the dancers' descendants. "Fear not, sweet lady," says one of the Gentleman

Dancers, "Our hands still mingle, though they do not touch. Fear not, sweet lass, for shadows are immortal."

Finally, *Cock-a-Doodle Dandy* (People's Theatre, Newcastle-on-Tyne, December 10, 1949). This was O'Casey's favourite among his own plays and of them all it shows most clearly the impact made by Yeats's dance plays on his imagination.

It is the closest to being an out and out dance play itself, for it is dominated by a dancer, the Cock in his brilliant colours of black, yellow and green, with his crimson crest and flaps and his "look of a cynical jester." He starts the action off by dancing round the stage house to the tune of an offstage accordion, and whenever he appears or his cheeky crow is heard, cracks open up in the façade presented to the world by the respectable bourgeoisie of Nyadnanave, the parish under the puritanical rule of Father Domineer.

For much of the time the stage is the Cock's domain and under his aegis the characters are mesmerised into revealing their minds, both the prudish distortions of view forced on them by their clerical mentor and also their hidden affinities with the Dionysiac visitant. The Cock is a jester, as O'Casey says, who performs practical jokes like a comic turn from a Crazy Show. He tricks them into confusing him with their sacred icon, the "silken glossified tall-hat" which is bandied about, shot at and battered until every scrap of dignity has been removed from it. This comic craziness, however, highlights a more serious kind. Life at Nyadnanave is dark where it need not be: a shadow is cast by the illusions which encourage the incurably ill girl to go uselessly to Lourdes and the priest to exert such tyranny; he causes a man's death and the final rejection of home and family by the young woman whom he tries to bully into conforming to his "crazy" sexual creed. In this darker sphere, the actor—or perhaps it should be dancer—playing the Cock has to suggest a super-subtle force, terrifyingly demonic to some, sympathetic and suggestive to others. He can be led on by the young Messenger on the end of a ribbon, perfectly docile and friendly: "Just a gay bird, that's all. A bit unruly at times, but conthrollable be th' right persons." He can also be uncontrollable, able at will, it seems, to summon up thunder and lightning and to release Father Domineer's parishioners from their inhibitions with a suddenness and violence which is comical but should also seem truly disturbing.

The "interior" effect is not limited to a single moment in this play. The characters struggle to maintain an impervious façade, but under the power of the Cock it is peppered with shots that open up startling views into the haunted abysses of their minds. Scene and sound take on the shapes of their fantasies: Michael has only to imagine his young wife's secret longings and the stage makes them real:

> MICHAEL: Up there in that room (*he points to the window above the porch*) she often dances be herself, but dancin' in her mind with hefty lads, plum'd with youth, an' spurred with looser thoughts of love. (*As he speaks, the sounds of a gentle waltz are heard, played by harp, lute or violin, or by all three, the sounds coming, apparently, from the room whose window is above the porch. Bitterly*) There, d'ye hear that, man! Mockin' me. She'll hurt her soul, if she isn't careful.

Under the lustful but timid eye of Michael and Sailor Mahan the pretty girls sprout horns, the whisky bottle glows a devilish red and the top hat becomes a focal point of wild confusion.

The fantasies explode in a physical outburst which is the most Dionysiac of all O'Casey's dances. It is unsentimental, in fact impersonal (the young women dance frenziedly with older men they have no real affection for) and aggressively sexual—the cock-like crest in the girl's hat rises higher as she dances. The dancing has a manic quality: it should not be possible to dismiss as simply absurd Father Domineer's rage when he interrupts them, shouting: "Stop that devil's dance! . . . Th' empire of Satan's pushin' out its foundations everywhere, an' I find yous dancin', *ubique ululanti cockalorum ochone, ululo!*" We should feel the power of the dance to do just what the priest suspects it will, destroy the desire for prayer or for work, weaken clerical authority, create a revolution.

The Cock who inspires such dances should have acquired by the end of the play, in his own mischievous style, something of the numinous quality of Yeats's Hawk Woman. Like her, he is dumb except for his bird cry, like her he seduces and terrorises with a dance, like her he irresistibly opens up the deep interior. There can be no doubt about the Yeatsian inspiration behind this play. O'Casey himself makes it very clear by having his Messenger introduce the cock with a quotation from *The Dreaming of the Bones:*

> Go on, comrade, lift up th' head an' clap th' wings, black cock, an' crow!

By the slight misquotation which inserts the word "comrade," O'Casey allies himself with the popular movements in the arts which he saw no incongruity in crossing with the Yeatsian strain. *Cock-a-Doodle Dandy*, it seems to me, is a triumphant demonstration of his ability to effect this new synthesis which has proved so attractive to subsequent playwrights, notably John Arden. Of course, like all the plays in the Yeatsian mode which use total theatre techniques to reveal the fantastic processes of the interior, O'Casey's plays depend to a very great degree on the ability not just of performers but of scene designers, musicians and choreographers and they present difficulties which Yeats's do not, being on such a big scale and demanding all the facilities of a proscenium set for the elaborate, artfully lit "pictures" which are a crucial element in the whole effect. So far he has not had much luck in [England] (though in France it is another matter). We cannot really know how these late plays work until we have a chance to see them properly staged: let us hope that in the context of today's theatre there will be new productions sufficiently bold and adventurous to realise the vision which was so far ahead of its time.

BERNICE SCHRANK

"You Needn't Say No More": Language and the Problems of Communication *in* The Shadow of a Gunman

From Boyle's repeated comment in *Juno and the Paycock* that "the whole worl's . . . in a terr . . . ible state o' . . . chassis" to the vision of Armageddon in act 2 of *The Silver Tassie*, O'Casey explores the theme of breakdown. *The Shadow of a Gunman* (1923), O'Casey's first full-length play to be accepted by the Abbey, reflects the dominant motif of the other early plays. Here too O'Casey examines the manifestations of chaos. The "troubles," the slum poverty, the religious hypocrisy, and the exploitative personal relationships contribute to the overwhelming sense of breakdown in this play.

O'Casey's presentation of breakdown in *The Shadow of a Gunman* is, no doubt, important in itself. It also provides the context for his treatment of language. For some critics, the colourful language of O'Casey's characters is one of the most remarkable features of an O'Casey play. But language does not float on the surface of an O'Casey play like a layer of cream in a cup of Irish coffee. The language the characters use in *The Shadow of a Gunman* is an integral part of the play's overall vision of chaos.

The characters have one of two basic problems with language. The majority—Gallogher, Owens, Grigson, Seumas and Donal—indulge in meaningless talk. In contrast to the talkers are Maguire and Minnie who act. But Maguire refuses to communicate his true purposes, while Minnie is unable to express herself in her own words. Maguire and Minnie do not adequately explain their actions and, as a result, these actions are open to some very unflattering interpretations. Maguire, in silently leaving the bombs, seems reckless and morally reprehensible. Minnie's "heroism" in

From *Irish University Review* 8, no. 1 (Spring 1978). © 1978 by *Irish University Review*.

removing the bombs, all the while believing they belong to Donal, can also be seen as an unheroic amalgam of illusion, sentimentality and second-hand patriotism.

From the examples of Gallogher, Owens, Grigson, Seumas and Donal on the one hand and Maguire and Minnie on the other, O'Casey demonstrates that words without deeds and the converse, deeds without appropriate words, are unsatisfactory. Both are essentially negative responses to chaos which give rise to new manifestations of breakdown. Both approaches to language will be examined in turn, beginning with the talkative characters.

II

Gallogher, Owens, Grigson, Seumas and Donal flood the play with a veritable Niagara of words. The politically and economically hostile environment of O'Casey's Dublin is more likely to stimulate talk than to produce constructive action. Should Seumas organize his fellow pedlars into a union of the unskilled and underemployed? Should Owens and Grigson really take sides and quite possibly get themselves killed? The point is that the kinds of actions which poverty and political turmoil suggest to the activist or social reformer—commitment and militancy—are unattractive or dangerous and are never seriously considered by these characters. All Gallogher, Owens, Grigson, Seumas and Donal have, then, is talk and they talk unceasingly to  insulate themselves from a destructive reality. By allowing them to project pseudoselves of heroism and brilliance, their talk relieves their sense of fear and their feelings of impotence. Unfortunately it also paralyses them. More than just insulating them, their talk, idiosyncratic, incoherent and egotistical, isolates them from meaningful communication with each other and from any hope of collective action. Thus the various distortions of normal speech that Gallogher and the others demonstrate, while superficially comic, are ultimately destructive because they are not only a response to, but a perpetuation of, the overall chaos.

Gallogher's ineffectual talk characterises the man and his situation as he is overtaken by the effects of breakdown. The unpleasant truth is that he is economically, politically and verbally impotent. In seeking help from the IRA, Gallogher shows how desperate life in Dublin's tenements can be and how distant that life is from the official channels of law enforcement. In requesting Donal's intervention, Gallogher illustrates his own incapacity to act. The situation is in fact doubly ironic because, by going to Donal who is himself unable to act, Gallogher demonstrates still further incompetence. Gallogher's utter powerlessness is summed up in his manner of lodging the complaint. Gallogher presumably initiates it, but he does not use his own words when he presents it. At first, a parrot-like repetition of Mrs Henderson's comments is the best he can muster. When he breaks free of her linguistic embrace, however, he does not discover his own voice. He proceeds to read his jargon-laden letter which strives for absolute precision through a dense array of misused legalisms and which achieves only bombastic incoherence. Finally, although his parting words to Donal are clearly unrehearsed, they do not so much resemble spontaneous discourse as badly studied affectation. On behalf of himself and his wife, Mr Gallogher thanks Donal for his "benevolent goodness in interferin' in the matter specified, particularated an' expanded upon in the letter, mandamus or schedule, as the case may be." This hodge-podge of jargon, malapropism and redundancy is Gallogher's unsuccessful attempt to create a super-self by manipulating language. He tries to disguise his powerlessness in pomposity, but the only people he takes in are himself and Mrs Henderson. To everyone else, what he says is so patently a pose that it only emphasizes his own impotence. Gallogher's fate is to be forever seeking the attributes of power in language because he cannot alter the basic powerlessness in fact.

Gallogher's verbal distortions are harmless when compared with those of Tommy Owens and Dolphie Grigson. The discrepancy between what these two say and what they mean is so great that their speech comprises a case study in the verbal art of noncommunication. Tommy's first words set the pattern of verbal perversion which will characterise his and Dolphie's entire performance. As Tommy enters in act 1, he observes Donal and Minnie kissing. Yet he insists that he has seen "nothin'—honest—thought you was learnin' to typewrite—Mr. Davoren teachin' you. I seen nothin' else—s'help me God." Now Tommy knows perfectly well that Donal and Minnie are not "typewriting," but he deliberately lies in order to curry favour with Donal, the presumed gunman on the run. If, in the process, Tommy converts Donal and Minnie's genuine display of affection into a sordid and dirty secret, trust Tommy not to be unduly concerned. Tommy's disjointed syntax is, moreover, the ideal medium for his perverted comments. By consistently avoiding connectives in his speech, he can jump from "typewriting" to self-praise to patriotic effusiveness without the slightest nod to the demands of logic and coherence. Furthermore, by suppressing the logical and verbal links, Tommy makes his speech resemble a series of explosions which suggest to the ear what has been plain to the mind, that political disorder and verbal dislocations are related.

For the most part, however, Tommy and Dolphie are not casual liars. Their lies are usually part of a calculated plan of self-promotion. As long as

it is cheap and fashionable to be patriots, Tommy Owens and Adolphus
Grigson swell with national pride, shout patriotic slogans and fill the stage
with patriotic songs. Their heroic posturing is based on the odds that their
rhetoric will never be tested by unpleasant facts. Thus, Tommy goes out of
his way to establish his patriotic credentials. He intentionally refuses to
understand Donal's straightforward statement that he "has no connection
with the politics of the day." Instead, Tommy chooses to hear in Davoren's
disclaimer a verbal code which confirms Tommy's fantasy that Donal is
indeed a gunman on the run.

> TOMMY: You needn't say no more—a nod's as good as a wink
>   to a blind horse—you've no meddlin' or makin' with it,
>   good, bad, or indifferent, pro nor con; I know it an'
>   Minnie knows it—give me your hand.
> > (*He catches Davoren's hand*).
> Two firm hands clasped together will all the power outbrave of
>   the heartless English tyrant, the Saxon coward an' knave.
>   That's Tommy Owens' hand, Mr. Davoren, the hand of a
>   man, a man—Mr. Shields knows me well.
> > (*He breaks into song*).
> High upon the gallows tree stood the noble-hearted three,
> By the vengeful tyrant stricken in their bloom;
> But they met him face to face with the spirit of their race,
> And they went with souls undaunted to their doom!
> MINNIE (*in an effort to quell his fervour*): Tommy Owens, for
> goodness' sake . . .
> TOMMY (*overwhelming her with a shout*):
> God save Ireland ses the hayros, God save Ireland ses we
> all,
> Whether on the scaffold high or the battle-field we die,
> Oh, what matter when for Ayryinn dear we fall!
> (*Tearfully*) Mr. Davoren, I'd die for Ireland.

Tommy uses language here not to communicate sincerely held beliefs, but
to stage an act in which a heroic Tommy Owens plays the lead. Tommy's
metamorphosis from slum dweller to sentimental star can be traced in the
syntax. As the disconnected clauses typical of the real Tommy Owens become complex and inverted rhetoric, a platform hero is hatched. Fortunately,
the verbiage becomes so overwrought that Tommy cannot keep it going
indefinitely. He soon collapses into the more natural and disconnected, "Mr.
Shields knows me well," and for a second the real Tommy is back. But the

illusory Tommy regains control of stage centre by bursting into song. From the moment Tommy grasps Donal's hand until he ends the song, he creates a verbal routine in which to project a bogus identity many times removed from his real self.

What Tommy does to language in act 1, Grigson perpetuates in act 2. Like Tommy, but even more frequently, he refers to himself in the third person, the unmistakeable sign for the *poseur* infatuated with the role he is playing. And like Tommy, Grigson fancies himself a hero, "Dolphus Grigson's afraid of nothin' creepin' or walkin'," and a patriot. Although he is an Orangeman and drinks to "King William, to the battle av the Boyne . . . an' to The Orange Lily O," he assures Donal, the supposed Republican gunman, of his unswerving loyalty in a burst of confused, intoxicated effusiveness. Grigson's comments here are as short on logical connections and inner consistency as Tommy's are. The syntactic disorder gives the same boost to Grigson's need for self-advertisement, to his penchant for rhetorical flights and to his love of heroic poses that it gives to Tommy Owens's very similar reflexes. For both Tommy and Dolphie, language is a plastic medium that can be moulded to the shapes of their egos and their illusions without the slightest regard for the demands of logic, grammar or reality.

Yet reality finds them out during the raid. When the Black and Tans put pressure on their patriotic sentiments, Tommy and Dolphie collapse into terrified submission. Both the easy bombast and the cringing about-faces are the responses of politically uncommitted characters caught in the middle of warring political factions and overcome with a sense of their own helplessness. Tommy and Dolphie create verbal smokescreens because no other action seems possible and their boasts and songs give them a false but needed sense of security.

The overriding sense of breakdown which encourages Owens and Grigson to develop their own private and idiosyncratic language, moreover, fosters still further breakdown. Their cowardice is a weakness; their reckless misuse of language and their wholesale illusion-mongering are much more serious matters because they intentionally cater to a tenement audience which is already prone to accept illusion for reality. It is understandable that Owens and Grigson resist going to the barricades themselves. It becomes morally damaging when, in glorifying the barricades, they help create the emotional climate that sends Minnie in their place. The talk of Owen and Grigson is not the harmless self-indulgence that Gallogher displays. In itself and, more importantly, in its consequences, it illustrates a very destructive form of breakdown.

Seumas Shields also distorts language. But unlike Tommy and Dolphie who use verbiage mainly to inflate their egos and unlike Gallogher who uses jargon as a defense against his own impotence, Seumas's rhetoric is sometimes intentionally anti-rhetorical. Frequently an ironist of penetration in dealing with others (he is as blind as everyone else in the play to his own failures), Seumas can deflate verbal pretensions with well-turned barbs of his own. His comment on Nationalist propaganda, "I draw the line when I hear the gunmen blowin' about dyin' for the people, when it's the people that are dyin' for the gunmen," is an effective putdown couched in nicely balanced clauses. He undercuts the romanticism of Donal's poetry with equal ease by reminding Donal of the realities of proletarian life.

But although Seumas understands and criticizes the rhetorical affectations of others, he has problems with language himself. His verbal awareness, subtler than Tommy's, Gallogher's or Grigson's, is nevertheless partial and flawed. Through his facile wordiness, which in moments of crisis degenerates into a nervous stutter, he too is caught in the Babel of tongues.

Side by side with his sensible observations about propaganda and poetry, Seumas has long-winded, bad-tempered and know-nothing opinions on religion, society and personality. In act 1, many of these opinions take the form of grandiose pronouncements that are, on closer examination, nothing more than glib generalisations. Seumas uses this bloated rhetoric to work off tension that might better be vented in action. Thus when Maguire is late for his appointment in act 1, Seumas relieves his annoyance by denouncing the entire population of Ireland instead of going off to peddle on his own. "No wonder this unfortunate country is as it is," he complains, ironically providing a good example in his procrastinating speech of the laziness he rails against. Again when the landlord threatens to evict Seumas, Seumas tries to dissolve the problem in words. Twice Donal asks Seumas what he intends to do and, although Seumas can offer no plan of action, he neither exits quickly as he promises, nor remains silent.

> DAVOREN: What are we going to do with these notices to quit?
> SEUMAS: Oh, shove them up on the mantelpiece behind one of
> the statues.
> DAVOREN: Oh, I mean what action shall we take?
> SEUMAS: I haven't time to stop now.

At this point, Seumas ought to rush for the door. He claims he has no time to deal with the matter at hand, yet he stays to denounce the landlord, to wish him and his tenement ill (which is enormously self-destructive in that it is Seumas's room that will be destroyed as Mulligan's "rookery"), and to sing a song, ending with the self-pitying largeness of "Oh, Kathleen ni Houlihan, your way's a thorny way." Then, and only then, does he actually leave. Now this generalisation, like the previous one about "this unfortunate country," is as irrelevant as it is comforting. Since neither points to specific and remediable problems, even though these problems exist, neither requires any action. The generalisations are, at least in act 1, agents of paralysis.

In act 2, Seumas's pronouncements seem on the whole more appropriate to the situation than they do in act 1. When he talks of Ireland as a "hopeless" country "gone mad," he acknowledges the political chaos that has overtaken it. But his pronouncements do not prepare him for the reality of chaos; quite the reverse. They incapacitate him, thus reproducing his situation in act 1. As he and Donal hear the Black and Tans approaching and simultaneously discover the bag of bombs, Seumas becomes terrified. He expresses his fear by repeating empty phrases: "Did I know he was a gunman; did I know he was a gunman, did I know he was a gunman. Did . . . Just a moment . . . Just a moment . . . Just a moment." It is as if Seumas were trapped in a circle of words. Clearly, wallowing in generalisations, even accurate generalisations, leaves Seumas verbally and mentally unfit to deal with the raid. But he almost always talks with little point, he cannot, in moments of crisis, get beyond his habitual verbal distortion and come to terms with the specific matter at hand. Worse, at these moments the verbal distortions intensify and become an overt stutter: repetitious and unmeaning noise which has ceased to even sound like real speech. Unable to improvise or verbalise any solution himself, he compounds the chaos by allowing Minnie to carry off the bombs.

Seumas is all talk until the raid; then ("Just a moment . . . Just a moment") language utterly fails him. His fate, like Gallogher's, Owens's and Grigson's, is to be imprisoned in compulsive noncommunication. They all share the same basic problem with language: they love empty, endless and ultimately destructive talk.

III

Donal's more skilled use of language ought to offer a positive counter-weight to the distortions of Gallogher, Owens, Grigson and Seumas. Ostensibly, Donal is a craftsman in words, the poet in residence. Both acts open with examples of Donal's poetic skills. The very first lines of the play are Donal's:

> Or when sweet Summer's ardent arms outspread,
> Entwined with flowers,
> Enfold us, like two lovers newly wed,
> Thro' ravish'd hours—
> Then sorrow, woe and pain lose all their powers,
> For each is dead, and life is only ours.

As poetry, these lines invite and justify Seumas's parody. They are imitation Romantic and badly done at that. The rhyme of "hours" and "ours" depends entirely on the eye. It is quite likely that the phrase "only ours" will be heard as "only hours," an unintended, if subconsciously appropriate, word-play. Donal's lines at the beginning of act 2 are more competent than those in act 1, but they too are highly imitative, showing the influence of Shelley's *Epipsychidion*, specifically the lines on "the cold chaste moon, The Queen of Heaven's bright isles" which Donal quotes just before he composes his own lines on the moon. But for all Donal's growing poetic competence, his jux-tapositioning of Shelley's lines with his own can only call attention to his amateurishness.

In the same vein, Donal's habit of alluding to major literary figures— to Shakespeare and to Milton as well as to Shelley—provides another bench-mark for judging Donal's poetic achievement. If Donal's poetry appears flimsy and imitative in its own right, the literary companionship of Shake-speare, Milton and Shelley can only diminish it further. Now the last thing the world of *The Shadow of a Gunman* needs, populated as it is by so many other windbags, is a second-rate, secondhand versifier.

Donal's persistence in spite of his limited inspiration and Seumas's acute criticism suggest that poetry serves very intense personal (and nonpoetic) needs for him. In fact, Donal's dedication to the Muse is an attempt to escape from the chaos that surrounds him. Donal is in terrified verbal flight from oppressive conditions. The operative word is "verbal" because Donal is physically inert. As the other characters pass across the stage, Donal tends, in striking contrast, to remain standing or sitting in place. Donal's poetry reflects the inertia of the poet. It makes nothing happen because it, like Donal, evades reality. Donal passively hides from life in Seumas's room; Donal's poetry ignores the existence of Seumas's chaotic room by projecting a fantasy world of perpetual summer.

And it is not merely the sordid tenement room from which Donal is trying to escape. Through poetry, Donal hopes to retreat from the totality of life. The last line of his verse in act 2 revealingly states that "all beautiful and happiest things are dead." By itself, that line suggests that Donal is at once horrified and fascinated by death. But there is other, perhaps more convincing, evidence. As Donal is finishing his rhyme in act 1, *"a woman's figure appears at the window and taps loudly on one of the panes; at the same moment there is a loud knocking at the door."* The room is besieged by voices at windows and door trying to awaken Seumas and simultaneously calling Davoren back from his dream world where "life is only ours," to the real world where "life is only hours." Donal perceives these invitations to life as an irritation and a threat. Such interruptions are sure signs to Donal that his attempts to escape from life are doomed to fail and that he is caught in the inevitable pattern of human decline. The unintentional Freudian play on "hours" captures Donal's flagging sense of life, his fear of growing old, and the degree to which his poetry, such as it is, is being made to pander to his middle-aged insecurities.

Donal's poetry certainly demonstrates a sensitivity to some of the possibilities of language. But insofar as his poetry expresses his fear of life and creates a fantasy world of "summer" to redeem the impossible conditions of poverty and undeclared war, Donal's poetry does not really set him apart from the other rhetoricians. It is as empty as Gallogher's legal jargon, Owens's and Grigson's patriotism, and Seumas's stutter.

Moreover, Donal's use of poetic language distorts his use of everyday speech. Donal tries to strike the same high tone here that he attempts in poetry. By introducing literary allusions, balance, poetry and a highfalutin word choice into ordinary discourse, Donal again tries to transform his sordid environment through words. Occasionally, Donal gets out a powerful sentence. For instance, when Seumas complains that nobody has bothered to wake him on time, Donal explodes: "Why, man, they've been thundering at the door and hammering at the window for the past two hours, till the house shook to its very foundations, but you took less notice of the infernal din than I would take of the strumming of a grasshopper." The grasshopper image, the internal rhythm and the logical relationship of the parts are all used to good effect. But Donal is also capable of the rhetorical pretentiousness of the following remark to Seumas and Mulligan, the landlord: "For Goodness' sake, bring the man in, and don't be discussing the situation like a pair of primitive troglodytes." Here the image is "literary" and weak.

Unfortunately, it is this weak literary style in Donal's speech that predominates. Speaking to Donal, Minnie praises Tommy Owens's melodeon playing. Donal cannot let things go at that. He comments that Tommy is "a gifted son of Orpheus." His success at communicating through that classical reference can be gauged by Minnie's response: "You've said it, Mr. Davoren: the son of poor oul' Battie Owens, a weeshy, dawny, bit of a man that was never sober an' was always talkin' politics." Donal might just as well be talking to himself for all the communicating he has done. But Minnie's lack of comprehension perversely stimulates more verbal fireworks. Donal goes on to call weeds "wild flowers," "wild violets," "*Arum maculatum*," "Wake Robin" and "Celadines." Minnie does not understand this gush any better than the reference to Orpheus. Clearly Donal's verbal affectations frustrate communication and isolate him in language. But like Gallogher,

Grigson, Owens, and Seumas, Donal enjoys misusing language for maximum display. No sooner has Donal finished naming the weeds than he bursts into poetry in much the same way that Tommy and Grigson burst into song.

> DAVOREN (*He quotes*):
>   One day, when Morn's half-open'd eyes
>   Were bright with Spring sunshine—
>   My hand was clasp'd in yours, dear love,
>   And yours was clasp'd in mine—
>   We bow'd as worshippers before
>   The Golden Celandine.
> MINNIE: Oh, aren't they lovely, an' isn't the poem lovely too! I wonder, now, who she was.
> DAVOREN (*puzzled*): She, who?
> MINNIE: Why, the . . . (*roguishly*) Oh, be the way you don't know.
> DAVOREN: Know? I'm sure I don't know.
> MINNIE: It doesn't matter, anyhow—that's your own business; I suppose I don't know her.
> DAVOREN: Know her—know whom?
> MINNIE (*shyly*): Her whose hand was clasped in yours, an' yours was clasped in hers.
> DAVOREN: Oh, that—that was simply a poem I quoted about the Celandine, that might apply to any girl—to you, for instance.

Donal's word games turn language into a vehicle for confusion, not a method of communication.

Clearly, Donal's talk leaves something to be desired. Inasmuch as Donal does nothing but talk and recite poetry, he lacks the habit of acting decisively. As long as no action is called for, Donal's rhetorical displays and romantic poetry seem harmless. But the Black and Tan raid is the same moment of truth for Donal that it is for Grigson, Owens and Seumas. Donal finds that he must act and cannot. His verbal escapism isolates him from reality, renders him impotent and forces Minnie to act for him. She takes the bag of bombs. Later, Donal blames himself for Minnie's death, calling himself a "poet and poltroon." But the relationship between Donal as poet and Donal as poltroon is never as clear to Donal as it should be to the audience: Donal is a poltroon because he is not the right kind of poet. Unlike his oft-quoted model Shelley who related poetry to political action in his life and in such works as *Pro-*

metheus Unbound (a poem, ironically, never far from Donal's lips), Donal remains a sterile and self-absorbed manipulator of language.

It would thus be wrong to think that Donal's recognition of his responsibility in Minnie's death changes him. In death, Minnie is still grist for Donal's word-mill. The first news of Minnie's death forces Donal to some measure of self-knowledge as he tells Seumas that the two of them precipitated the tragic event by their inaction.

> DAVOREN: Do you realize that she has been shot to save us?
> SEUMAS: Is it my fault; am I to blame?
> DAVOREN: It is your fault and mine, both; oh, we're a pair of
> dastardly cowards to have let her do what she did.

But Donal's recognition of responsibility does not linger long. His final words are a return to the *status quo ante*, a triumph of rhetoric over reality. Minnie's memory and Donal's sense of complicity both fade as Donal takes stage centre for a final thrust of words.

> Ah me, alas! Pain, pain, pain, ever, for ever! It's terrible to think
> that little Minnie is dead, but it's still more terrible to think that
> Davoren and Shields are alive! Oh, Donal Davoren, shame is
> your portion now till the silver cord is loosened and the golden
> bowl be broken. Oh, Davoren, Donal Davoren, poet and pol-
> troon, poltroon and poet.

Not only are the phrases more measured and poetic here than they were in the previous exchange with Seumas, but the pronouns of Donal's previous speech have been translated into nouns. Rather than Donal expressing himself, Donal the poet is watching Donal the man expressing himself. And he pulls out all the stops. His favourite quotation from Shelley's *Prometheus Unbound*, "Ah me, alas! Pain, pain, pain, ever, for ever," is heightened by biblical allusions to silver cords and golden bowls. Minnie is mentioned only once at the beginning which strengthens the feeling that Donal is now chief in Donal's mind. As Donal's immediate response gives way to aesthetic distancing, as ordinary discourse becomes highly allusive and alliterative, Donal refashions Minnie's death into a lament for himself, "Davoren, Donal Davoren, poet and poltroon, poltroon and poet." That this lament is a more satisfying conclusion to Donal than his straightforward recognition of responsibility is understandable because once again the flood of words dissipates any need for action.

It is surely ironic and sad that Donal, who has a talent for words, who

is sensitive to prose construction and who appreciates poetic creation, succumbs to the verbal chaos. Yet neither Donal's poetry nor his ordinary speech
suffers a counterweight to the verbal distortions of Gallogher, Grigson,
Owens and Shields. Donal's misuse of language may be more sophisticated
than the others, but it ultimately degenerates into the same empty rhetoric.
Typical of all of them is the pattern of words without deeds. They also share
the isolation, the inflation of ego, and the illusions which such a pattern
provokes and sustains. Finally and most importantly, the accumulated weight
of all their words and inaction contributed to Minnie's death.

IV

If Donal, Seumas, Owens, Grigson and Gallogher live in a world of
words, Minnie and Maguire exist in the realm of action. Neither has much
to say. Unlike that of Donal and his group, Minnie's language is consistently
unaffected and plain. In her conversations with Donal, the two are often at
cross-purposes because Donal insists on "literary" words and Minnie cannot
understand him. Minnie talks about "weeds" whereas Donal talks about "wild
flowers"; Donal recites poetry and Minnie gets the mistaken impression that
he has another girlfriend. When Minnie takes the bombs, she remains true
to her own voice and does so without song, dance or rhetorical show. Minnie
matter-of-factly states, "I'll take them to my room; maybe they won't search
it, if they do aself, they won't harm a girl," and exits. Maguire, like Minnie,
hardly speaks at all. He flits across the stage, deposits the bag, and flits off
again to meet a bullet at Knocksedan.

That neither Maguire nor Minnie says much does not mean that what
they say or do is inadequate. Maguire's remark about catching butterflies is
a transparent lie, an intentional failure to communicate. The bag of bombs
he casually leaves behind makes the whole tenement vulnerable during the
Black and Tan raid and contributes to Minnie's death. He never explains
his patriotic motivation, so his own death seems unnecessarily meaningless.
In acting without stating his true purposes, Maguire collaborates in the
overall drift to chaos and destruction as surely as the more talkative and less
active characters.

While Maguire is one of the play's prime movers, a major cause of the
closing plot complications, Minnie reacts. Her last words and actions are
the results of the endless babble, the verbal obstructionism and the prior
actions of others. Thus, when Minnie is arrested, she is heard "*shouting
bravely, but a little hysterically, 'Up the Republic.'* " That Minnie's commonsense
approach to language should be channelled into an empty slogan first spewed

out by Tommy Owens in act 1, a slogan, moreover, that Minnie gives no previous indication of supporting, is as much a measure of how contagious the verbal distortions of the others are as of her own fright.

Minnie's actions are no more satisfying than her slogans. Taking the bombs is a selfless gesture, but it is also an impulsive and irrational one. Her comment that "they won't hurt a girl" fails to take into account the callous nature of the political turmoil. The ruthlessness of both sides and the large role accident plays are facts that Minnie ignores or never really appreciates. So the Black and Tans arrest her, the IRA open fire at the Black and Tans, and in the confusion a stray bullet from one side of the other kills Minnie. Her seemingly decisive and heroic action in taking the bombs is, thus, compromised by her inability to perceive the consequences of her actions. Part of her apparent decisiveness is surely based on her lack of political consciousness.

Yet accident and faulty analysis are only partial determinants of Minnie's fate. As important is the recognition that Minnie's death is the end product of a collective failure—Maguire's, Tommy's, Grigson's, Seumas's, Donal's and the sociopolitical fabric's—to establish the proper relationship between language, thought and action.

It seems fair to say that, in *Shadow of a Gunman*, acts divorced from rational and articulate thought are no more meaningful than words without deeds. Neither Minnie nor Maguire sets things right by his/her actions. In fact, Maguire's actions lead to his own and Minnie's deaths. Maguire's wilful silence and Minnie's inarticulate action are further illustrations of the overall language problem in *Shadow* and just as potent forces for creating chaos as the rhetorical strategies of Grigson, Gallogher, Seumas, Owens and Donal.

V

Thus *Shadow* offers no solutions to the language problems it dramatises in such careful detail. All the characters have difficulties with language. Their distortions vary greatly and some of their verbal pyrotechnics are hilarious. But a closer analysis proves them all dangerous. The breakdown in communication has dire results: it eventuates in Minnie's death. As she is one of the most vital characters in the play, her death seems tragically unnecessary. To the degree that the verbal perversions contribute to Minnie's death, they may be viewed as instruments of murder. It is not accidental that Owens's explosive rhetoric and Seumas's stutter sound like guns going off. Yet, it would be unfair to blame the characters entirely for their verbal distortions without noticing that the characters in *The Shadow of a Gunman* are terrified as well as terrifying. They may perpetuate chaos, but they rarely initiate it. They exist in a hostile and chaotic world not of their own making and their verbal manoeuvres are, in one sense, only an unsatisfactory adaptation to that world.

ROBERT G. LOWERY

Sean O'Casey and Socialist Realism

O'Casey's experiments with expressionism in [*The Silver*] *Tassie*, with poetic symbolism in [*Within the*] *Gates*, and with the stream-of-consciousness in *I Knock at the Door* would seem to run counter to the dominant mode of revolutionary drama and writing of the turbulent 1930s (hence Greaves's charge of "artistic elitism"). Although parts of *Tassie* and *Gates* had scenes with techniques popular with the agit-prop and socialist realist dramas of those years (such as the Mass chant and choral arrangements), O'Casey had been moving increasingly away from the realism of his Dublin period: a realism so strong that he was labelled a "photographic artist." Beginning in the early thirties his essays denounced realism as an outmoded and worn-out style of writing, a conviction he held the rest of his life. In 1934, the year socialist realism was institutionalized, he wrote:

> Realism, the portrayal of real life on the stage, has failed, for the simple reason that real life cannot be shown on the stage; realism has always failed to be real. Nothing can be more artificial than the play that claims to be true to life. In setting out to gain everything it has lost all. Realism died years ago and the sooner we bury the body the better.

In 1960, he complained that "present-day drama is beset by the worship of realism," which O'Casey believed was never enough to capture the magic

From *Sean O'Casey Centenary Essays* (Irish Literary Studies 7), edited by David Krause and Robert G. Lowery. © 1980 by Robert G. Lowery. Colin Smythe, 1980.

of life. Taken alone, these statements suggest that O'Casey and socialist realism were never together long enough to part company.

In a characteristically frank letter in 1955, O'Casey stated categorically that he did not believe in socialist realism. He also confessed that he did not know what socialist realism was. O'Casey's confusion was not singular. Many writers of the 1930s who were sympathetic to Communism felt an ambiguity toward this new doctrine. On one hand they deeply believed in the Soviet revolution and its goal of socialism. On the other hand they believed in their own artistic talents. To begin writing in a new form would bring problems that negated much of their power and artistry.

This ambiguity was compounded by an uncertainty of definition, for the definition of socialist realism varied from writer to writer, country to country, and even from year to year. It was a poor ideology insofar as being imposed or universally accepted. As formulated by Maxim Gorky at the 1934 Soviet Writers Congress, socialist realism was literature which was realistic in content, socialist in politics and affirmative in tone. This, however, was subject to interpretation of the nature of realism, the nature of socialism, and the nature of affirmation. As an example, the French Communist Party did not accept Brecht until the late 1950s, long after the dramatist found acceptance in other socialist countries and Communist parties. On the other hand, the British Party seemed to have no criteria for judging socialist realism and accepted humanists of all stripes. The French/Brecht/British dichotomy was by no means peculiar. Picasso, O'Casey, and many other writers and artists traversed the same path of acceptance in one country and nonacceptance in others. Some Communists liked them; some didn't.

Even the best known theorists, Brecht and Georg Lukacs, could not agree on a definition. Both laboured for years and came to diametrically opposite conclusions as to what constituted socialist realism. At the same time, the apodictic Zhdanov in the Soviet Union seemed to have no theory at all and appeared to be arbitrary and capricious. Writers who were praised in the 1930s during the United and Popular Front periods found their same works condemned during the Cold War period of the 1940s. The confusion O'Casey felt, then, was appropriate.

Most theorists believed that socialist realism was an application of Marxism. Though neither Marx nor Engels wrote a study of literature both were well-read and balanced in their approach to the arts. Marx was very familiar with literature; his favourite authors were Shakespeare, Balzac and Heine. Indeed, Shakespeare appears to have been as important an influence on Marx as he was on O'Casey. Marx was so fascinated by the dramatist that he once embarked on a study of the playwright's originality. Moreover, Shakespeare was a valuable aid to Marx's efforts to learn the English language. He knew the dramatist's works by heart in German and it was a logical step to tackle them in English. To both Marx and Engels art was viewed axiologically rather than ontologically. Art had no history of its own other than the particular milieu out of which it grew. Personally, they both preferred realistic works, such as those by Balzac who, though a staunch Catholic and rank royalist reactionary, was in Marx's eyes a superb writer and a chronicler of the follies, decadence and weaknesses of the bourgeois class. But both Marx and Engels also detested propaganda novels which Engels termed "tendentious." It was not enough or even important to have the "correct" opinions. Indeed, "the more the author's views are concealed the better the work of art." (One thinks of Yeats's advice to O'Casey that the author's opinions should be burned up in the action of the play.) To Engels, whatever social significance a work had should flow from the development of the narrative rather than be imposed by the author.

The stature of Marx and Engels as revolutionaries and their choice of realism naturally put them on the side of the "art is a weapon" school of the 1930s. There is some question whether they would have concurred with this, though they did give every indication of not believing in the concept of art for art's sake. To both, art was a tool for learning about and understanding the past and for imparting the knowledge of today. To many critics, though, the main problem of the 1930s and beyond was not with the concept of art as a weapon as it was with the belief that every literary weapon was art. The early stages of socialist realism seemed to revolve around the deduction that since both socialist realism and art were weapons, then socialist realism was art. It was a golden age for tendentious writers.

In the Soviet Union, the campaign for realistic art was enlisted in the service of eliminating illiteracy. In this regard, the makers of the first socialist state faced enormous odds. An entire generation had suffered through world war, revolution, and a devastating civil war. This condition was added to the already dismal state of the Russian working class and peasantry whose education ranked low on the Czar's priorities. The problem was compounded by the diversity of languages in the Soviet state—180 by one count—many of which were not written languages. Realism was considered the most appropriate tool for education, and literature took the form of folk pageants and socialist novels whose primary task was to educate, encourage and inspire. Undeniably, this democratization of culture had an effect on the quality of literature and drama. Equally undeniable, art became more utilitarian and served a greater purpose to a larger number of people than it ever had in the past.

But there was another side to socialist realism. It should not be supposed that all theorists laboured to justify folk pageants and socialist novels, important though they may be for education. In the Soviet Union, for instance, Anatoly Lunarcharsky differed with Zhdanov's version of socialist realism. Lukacs and Brecht, while disagreeing with each other, agreed on their dislike of Zhdanov. From some writers, such as C. Day Lewis, came the theory that any great work of art, socialist realist or not, was a plus for Communism, a view O'Casey partially shared. O'Casey's friend, Hugh MacDiarmid, placed his faith in a relatively obscure party resolution from a 1925 Central Committee meeting:

> The party must combat attempts at pure hot-house "proletarian" literature. . . . Marxist criticism must decisively expel from its midst any pretentious, semi-literate and smug communist conceit. . . . While gaining a deep and unerring knowledge of the socioclass content of the literary streams, the Party can in no way bind itself in adherence to any one direction in the sphere of artistic form. . . . The Party must completely eradicate attempts at crude and incompetent administrative meddling in literary affairs.

O'Casey always believed that Communists were selling themselves short by applauding simple and didactic forms of realism. Life, he felt, was complex and, like art, could not be reduced to a formula. Though he denounced realism, he never denied that his own works were realistic, but he always insisted they had other ingredients, such as fantasy and stylized imagination, which heightened the realism. Indeed, it is clear that the dramatist did not denounce *all* forms of realism; just those which did not allow for a more truthful, imaginative, and deeper expression of life, as he saw it. In the 1934 essay, he wrote: "the veneration of realism, or, as Archer calls it, pure imitation, must cease, and imagination must be crowned queen of the drama again." And in 1950, he reiterated this belief: "A lot think that anything fiery fierce or commonplace is realism, but realism is but a form of writing in which imagination has no place. It is the setting down of things and characters as they are, without change, selection, modification, or arrangement." To O'Casey, fantasy and imagination must be a part of any living play for both were part of the living world.

In this regard, O'Casey was in accord with the more sophisticated theorists of socialist realism. Lunarcharsky, for instance, wrote:

> The revolution is bold. It loves brightness of colours . . . revolution gladly accepts those extensions of realism that are indeed

in its sphere. It can accept fantastic hyperbole, caricature, all sorts of deformations. . . . If effective presentation demands depicting a certain social feature in a distorted or caricatured fashion to reveal what is hidden behind an appealing or nondescript exterior, then this device is, of course, profoundly realistic.

Later, he wrote: "Writers and, in particular, playwrights belonging to the movement, to the school, to the era of socialist realism, can create their works in highly diverse styles." Moreover, fantasy, the grotesque, and caricature are fully appropriate for realism if "their role is to deepen reality, to illuminate its artistic interpretation."

Lukacs took the same approach, writing, "Marxist aesthetics is clearly opposed to any trend which limits itself to the photographic reproduction of the immediately perceived surface of the outer world." It takes no stretch of the imagination to link Lukacs's comments to O'Casey's works:

even the most extravagant play of the poetic imagination [*Within the Gates*], even the fartherest reaching fantasy [*Cock-a-Doodle Dandy*] in the representation of phenomena, is completely compatible with the Marxist concept of realism. It is no accident that some fantastic tales of Balzac or E. T. A. Hoffman count among the works which Marx rated very high.

Lukacs concluded that "the fantastic tales of Balzac and Hoffman constitute high points of realist literature since in them, precisely with the help of imaginative representation . . . essential forces are portrayed."

Today, it is this view which prevails among socialist realist critics. A Soviet critic recently concluded:

It is irrelevant to set down which structure, which form [literature] uses. It is possible to give a true view of the world through the use of inner monologue or literary montage, but it is also possible to distort it, and the same applies to the Aristotelian dramatic rule versus the non-Aristotelian. What matters is that a work of art, to quote Brecht, "while laying bare the social casual nexus, should give an insight into the social machinery."

The question of form in O'Casey's plays, therefore, is of no consequence insofar as socialist realism is concerned. The expressionism of *The Silver Tassie*, the poetic symbolism of *Within the Gates*, and the fantasy of *Cock-a-Doodle Dandy* are all compatible with Marxist aesthetics. Indeed, from the perspective of theorists like Lukacs and others, what has been of utmost

importance in socialist realism has not been technique but "the expression
of a personal world view" and "a creative attitude toward life." This world
view is not Oswald Spangler's "Man is a beast of prey, I shall say it again
and again." Rather it is Gorky's "Man is more miraculous than the miracles
he accomplishes." It is the world of the old versus that of the new. Valderman
von Knoeriger wrote: "The basic area of contradiction, which cannot be
resolved and which divides both worlds, is the essence of man, his internal
essence. It is the battlefield on which the future of mankind must be determined." The Soviet critic, Anatole Ovcharenko, commented: "We are saying
that because the artists of the new world have an unshakeable faith in man,
in his final triumph, they can depict the world more profoundly, more
fearlessly."

This "unshakeable faith in man" is the socialism in socialist realism. By
definition it is affirmative. It implies a progressive view of history, an understanding of the multi-layered political and economic forces in capitalist
society, and belief in the ability of mankind to shape, control, or determine
its own destiny. In short, it is the artist's view of life that carries the most
weight with socialist critics. Lukacs wrote: "Marxist aesthetics requires only
that the essence conceived by the writer should not be represented abstractly,
but as the essence of the phenomena in which surging life is organically
hidden and out of which it grows." Another critic said:

> The socialist realist cannot be only concerned with an interpre-
> tation of reality. For him reality has many layers; it is constantly
> evolving. For his point of view, which corresponds to the dialectic
> of life, not everything has the same value, the same specific
> weight. In real life, the new and the old, what is becoming and
> what is decaying, coexist, often within the same social
> phenomenon.

O'Casey instinctively understood all these concepts and said much the
same thing (though a little more poetically):

> I have always aimed . . . at bringing emotion and imagination on
> to the stage, in the shapes of song, dance, dialogue, and scene;
> each mingling with the other, as life does, for life is never rigid
> . . . nothing changes so often, so inevitably in city and country,
> in field, factory, workshop, and home.

For Lukacs's "organically hidden surging life," O'Casey could write as far
back as 1934: "There is a deeper life than the life we see and hear with the
open ear and the open eye, and this is the life important and the life ever-

lasting." Finally, of all O'Casey's criticisms of literature, none is so pervasive as his objections to those works "in which man is arrayed against forces stronger than himself, completely beyond his control, and the characters . . . invariably set down on the animal plane." This theme was the basis for his criticisms of the "great galaxy of darkened stars dulling the human sky": Kafka, Ionesco, Greene, Eliot, Genet, Orwell, and, to a lesser degree, Beckett ("though Samuel Beckett wears his rue with a difference. He is a poet, and there is sly humour as well as music in his writing"). O'Casey's "unshakeable faith in man" also formed the basis for those writers he championed: Shakespeare, Burns, Shelley, Whitman, Gorky, Shaw, and Yeats. For, like himself, these exceptional souls championed his creed:

> Man is the only form on earth that can see its form and love its grandeur; he has enriched the world, for without him it would have no meaning and look dead; it would be death. He has ennobled the star we stand on; exceptional souls give things exceptional beauty.

If the form and content of O'Casey's plays were not antagonistic to Marxist aesthetics, what about other factors? Critics have maintained that the case for O'Casey's Marxism is weakened by important distinctions, all of which are termed "unorthodox." The critics include the use of religious symbols and language in his works; his independence which was so strong as to negate any observance of Communist orthodoxy; and his romanticism which was not in accord with the "steel-like" discipline of Communists.

The charge that O'Casey professed an unorthodox brand of Communism is tricky. I have tried to show in ["Sean O'Casey: Art and Politics"] that orthodoxy and unorthodoxy in the Communist movement were relative terms. Communists rarely used them, for obvious reasons. One can easily grant that all great writers and artists who at some time in their career professed sympathy for Communism, were unorthodox. By definition they were so. Greatness in any artistic sphere is the product of an unorthodox mind. Just as they were able to perceive and re-create the world in their own distinctive way, so too did they perceive Communism in a special manner. But this is not extraordinary. The tailor, the baker, the farmer, and the electrician who believe in Communism all bring their own perspective to politics, a perspective more often than not determined by how they earn their living and by the problems incurred at the workplace. Their perception is also unique and distinctive. While the artist and the worker may differ on a vision of reality because of their differing experiences, both have in common a shared vision of what the world can be. Further, no purpose is served by setting up dual standards for artists and workers. Competency in an artistic area does not negate competency in the political arena. It is, after all, one of the principles of democracy that an educated people, who are usually competent in their occupations, will be able to render fair political judgements. The critics' problem has been in accepting that Communism is a fair political judgement.

Organized religion was frequently the *bête noire* in O'Casey's plays, yet he never tired of using religious allegory and biblical rhetoric for illustrative purposes. Some critics have seen this as a primary reason why O'Casey cannot be considered an "orthodox" Communist. Saros Cowasjee, for instance, wrote in two places of O'Casey's play, *The Star Turns Red:* "The Communists feel that O'Casey is unnecessarily recreating a God that they have killed" and "Some Communists may not approve of O'Casey's enthusiasm for God and religion." Disregarding the fact that Cowasjee doesn't quote a single Communist authority for his statements, his confusion is apparent. For to come to Communism by way of Christianity or to infuse Christian symbols may seem strange in view of Marx's often misquoted statement: "religion is the opinion of the people" (found first, incidentally, in Charles Kingsley).

Yet it is not so strange. The symbolism of Christ as "the first Communist" or counterposed against capitalism, and of Christianity as the basis for Communism is pervasive throughout socialist and non-socialist literature. Its imagery is frequently found in twentieth-century Communist writings and the whole idea was the basis for the Christian Socialism of the nineteenth century. One of the most famous works in which the Christ symbol is used is Alexander Blok's poem *The Twelve*, where Christ is portrayed leading the revolutionary proletariat, the modern twelve apostles. In Henri Barbusse's poem *Jesus*, Christ is a Communist and an atheist whom the capitalists nail to the cross. In the first Soviet play, *Mystery-Bouffe* by Mayakovsky, produced on November 7, 1918, in celebration of the first anniversary of the October Revolution, Christ is the symbol of the Man of the Future. Replete with a Sermon on the Mount, this Christ of Communism tells his listeners that there is no heaven, that the only real heaven is the one built by human hands on earth. Other examples include Art Young, a leading Communist artist for the *Daily Worker*, who drew the highly-popular "Wanted" poster of Christ, satirizing the capitalists' fear of those like Jesus who preached dangerous social ideas. Day Lewis was moved to write a "Marxist morality play," *Noah and the Waters*, using the biblical story to present a conflict between Noah—the life of capitalistic exploitation—and the new life of the Flood (as O'Casey may have used the Flood at the end of *Purple Dust*). The list could go on and on, for many Communists have not hesitated to use the Christ symbol as a symbol of Communism or as a protest against capitalism. How effective it has been artistically is another question, but the symbol is in no way anathema to Communist writing.

Like Marx and other Communist writers, O'Casey used the language and cadences of religious expression as a weapon and as a tool for satiric and dramatic purposes. Compare, for instance, the language he used in one passage in *Inishfallen, Fare Thee Well* with two Communist works: Mike Gold's classic *Jews without Money* and Wangenheim's *Chorus of Work:*

> (O'Casey) Morning star, hope of the people, shine on us! Star of power, may thy rays soon destroy the things that err, things that are foolish, and the power of man to use his brother for profit so as to lay up treasure for himself where moth and rust doth corrupt, and where thieves break through and steal. Red Mirror of Wisdom, turning the labour in factory, field, and workshop into the dignity of a fine song; Red Health of the sick, Red Refuge of the afflicted, shine on us all. . . . The sign of Labour's shield, the symbol of the people's banner; Red Star, shine on us all!

> (Gold) O workers' Revolution, you brought home to me, a lonely suicidal boy. You are the true Messiah. You will destroy the East Side when you come, and build there a garden for the human spirit. O Revolution, that forced me to think, to struggle, and to live. O great beginning!

> (Wagenheim) Our Communism
> Which art in deed
> Hallowed be your name
> Your kingdom come on earth
> Not in heaven . . .
> For thine is the kingdom
> The power and the humanity
> May this be granted
> By the Comintern
> And the KPD.

None of these passages will live forever. Nor should they. But for O'Casey at least, this method of writing had a utilitarian purpose. In a letter to Timofei Rokotov, he wrote of those in religious organizations he wished to reach. It is a good thing, he said, "to try to confound them with the words that come out of their mouths. . . . Were Red Jim [in *The Star Turns Red*] to speak as a Marxist, the audience here or in America . . . would take no notice; only those converted, those already Marxists would listen."

There is no doubt, of course, that religion was an important influence in O'Casey's life, however much he may have used it as a weapon or literary device. But this fact alone puts him in the company of many other Communists and in no way does it single him out as exceptional. André Gide wrote: "What leads me to Communism is not Marx but the Gospels." Day-Lewis saw his Communism having a "religious quality." Rockwell Kent reflected that in his youth he was an ardent reader of the New Testament. One can only guess the number of nonwriting socialists and Communists who started with a belief in Judaism or Christianity, who saw in Christ a powerful revolutionary figure, and who found themselves immersed in the ideals of the early apostles. Indeed, to some, there was a quality about Christianity that led them to Communism, as illustrated by a conversation between the Dean of Canterbury and Paul Robeson in which the Dean said:

> There is nothing more fundamental about Christianity than the one brotherhood of man. Grant that, and the demand for justice, freedom, and abundance of creative life for each individual together with an ever-widening fellowship, follows as day follows night. Grant that, and an economic order, which not only frustrates science but produces and tolerates wealth beside poverty, creates and perpetuates class distinctions, and fails to provide opportunity for all in the matter of work, leisure, education, or security, stands condemned.

The religious influence on individual Communist writers must, however, be kept in perspective. There is no general rule that applies to all. Sometimes Communism successfully picked up where religion left off, exchanging one set of values for another. Other times, and less successfully, Communism was just an extension of religion, as in the case of Gide and Day-Lewis, incorporating one set of values with the other. Often, as expected, the two values clashed, especially if each was carried to its logical conclusion and promoted the examination of man's relationship to the world around him. To Marxists, man's existence was social and with his fellow man, while religion was essentially individualistic and egoistic, separating man from his communal existence. Christianity was a religion, a relationship between God and man in which man acknowledged the supremacy of God. Christianity saw itself as an answer to man's fate on earth but only in the light of God. Marxism denied all transcendence and metaphysical questions.

One believed that all was knowable; the other believed that the essential spirit escaped human knowledge. To Marxists, only that which denied mystery made science possible, for to admit that reality was unknowable was a view which limited man's potential and capacity to control and conquer it. Given the choice between a religious and a scientific view of reality, Marxism chose science. And to O'Casey, science was everything:

> What is beyond us outside the world of what we see, hear, smell, taste, and touch, we don't know. Not one of the philosophies that have tried to hem us in or bring us out has told us, or can tell us anything outside of ourselves and the world. Science has told us a lot, will tell us more, and we must wait for science to tell us all.

But to Gide, Day-Lewis and others who tried to religionize Marxism, it was a God that failed. O'Casey's strength was that he never worshipped at the altar.

Robert F. Aickman posed a dichotomy once by writing: "Mr. O'Casey is a Communist. A romantic Communist, of course." In this way he both described and negated the dramatist's political views in a mere ten words. To describe O'Casey thusly quite naturally led people to believe that O'Casey was a hopeless utopian, lost in a world of his own. On one hand was O'Casey, the passionate romantic; on the other were a band of steely-eyed Bolsheviks led by the bloodless theories of the equally steely-eyed Marx and Lenin. Once again though, the critics misread both the theoretical and practical content of Marxism.

Marxism has always had within it two currents of revolutionary activism, the theoretical and the romantic, described by Ernst Bloch as sobriety and enthusiasm and alluded to by many Marxists. Bloch wrote: "Nothing is more distant from true Marxist sobriety than common sense, which is not so healthy and not so human, but is more likely to be replete and petit bourgeois prejudices. On the other hand, nothing is closer to genuine sobriety than the quality of *bon sens*, as found in Marxist enthusiasm." These warm and cool currents of Marxist thought have been and are present in nearly all Communists, from the rank-and-file to the leadership, but they vary in degree of dominance. Whether one is a sober or an enthusiastic Marxist depends, to a large extent, on the personality of the believer. A relative few have a predilection for intellectualism and cool realism. But the vast majority of Communists have not mastered the theoretical intricacies of Marx and Lenin (few have) and they are distinguished by their passionate and romantic enthusiasm, corresponding to the dynamic *élan* of society. This is not to imply that one facet is superior to the other; only that from a Marxist view one is not contradictory to the other. Indeed, Marxists such as Bloch see as the strength of Marxism its ability to harmonize the two. "Marxism," he wrote

> overcomes the rigid antithesis of sobriety versus enthusiasm by bringing them both to a new state, and enabling both to work together for precise anticipation and concrete utopia. It is not the function of sobriety merely to remove fantasy, and it is not the function of enthusiasm, precisely as imagination in action, to operate exclusively with absolutes, as though revolutionary romanticism coincided with quixotism.

It takes a stretch of the imagination to accuse O'Casey of not having a realistic view of life and of being overly romantic. He spent the first forty years of his life in decidedly unromantic poverty and financial insecurity, existing on meagre wages, the dole, and whatever else was available. He spent years as a labourer on the unromantic scrap-heap of capitalism, learning the value of his and others' labour. He devoted a considerable number of years to political movements, learning and teaching the tactics of trade unions and revolutionary parties. He was, by all accounts, a voracious reader on a wide variety of subjects, ranging through drama, history, literature, nature, politics, and economics. What has been termed O'Casey's romanticism is nothing more than the dramatist's view of reality and his conviction that, despite its woes, life has a richness and a fullness that are not adequately recognized. To him and to most other Communists, the *élan* of society was quite real. It was the dynamism in every home, factory, field, and workshop. It was in the lives of the lowly as well as in that of the mighty. It was song and sorrow, love and beauty, comedy and tragedy. It was far in advance of the understanding of even the most revolutionary parties, and yet it was the oldest subject for artist and writer who tried for centuries to capture it on canvas and paper. Lenin recognized the same force, writing:

> History generally, and the history of revolutions in particular, is always richer in content, more varied, more many-sided, more "subtle" than the best parties and the most class-conscious vanguards of the most advanced classes imagine. This is understandable, because the best vanguards express the class consciousness, the will, the passion, the fantasy of tens of thousands, while the revolution is made . . . by the class-consciousness, the will, the passion, and the imagination of tens of millions.

The "imagination of tens of millions" that Lenin wrote of was of seminal importance to O'Casey. In his essay "Art Is the Song of Life," he wrote:

imagination is all: it is the focus of all achievements by man, it sparked off the American Revolution, it began the discovery of Evolution in the mind of Darwin, it flamed forth from the mind of Lenin, inspired Shakespeare's plays and all his songs; and is the burning core of form and eloquence which is present in a fine play, novel, painting, or musical creation.

All these moments of greatness were to O'Casey the foundation of Communism, the historical heritage to which Communism must pay tribute. They were the blocks on which society was built, on which it thrived, and which gave it life. It was a dream handed down from generation to generation and passed on from father to son and from mother to daughter. It was no contradiction to Marxism nor was it overly romantic for O'Casey to believe that

> Communism isn't an invention of Marx; it is a social growth, developing through the ages, since man banded together to fight fear of the unknown, and destroy the danger from mammoth and tiger of the sabre-tooth. All things in science and art are in its ownership, since man painted the images of what he saw on the wall of his cave, and since man put on the wooden share of his plough the more piercing power of iron or of bronze.

It was no contradiction because Marx said the same thing himself in 1843.

> It will be shown . . . that the world has long possessed in dream form something of which it need only become conscious in order to possess it in actuality. It will then be evident that it is a question not of a great and theoretical gap between past and future, but rather of realizing the ideas of the past.

DAVID KRAUSE

On Fabrications and Epiphanies
in O'Casey's Autobiography

3 The road of excess leads to the palace of wisdom.
4 Prudence is a rich ugly old maid courted by Incapacity.
44 The tygers of wrath are wiser than the horses of instruction.
57 Damn braces. Bless relaxes.
                    —WILLIAM BLAKE, "Proverbs of Hell"

*Its soul, its whatness, leaps to us from the vestment of its appearance. The soul
of the commonest objects, the structure of which is so adjusted, seems to us
radiant. The object achieves its epiphany.*
                    —JAMES JOYCE, *Stephen Hero*

*He was at home among the mortals. His epiphany was the showing forth of
man to man. Man must be his own saviour; man must be his own god.*
                    —O'CASEY on Shaw, *Sunset and Evening Star*

Autobiography no less than fiction is the art of supreme fabrication, and
it is therefore as a supreme fabricator of his life that I wish to consider Sean
O'Casey's creation of himself and his world in his autobiography. Since no
deep portrait of a life, and certainly no self-portrait of the artist, can be
reduced to a realistic mirror-image, whether in an autobiography or a novel,
the symbolic Johnny Casside must be seen as a fabricated or mythic expansion
of the living O'Casey, just as the symbolic Stephen Dedalus must be seen
as a fabricated or mythic expansion of the living Joyce. What this means is
that these two Irish writers, working with similar transmutations in different

From *Essays on Sean O'Casey's Autobiographies*, edited by Robert G. Lowery. © 1981
by David Krause. Barnes & Noble, 1981.

but related genres, were compelled to invent their lives in extravagantly fictive terms in order to achieve the aesthetic distance which distinguishes art from life. It also means that in the Irish experience, where reality is often a nightmare and the truth must be mythologised before it can be recognised, everything must be transmuted if it is to be endured, with the result that most fiction is autobiographical and most autobiography is fictional. Fabrication is sublimation in Ireland. In autobiography as well as fiction, the vital statistics of life are less significant than the vital imagination of art; the creative process must function as more than a reflex mirror for the imitation of life. The artist as fabricator makes something that did not exist before; he invents a new vocabulary, a new form. And when he reconstructs his own life, which presumably did exist before, what he makes is a symbolic projection of that life which has not yet been seen, which was waiting to be discovered.

In subject nations like Ireland where the historical betrayals have produced an excess of human misery, the impulse to fabricate or create new forms can be urgent, and the literary transmutations of necessity mitigate and even supersede the grim realities of life. Since the pervasive mood of Irish fatalism is a state of mind conditioned by seven centuries of frustration, it is no accident that the folk imagination has fabricated the second law of thermodynamics into Murphy's law or the Celtic version of entropy: if things can possibly get worse, they always will. Perhaps the intensity of the national anguish provoked the Irish people, consciously and unconsciously, to fabricate, to wear ironic masks in order to fool John Bull and the lord of the big house. In the relevant terms of R. D. Laing, the Irish have consistently had to invent survival games, fabricated strategies "in order to live in an unlivable situation." When nations like Ireland develop advanced symptoms of frustration and fantasy, and the people have difficulty trying to hide their centuries-old repressions and daily illusions, they may seek relief in acts of physical aggression, or they may turn to the artistic process which, by providing a compensatory release of verbal aggression, becomes an act of faith in a fatalistic world. Under the yoke of an unrelieved history of master-slave relationships, then, and while abortive political attempts to liberate the nation offered only compromises and defeats, the Irish people were forced to create a superabundance of sublimating oral and written literature which helped to transfigure and disguise reality. The uninhibited glory and freedom of words became the primary ritual of catharsis for the country.

The fine art of verbal fabrication has always been a sword of the spirit in Ireland, and I would therefore venture to suggest that psychologically the transubstantiated words of literature have for centuries functioned as a secular Mass, or a liturgy of Joycean epiphanies. In the beginning there was always the liberating word in Ireland. I call upon Blake, as well as Freud and Joyce and O'Casey, to guide me here, the apocalyptic Blake who in his towering epic *Jerusalem* celebrated the sanctity of art as an aesthetic gospel when he wrote:

> I know of no other Christianity and of no other Gospel than the liberty of both body & mind to exercise the Divine Arts of Imagination, Imagination, the real & eternal World of which this Vegetable Universe is but a faint shadow . . . What is the Divine Spirit? is the Holy Ghost any other than an Intellectual Fountain?

I would only add that in Ireland, even more than in Blake's Albion, the Holy Ghost is the Fountain of Art.

The extreme tensions of life in Ireland have always demanded extreme fictions. It is therefore emblematic that the twin artifices of talking and writing creatively should have become the divine instruments of psychic release in a disordered world. The compulsive appeal of words to the eye and ear, the two spiritual senses, as they have been called, helped the people survive in a frustrated and paralysed nation, a nation in "a state o' chassis." No one understood and dramatised these symptoms of frustration in the national character more effectively than the modern Irish fabricators, Joyce and Yeats, Wilde and Shaw, George Moore and Lady Gregory, Synge and O'Casey, Fitzmaurice and Behan, Clarke and Kavanagh, O'Connor and O'Faolain, Flann O'Brien and Edna O'Brien, all of whom, along with many of their fellow countrymen and women, in fiction, poetry, drama and autobiography, invented the extravagant and redemptive literature of Ireland. In that country a powerful or poetic word has invariably been a weapon worth a thousand pictures.

Ireland is now a partially independent but still partitioned and beleaguered nation, and the racial memory of seven hundred years of subjugation cannot be rubbed away in a generation. Even De Valera's republic of frugal shopkeepers, who after the sacrificial rhetoric and bloodshed of 1916 somehow managed to preempt Connolly's mad vision of a Workers' Republic, to add yet another frustration, were unable to forget that Irish art is always superior to Irish life. The mythic art of the word is the unreal McCoy in Ireland, where the vegetable universe of reality is but a faint shadow of the divine art of the imagination, and this phenomenon may help to explain why Irish life endlessly strives to imitate Irish art.

Perhaps no one understood the mysterious relationship between art and life more shrewdly than Oscar Wilde, that supreme fabricator and most flamboyant Dubliner of them all, Wilde who proclaimed what Blake and most Irishmen knew when he insisted that the divine gift of lying was the essence of all art. In his brilliant dialogue "The Decay of Lying"—a decay which may have begun to fester in England but has seldom been evident in Ireland—Wilde stated that "No great artist sees things as they really are. If he did, he would cease to be an artist." The artist's mendacious and unfettered imagination, therefore, must liberate him from what Wilde called "the prison-house of realism"; it must help him find the vision beyond reality, the Yeatsian mask or anti-self, the aesthetic vision that can only be discovered through the mythic power of lies or fabrications. Art is a magic "veil" not a reflex "mirror," Wilde argued, and along the way he corrected a common misconception about Hamlet:

> They will call on Shakespeare—they always do—and will quote that hackneyed passage about Art holding the mirror up to Nature, forgetting that this unfortunate aphorism is deliberately said by Hamlet in order to convince the bystanders of his absolute insanity in all art-matters.

Hamlet himself was an artist in his calculated fabrication of madness, and literalists who take delight in his aphorism, or take his disguise as a mirror of life, are no more reliable than Polonius in their failure to distinguish between art and reality.

Artifice in Elsinore and Ireland is not "the real thing," it is the thing beyond reality, the most ingeniously fabricated thing. Ireland like Elsinore was tainted by tyranny, and the Irish artists play variations of Hamlet's game of fabrication and disguise, though without his consummate resolution. In the extension of Wilde's illuminating symbolism, which echoes the aesthetic mythology of Blake and Yeats, the "forms" of art are "more real than living man," they are "the great archetypes of which things that have existence are but unfinished copies." It is in precisely this paradoxical sense that those two supreme fabrications, Dedalus and Casside, are the archetypes of the living and therefore unfinished shadows of Joyce and O'Casey. And the symbolic Dublin that both writers fabricated in their works was the archetypal city, of which the geographical city was but an unfinished copy.

Dublin was the uncommon denominator for both men, the uniquely irreducible focus, and their conceptions of the city grew out of similarly ambivalent attitudes of love and hate, compassion and arrogance, kinship and alienation. Again we must return to Blake for his theory of creative contraries to account for the ironic reconciliation of these opposites: "Without Contraries is no progression. Attraction and Repulsion, Reason and Energy, Love and Hate, are necessary to Human existence." All contraries are necessary for existence in dear, dirty Dublin. The paradoxical impulses of attraction and repulsion prevented Joyce and O'Casey from succumbing to the easy temptations of the Celtic twilight or nationalist moonshine that always threaten to sentimentalise the frustrated Irish, and therefore both men were free to fabricate the life of their city with a gritty tone of sceptical reverence. They revealed all the profanations and epiphanies of their holy city; Joyce in his tragic-ironic short stories and symbolic novels, O'Casey in his tragicomic plays and epic autobiography.

There were also many contraries between Joyce and O'Casey which separated and united these half-blind and percipient, raging and affirming giants. Joyce's milieu was middle-class Dublin, O'Casey milieu was working-class Dublin, and therein lies a social and economic distinction that partially accounts for the contrasting methods they used to take the measure of their city. University-educated and already a self-conscious artist in his twenties, the Thomistic and agnostic Joyce was an intense aesthete with his pedantically neoclassical principles all mapped out, a literary mandarin in complete control of his lyric and comic destiny. A self-educated common labourer not fully conscious of himself as an artist until he was in his forties, the Marxist and agnostic O'Casey was an intense socialist with what could only vaguely be called Romantic or Promethean principles, a literary primitive who had to improvise his dramatic and comic destiny. In their various mock-heroic ways both men profaned the excessive pieties of Cathleen Ni Houlihan and attempted to recreate the conscience of their people. And although they were both alienated figures while they were living in Dublin, similarly alienated by church and state politics, their Dublin roots were never more evident than when they left the city in self-exile and pursued their indomitable Irishry on foreign soil.

Joyce was the pure artist: his genius was a calculated, finely controlled instrument which seldom played a wrong note, and he always knew where he was going with his cunning craft. O'Casey was the impure artist: his genius was an instinctive, roughly hewn instrument which sometimes played outrageous notes, and he had to make his artistic discoveries by trial and error. Joyce's bold and innovative techniques made him a more significant figure of universal influence, as the groping O'Casey himself was often quick to acknowledge. Nevertheless, there are many instances where O'Casey is at the top of his fictional form in his autobiography, for example, in the way he exploits the strategies of comedy and epiphany and invents a flexible structure of picaresque fabrications to accommodate the adventures and initiations of Johnny and Sean Casside. In his autobiography as well as in his plays, O'Casey revealed that, like Joyce, he was a master of comic irony and had few peers in his rendering of the mock-heroic absurdites that frustrated his vainglorious countrymen.

I am not at the moment concerned with O'Casey's giddy attempts to play with Joycean puns and neologisms, in which comic and satiric extravaganzas he can sometimes parallel the master and sometimes sound like the sorcerer's apprentice. Specifically, what I have in mind are the instances when O'Casey in his autobiography successfully adopted and modified for his own purposes the technique of the Joycean epiphany. In the penultimate chapter of *Stephen Hero*, Joyce defined the literary epiphany as an attempt to reveal the "*quidditas*" or "whatness" of an unexpectedly luminous experience, the very quintessence of the mysterious thing itself. Stephen explained it in the following manner:

> By an epiphany he meant a sudden spiritual manifestation, whether in the vulgarity of speech or gesture or in a memorable phase of the mind itself. . . . The moment the focus is reached the object is epiphanised. . . . Its soul, its whatness, leaps to us from the vestment of its appearance.

The spark that ignites the epiphany is always something unpredictable, something outside the artist, or something hidden in his mind, something he hears or sees, a vulgar colloquy or fragment of speech overheard, a gesture or object observed in a room or in the street; and suddenly, miraculously, there it is, the heart of the encounter, the thing in and beyond reality is epiphanised as the artist looks *into* rather than *at* something or someone. Wilde might have insisted that all art epiphanises life through the divine process of lying or fabricating. Blake might have seen the epiphany as the creative force that is radiated by a divine excess of love and wrath, wisdom and folly. Yeats might have caught the flash of an epiphany at critical moments in his poems or whenever he responded to the vibrations of his daimonic anti-self. O'Casey would have agreed with all of them, but he was not consciously imitating them when he was instinctively touched by the Holy Ghost and created his own variety of epiphanised experiences.

What distinguishes O'Casey's use of the epiphany is the astonishing degree of visual imagery which he brings to his moments of illumination. He is a word-painter in contrast to Joyce as word-poet. He is so graphically visual he often thinks in dream-pictures, he seldom hides his verbal brush strokes, and he creates a powerful sense of dramatic movement and immediacy on the page. Joyce, on the other hand, transfixes his epiphanies, freezes them into images of stasis and imbues them with a powerful sense of eternity.

In his introduction to the first edition of *Stephen Hero*, Theodore Spencer pointed out the static and timeless aspects of Joyce's theory of the epiphany:

> A theory like this is not of much use to a dramatist, as Joyce seems to have realized when he first conceived it. It is a theory which implies a lyrical rather than a dramatic view of life. It emphasises the radiance, the effulgence, of the thing itself revealed in a special moment, an unmoving moment, of time.

Spencer was right about Joyce, but he was apparently not aware that someone like O'Casey, a playwright working in a fictional form of autobiography, could open the theory to dramatic as well as lyric possibilities.

Now, before going on to examine some of those possibilities, those heightened moments of dramatic *quidditas* in O'Casey, I want to suggest a theory about how I think his verbal and visual techniques are structured by acknowledging a special debt to the noted art historian and iconologist E. H. Gombrich. In a luminous discussion of sensory symbolism in painting, Gombrich points out some synesthetic correspondences between technique and taste in art by suggesting that what goes on the palette or paint-mixing board is directly related to the response of the palate or taste buds. In order to illustrate how these correspondences work, Gombrich introduces two metaphoric and catalytic agents that are always available to the painter, and I believe that similar agents are available to the writer, especially to Joyce and O'Casey. The first agent is a distorting surface of wobbly or rolled glass, the second is an abrasive surface of crunchy or gritty texture. Believing with Wilde that the artist is an image-maker not an imitator, one who constructs fabrications rather than representations, Gombrich asserts that the working artist, in the first instance, figuratively holds a sheet of wobbly glass in front of his canvas to wrench or distort the natural and symmetrical shape of things, to avoid what is too representational and predictable. In the second instance, which is part of and overlaps with the first, the artist includes a texture of crunchy or gritty pigments and brush strokes to break up the soft or smooth surfaces, to avoid what is too literal and sentimental. In both instances the artist tries to liberate himself from everything that is too facile in order to achieve an aesthetic distance from reality. He has, in Gombrich's words, struggled "to get away from skill and sentiment," and as a result "we are constantly brought up against tensions and barbs, as it were, which prevent our eyes from running along smooth lines."

In support of the artist's need to create visual tensions and barbs, Gombrich cites the Browning poem in which the too smooth and too realistic

Andrea del Sarto, trapped by the fault of his faultlessness, tries to correct a purposely misdrawn or wobbly arm by Raphael. Then, in a direct experiment Gombrich takes an "atrocity" or realism painted by Bonnencontre, the excessively sentimental and symmetrical *Three Graces*, and holds a sheet of wobbly glass in front of it, suddenly transforming a tasteless piece of "sloppy mush" into a symbolic image that is gratifyingly vigorous and crunchy. Thereafter Gombrich goes on to point out the metaphoric varieties of wobbly glass and crunchy texture in modern art, in the paintings of the French Impressionists, in the violent and primitive distortions of Van Gogh and Gauguin, in the tensions and barbs that emerge in Cezanne, in the passionately savage and sophisticated canvases of Picasso.

I believe, therefore, that there are significant connections between the visual and verbal art forms, that similarly metaphoric constructs of wobbly glass and crunchy texture can be found in the symbolic prose of O'Casey's autobiography. In spite of the fact that O'Casey the dramatist is often put down as a naturalist or realist, a misleading critical platitude that is unfortunately evident in most anthologies and surveys of drama, he is in everything he wrote a verbal and visual image-maker who brings the passionately savage eye of the modernist painter to the printed page. All his work, from his early journalistic and historical essays to his late farcical fantasies, was fabricated through a symbolic conceit of wobbly glass with tensions and barbs of crunchy comedy and irony. The Daumier-like scenes of the ragged poor of Dublin during the 1913 General Strike in *The Story of the Irish Citizen Army* are distorted with contraries of pain and hope. The tone and structure of the Dublin trilogy are calculated to break down the lines of smooth and symmetrical action, and the mock-heroic language of the characters is limned with rough and gritty strokes that deny stock responses to historical events. The surrealistic second act of *The Silver Tassie*, the park-world metaphor in *Within the Gates*, the comic disintegration symbolism in *Purple Dust*, the miraculous transformation scene in *Red Roses for Me*, the cock-catalyst revolt in *Cock-a-Doodle Dandy*, the sardonic Prerumble in *The Drums of Father Ned*—all of these asymmetrical and apocalyptic, savage and farcical fabrications are designed to reach far beyond "the prison-house of realism" in order to create verbal and visual correspondences.

Now I want to examine some of those synesthetic correspondences in the autobiography by concentrating on two types of fabrication that are directly associated with the initiations and discoveries of Casside, the secular epiphanies. The first type is the introspective moment when O'Casey looks at himself and creates personal epiphanies for Johnny or Sean. The second type is the perspective moment when he looks at Ireland or the world and creates historical epiphanies for us. There are many ways to read a work as complex and multidimensional as the autobiography, and for my present purposes I have chosen to read it as a book of revelations, a wobbly and gritty kaleidoscope of private and public visions.

If epiphanies, like discoveries, only come to those who are looking for them, young Johnny Casside finds them even before he has reached the age of full understanding because he is so eager to confront the strange and hostile world around him. For example, his first confrontation with death came when he was six and his father died. After the funeral, while the mother sorrows in silence, the sister and the brothers get into a series of sharp arguments, with one another about Parnell, and with the innocently irreverent Johnny who sings about the death of cock robin and asks interminable questions about which colour God likes best. The impact of their grief is deflected by the heated arguments, until the others leave angrily and Johnny is left alone with his mother. O'Casey sets up the moment of epiphany with a comic crunch when Michael, just before he leaves for the pub with Tom, aims some mocking barbs at little Johnny:

> I wonder, said Michael, how you'd get to know whether God Almighty likes blue, green, yellow, or red the best?
> Oh, shut up, Mick, said Tom, and let the kid alone.
> Red, I think, went on Michael, red like the red on a monkey's arse.
> No more talk like that in front of the kid, said Tom tittering.
> Oh, shag the kid! said Michael, he'll have to learn about these things some day.

And Johnny begins to learn about some of these things as he looks out of the window and watches them leave, watches the lamplighter creating a string of yellow lights in the street, and finally sees the first sign of his mother's grief in the reflection of the fire in her tears:

> Johnny watched the little lamplighter running, with his little beard wagging, carrying his pole, with a light like a sick little star at the top of it, hurrying from lamp to lamp, prodding each time a little yellow light into the darkness, till they formed a chain looking like a string of worn-out jewels that the darkness had slung round the neck of night. His mother returned to the room as he was stretching to see how far he could see down the street, and how many of the lights he could count. Going over to the fire, she sat down, and gazed steadily into the blaze.

I was thinking, Mother, he said, that green must be a great favourite of God's, for look at the green grass, and the leaves of bushes and trees; and teacher said that green stands for life, and God loves life.

He waited, but his mother did not answer him. He turned, and saw her gazing steadily into the blaze of the fire. He stole over and sat down beside her, and took her hand in his. And there they sat and stared and stared and stared at the flame that gushed out of the burning coal. Suddenly he looked up and saw the flame from the fire shining on tears that were streaming down her cheeks.

Johnny has shared a sudden moment of communion with his mother by innocently releasing her pent-up grief. Without realising it he prepares himself for the epiphany by watching the grotesque little lamplighter create a string of yellow lights in the darkness outside, and then by wondering if green is God's favourite colour since it represents the life that God creates. At that point, as she stares at the red flame of the fire, the stricken widow's reverie is broken by her son and she finally seems to realise that she has been touched irrevocably by death not life. The sudden stab of grief is epiphanised for mother and son. And more, it is totally visualised for us in finely etched nuances of darkness and light. If Johnny sees more than he entirely understands in that reflection of the fire in his mother's streaming tears, he has come face to face with one of God's mysteries that will touch him often in the years ahead. He has shared a sacred moment with his mother, the sheet-anchor of his life, and he has played out with her the theme of the song he was humming at the start of the chapter, "We all go the same way home," the song in which all mankind clings together, the symbolic song that gives the chapter its title. The whole chapter is a fabrication of dramatic barbs and lyrical dissonances which O'Casey couldn't have remembered realistically from his childhood, but which he has invented with brilliantly contrasting tones of visual imagery, all seen as through a wobbly glass darkly. This chapter, as a work of supreme fiction, like so many others in the autobiography, could well stand beside the finely wrought stories of lyrical and gritty paralysis in Joyce's *Dubliners*. It should be apparent that, like Joyce, O'Casey could be the pure artist as word-poet as well as word-painter when the fictive moment demanded his total effort.

Now I want to shift to the more crunchy and comic O'Casey, to look at another early chapter just before Johnny's unusual encounter with a tired cow on the North Circular Road, and I only want to examine two paragraphs at the start of the episode. It is a typical day of unrelieved pelting rain in

Dublin and Johnny, whose impressionable mind is full of Bible stories, wonders if the deluge of rain is a sign that God has decided to punish wayward mankind with an annihilating flood. This time the whole incident takes place in Johnny's uninhibited imagination and we get an extended interior monologue in the vivid lingo of a shrewd Dublin "chiselur" who is convinced that he has witnessed a miracle, the imminent damnation and suddenly merciful salvation of the world in a comic epiphany of joy:

How 'ud it be, thought Johnny, if God opened the windows of heaven, an' let it rain, rain like hell, for forty days an' forty nights, like it did when the earth was filled with violence, an' it repented the Lord that He hath made man, causin' a flood till the waters covered the houses an' the highest tops of the highest mountains in the land? There'd be a quare scatterin' an' headlong rushin' about to get a perch on the highest places, to sit watchin' the water risin' an' risin' till it lapped your legs, and there was nothin' left to do but close your eyes, say a hot prayer, slide in with a gentle splash splash, an' go to God; though you'd hardly expect to find a word of welcome on the mat in heaven, if God Himself had made up His mind you were better dead. But that could never happen now, for God had promised Noah, a just man and perfect in his generation, there'd never be anything like a flood anymore; and as proof positive, set His bow in the cloud as a token of a covenant between Him and the earth, for Noah to see when, sick an' sore, he crept out of the ark to start all over again with what was left of himself an' family, with the beasts of the earth, all creeping things, and all the fowls of the air, male an' female, that he had carried with him all the time the flood remained over the surface of the earth.

There was the very rainbow, now, sparklin' fine, one end restin' on the roof of Mrs. Mullally's house, and the other end leanin' on the top of one of the Dublin Mountains, with the centre touchin' the edge of the firmament; an', if only our eyes were a little brighter, we'd see millions an' millions of burnished angels standin' on it from one end to the other, havin' a long gawk at all that was goin' on in the earth that God made in the beginnin', an' that had to make a fresh start the time that Noah an' his wife, an' his sons, an' his sons' wives came outa the ark with the elephants, the lions, the horses, and the cows that musta given Noah the milk he needed when he was shut off from everything, till the dove came back with the olive branch stuck in her gob.

It could only be achieved with a grand design of wobbly glass and crunchy texture. It could only be constructed by one of the merry monks who might have illustrated the Book of Kells with a fantastic procession of angels and animals, or perhaps by the visionary Blake as he contemplated a child's dream of the salvation of man, or yet again, on a vast allegorical canvas by a Picasso or a Chagall. Only such divinely inspired fabricators might have matched O'Casey's cosmic mural of damnation and salvation as it took shape in the comically transcendent mind of Johnny Casside, from the hand of God to the rainbow crowded with millions of angels gawking in amazement at the earth, to the ark of Noah and all his animals, to the mountains and streets of Dublin and the roof of Mrs. Mullally's house, to the dove of peace arriving "with the olive branch stuck in her gob."

But all things move by contraries for O'Casey and that is only the beginning of his parable, which ends on a dark note when Johnny is soon confronted by a tired and stray cow who wasn't saved in the ark, a rebellious cow who refuses to follow the herd in the frantic run through the Dublin streets from the cattle market down to the pens at the North Wall from where they would be shipped to the slaughter houses in England. That stubborn and weary Irish cow, Johnny thinks, has apparently been abandoned by God: "a sthray cow lyin' on a rain-wet street is not enough to make God bother His head to give a thought about it." So we move from a song of innocence to a song of experience as O'Casey rings the changes on the recurring motif of Irish aspiration and frustration, and finally paralysis in the image of that tired and lost cow. The private nature of Johnny's original epiphany broadens to become a hint of an historical epiphany for us, with more to come later on the symbolic fate of Ireland. The angry drovers who have kicked and beaten the cow to no avail finally go after the rest of the herd, leaving Johnny to guard the stubborn beast. He feels a strong sense of empathy for the poor animal but he can't help or save it in any way, and since night is falling he must run home to his mother. The fate of the lost cow, like the fate of Ireland, remains unfinished, unresolved, as the departing Johnny looks back and transfixes a scene of epic sorrow in a forsaken cow:

> At the end of the road he looked back, and, in the purple of the twilight, he saw the dark mass of the cow still lyin' on the path where everybody walked, starin' straight in front of her as if she saw nothin', while the rain still kept fallin' on her softly; but the sun had stopped her shinin', and the rain was no longer golden.

This pattern of epiphanised contraries runs throughout the autobiography; for example, in *Pictures in the Hallway*, in the chapter on the hawthorn tree where the spicy scent of the hawthorn blossoms collides with the filthy work of the dung-dodgers, and Johnny proudly holds his sprig of creamy hawthorn as a sacred emblem in the battle of Dublin's poor against the inevitable slime and ashes of life. Again, in the final and title chapter of this volume the teenaged Johnny discovers the world of painting in an epiphany of bright colour and design amid the grimy smoke and cinder heaps of northside Dublin:

> Colour had come to him, had bowed, laughing, and now ran dancing before him . . . now that colour had come to him, he longed to be a painter, and his very bowels yearned for the power to buy tubes of cobalt blue, red lake, chrome yellow, Chinese white, emerald green, burnt sienna, and a deep black pigment.

But he cursed the poverty that prevented him from becoming a painter and he had to be satisfied with looking in a shop window in Dawson Street at some watercolours that ravished his eyes; and in a secondhand book barrow he discovered and bought for a few pence two old books that illustrated the paintings of Fra Angelico and Constable, and it was "like a sudden burst of music" for Johnny, a revelation of heaven and earth seen through a wobbly glass lightly:

> With all he had learned from the Bible and the Prayer Book it was but an easy jump into the brightly-tinted world of Angelico; and from the little church of St. Burnupus, in its desolate seat among the dust of the dowdy streets, the cinders of the bottle-making factory of North Lotts, for ever pouring out its murky plumes of smoke, the scarred heaps of mouldering bark and timber chips round Martin's timber yard, the dung of the cattle, passing in droves down to the quays, the smell of the beer-soaked sawdust, floating out from the wide-open doors of the pubs, blending its smell with that of the foul rags of the festering, fawning poor, Johnny ferried himself safely to the circle of delicate blue showing forth Angelico's golden-haired Saviour clad in a robe of shimmering creamy grey, a shining orb in a beautiful left hand, a halo of heavy gold, transversed with a crimson cross, encircling His heavenly head; or, there He was, standing in a purple arch of the heavens, staff in hand, looking with love on two Dominican brothers, one of whose hands timidly touched

the Saviour's, the two of them dressed in robes tenderly cream, covered with sombre black cloaks cunningly tinged with green, standing there gazing at Christ with a look that reverently called God their comrade. Again, with Angelico, he wandered through clouds of angels, a little stiff with innocence, thronging the skies like gaily-coloured Milky Ways, crimson or green or blue-gowned, powdered with stars or roses or golden fleurs-de-lys. Sometimes he chanted hymns softly to himself, strolling towards heaven through a field of pinks and roses, meeting often on his way more lovely angels, blowing with fattened cheeks through golden trumpets, or stringing delicate white fingers over graceful psalteries or zithers, sounding in honour of the Blessed Virgin, while her Son fixed another gem in her crown of glories.

Again, under the green, sunlit, or dewy trees, planted by Constable's imagination, giving shade and gracefulness to an eager sun, he wandered afield; or looking down where the ripening corn was striding upward to a golden grandeur, he wandered down quiet paths rimmed with vivid green, touched in with lavish blossoms, shyly forcing forward to kiss a greeting to the careless passer-by; while red-brown cattle, drowsing in the field beyond, stood knee-deep in the sappy grass, the honeyed smell of clover brooding delicately over the sleepy meadow, soothing the sweating brows of boatmen poling barges down the placid river full of sunny nooks making the green shades greener; gentle houses peering out from among the stately elms, the plumy poplars, and the proudly-nurtured ash with its sweeping foliage, moving in the wind, like a dancing Fragonard lady, coy with pride, and fancying herself the gem of the world around her; and over all the greying silver and the tender blue of a fresh and beaming sky.

So, through these two men, beauty and colour and form above and beside him came closer; came to his hand; and he began to build a house of vision with them, a house not made with hands, eternal in his imagination, so that the street he lived in was peopled with the sparkling saints and angels of Angelico, and jewelled with the serene loveliness Constable created out of the radiance of uncommon clay.

This may well be the seminal passage on the synesthetic technique of visual and verbal fabrication O'Casey used in the autobiography, for it is apparent here that he intended to create his story with the magic of words

as pigments, building his own house of vision out of the uncommon clay of
Dublin, from the mouldering dust and smoke and cinders to the epiphanised
glory of something akin to Angelico and Constable. But the glory is usually
tempered in the gritty contrast of poverty and radiance. In an early chapter
of *Drums under the Windows*, when the grown-up Johnny, who has now
become Jack to his labouring comrades and Sean to his Gaelic friends, is
mixing cement on a railway job and finds himself in the country for the first
time. Amazed at the golden sea of growing corn, and the sharp sweet smell
of new-mown hay, he immediately thinks of "the glory of Constable's *Corn-
field*," and he fancies he can see "Ruth standing there in that field, up to her
middle in the corn, a creamy face, rosy cheeks, and big brown goo-goo eyes
staring at poor Boaz." His imagination runs wild as he next sees Jesus strolling
through the corn field, chewing grains of corn as he thinks about some
parable, while the Scribes and Pharisees are hiding and whining behind the
hedges. Suddenly his reverie is interrupted by a horrible cry, a repeated cry
of lost and mad laughter that comes from the nearby Portrane Asylum, and
this quickly brings to his mind the image of his poor sister Ella whose life
is being destroyed by her mentally deranged husband now locked up in the
Dublin Asylum at Grangegorman:

> Out there, now, right in the centre of the corn, just where Jesus
> had passed a few moments before, floated the face of Ella, a white
> face, a face of settled fear, tightened with a stony smile that had
> a seed of wild weeping in it. He went back to his work of tem-
> pering the mortar and of carrying his hod of bricks to the mason;
> but whenever he turned his eyes to the growing corn, there was
> that damned white face, stony with fear, a swaying stem of corn-
> cockle at times empurpling an eye, or the scarlet shadow of a
> poppy giving it a bloodily splashed mouth, watching his work;
> watching, watching him work.

So often something terrible and irrevocable is happening at the same
time that something simple and glorious is taking place. During the "terrible
beauty" of the Irish Civil War in 1922 when Free Staters and Republicans
were savagely killing one another for the greater glory of Ireland, O'Casey
damned both sides and remained loyal to the lonely flag of labour, the Plough
and the Stars. In the chapter titled "Comrades" in *Inishfallen, Fare Thee Well*,
O'Casey records one episode of the ritualistic slaughter with an ironic detachment that heightens the revelation of horror. While Sean sits on a bench
in Stephen's Green watching the ducks on the lake, he meets an old friend,
drover Mick Clonervy, a man who had regularly helped his father herd his

cattle down the North Circular Road to be slaughtered in England. Mick is now Colonel Mick, dressed in the uniform of the Free State army, and he is slaughtering Republicans, who are slaughtering Free Staters. While he and Sean talk a Republican on a bicycle suddenly throws a bomb at a nearby building along the Green where Free State troops are being quartered, and in the midst of the explosion a wild chase begins as the colonel leaps on his bicycle and, with the help of two plainclothes men, sets out in frantic pursuit of the bomber, whom he recognises as Kevin Lanehin, a young lad who only a few years earlier served with him when they were both under the same flag and cheerfully killing Black and Tans. After an ambulance arrives to take care of the dead and wounded, "Sean hurrie[s] into the Green to sit in serenity beside the lake to try to sort out things, too, among the indifferent ducks and drakes."

At this point in the narrative O'Casey adopts a double focus, alternately showing us how Sean uneasily watches the mating ritual of the ducks at the same time that Clonervy gets ready to perform the ritualistic execution of Lanehin. The terrifying chase leads out towards Rathfarnham and the Dublin hills, with innocent children cheering as the mad cyclists go racing by, and Lanehin's "life rolled off behind him like thread unwinding from a turning spool"; and at the same time *The brown duck, like a maid hid in a Franciscan habit, spurted forward when she felt the pursuer coming too close.* Finally, O'Casey fabricates a double confrontation for us as Lanehin, exhausted and cornered in the hills, begs for mercy; as Sean, tense and abstracted, watches the ducks come together; and suddenly there is a grotesque consummation of death and life;

> I'm an old comrade of yours, Mick, the young man pleaded.
> Sure I know that well, said the Colonel heartily, and I'll say this much—for the sake of oul' times, we won't let you suffer long.
> Jesus! whimpered the half-dead lad, yous wouldn't shoot an old comrade, Mick!
> The Colonel's arm holding the gun shot forward suddenly, the muzzle of the gun, tilted slightly upwards, splitting the lad's lips and crashing through his chattering teeth.
> Be Jasus! We would, he said, and then he pulled the trigger.
> *Looka, Ma! shrilled a childish voice behind Sean; looka what th' ducks is doin'!*
> *Sean turned swift to see a fair young mother, her sweet face reddening, grasp a little boy's arm, wheel him right around, saying as he pointed*

out over the innocent lake: Look at all the other ducks, dear, over there
on the water!

The drake had reached a goal, and he was quivering in the violent
effort to fulfil God's commandment to multiply and replenish the earth.

It isn't only the fact that the shocked and amused O'Casey is on the
positive side of the ducks and drakes here, but that he understands how the
destructive and creative impulses exist side by side and reveal the tragicomic
cycle of life. This ironic revelation is strikingly similar to the one presented
in Auden's poem "Musée de Beaux Arts," where the tragic fall of Icarus in
Brueghel's painting takes place while the dedicated ploughman goes about
making his fields fertile, and "a boy falls out of the sky," just as an Irish lad
crashes in the Dublin hills. Auden and Brueghel and O'Casey, they knew
all about it:

> About suffering they were never wrong,
> The Old Masters: how well they understood
> Its human position; how it takes place
> While someone else is eating or opening a window or just walking
>   dully along;
> How, when the aged are reverently, passionately waiting
> For the miraculous birth, there always must be
> Children who did not specially want it to happen, skating
> On a pond at the edge of the wood:
> They never forgot
> That even the dreadful martyrdom must run its course
> Anyhow in a corner, some untidy spot
> Where the dogs go on with their doggy life and the torturer's
>   horse
> Scratches its innocent behind on a tree.

But how did it come to all this in Ireland, the debauch of dreadful
martyrdom ironically mocked by the innocent ducks or dogs, going on with
their ducky or doggy life in the midst of suffering, why did it happen?
O'Casey is seldom slow to answer such questions. He not only understands
suffering, he can roar out his wrath about it, he can make gritty observations
on it that are calculated to cut deeply into the conscience of those who caused
the suffering; and when he comes to the causes of the fate of Ireland the
outrageous folly of the Irish is only superseded by the even more outrageous
folly of the British. In the title chapter of *Rose and Crown* he happens to meet
Stanley Baldwin in London, and after teasing him with slyly irreverent

comments that bewilder the "toby-jug mind" of the Prime Minister, and "Sean's belly fill[s] out with the ecstasy of secret mischievous laughter," it is the time for an O'Casey drum-roll of injustices, an historical epiphany for Baldwin and England and all of us, an ultimate revelation of why the Irish have always been forced to play slaughter games while the animals play at ducks and drakes. "There is in Ireland, sir, a political catechism as well as the one coined by the Council of Trent," O'Casey begins with a rumble; and he goes on, with a devastating wobble and crunch, to paint an indicting mural that could be an Irish version of Picasso's *Guernica:*

> The ministers of the Rose and Crown have never known, and known not now, anything about the ways and means that have made the Ireland of today. Knew nothing, know nothing, about her folk-art in story, song, music, legend, and dance; know nothing about her struggles to perpetuate her life with something else besides a potato; know nothing even about the later things that tingle the Irish nerves, fire the Irish blood, provoking one section into wearing an orange sash, and another into wearing a green one. . . .
>
> Yet the predecessors of these men ramped over the land for hundreds of years; shot, hanged the leaders of the Irish who couldn't agree with them, and jammed the jails with the rest; when every tenant-farmer in the land lost the right to live; when hunger rose up with them in the morning and went to bed with them at night; when, at one go, in one place, seven hundred people were flung from their homes, poor mud-made homes at that, but homes all the same, by an absentee landlord, because the tenants couldn't give him enough for an extra fit of whoring; when the peasants were bound to pay six pounds an acre rent and work for their landlords at fippence a day; when an English earl was forced to explain, *If the military force had killed half as many landlords as it had the revolting Whiteboys, it would have contributed more effectually to restore quiet;* when in eighty-five years eighty-six coercion acts were passed to keep the Irish peasants toeing the landlordian Christian line; when to have a pike, a lance, or a knitting needle constituted an offence worth a term of transportation for seven years; when everyone or anyone found walking the roads, or standing at a corner, an hour after sunset in a proclaimed district was liable to the long holiday of fifteen years' transportation; when every judge to be a judge had to be a land-

lordian lover, and, finally all were made to act as jurymen as well as judges; when the catholic peasant of the south and the protestant peasant of the north of Ireland spent their lives sowing their own graves that stretched from the river Lee and the river Boyne to the shores of Lakes Ontario and Erie and far beyond them; when every government minister, every privy councillor, every magistrate, was a landlord, or a landlord's brother, or a landlord's friend; so that the threat, as recorded in the holy Bible, made by the King of Assyria to the people of Israel that he would reduce them to eating their own dung and drinking their own piss, fell upon the catholic peasant of the south and the protestant peasant of the north; while the perfumed voice of Lord Beaconsfield applauded, and Lord Salisbury declared, with a clapping of cold hands, that very soon the Kelt in Ireland would be as scarce on the banks of the Shannon as the Red Indian on the banks of Manhattan.

Contrary to the common view still prevalent in Ireland and elsewhere that O'Casey left the source of his genius behind him when he went into self-exile, the mighty anger etched in this pictorial scroll of his nation's anguish indicated that he could never forget his Celtic roots. On every page of the autobiography there is evidence that although all six volumes were written in England, he never really left Ireland. In so many special and symbolic ways the autobiography is an epiphany of Ireland itself, and particularly working-class Dublin. His Dublin memories always come back no matter where he is. When he and his wife try to enroll their son in a convent school in England and are turned away because they haven't enough money, he invokes the spirit of Fluther Good with a touch of comic grit:

Imagine Fluther Good, if he happened to be a father, going up this drive, his heavy hand holding the light one of his son; Fluther's shoulders squared, his walk a swagger, his lips forming the words of *The Wedding o'Glencree;* on his way to interview the reverend mother.—How much, ma'am for this little fella? How much? Jasus, ma'am, that's a lot to charge a chiselur for his first few lessons, an' makin' him into an ordinary, orderly Christian man.

When he is in Devon brooding about original sin—"Original sin has got us all by the short hairs"—he looks at the red earth of Devon and remembers something from his childhood in Dublin and invents a wobbly and crunchy

scene that only a lively little Dublin "chiselur" could have fancied on the
fall of man:

> Here, in Devon, they were anchored on the real red earth, rich
> earth, and very fruitful. Here, maybe, Adam was made, for in
> a bible Sean had had when a kid, he remembered a marginal note
> telling the world that Adam meant red earth; so here, maybe,
> Adam was needed into life. Adam filled a vacuum. All he had to
> do was keep his feet, and all would have been well, and all would
> have gone on living. God, what a grand world it would have
> been! The brontosaurus would have been a pet, and pterodactyls
> would have been flying in and out of our windows, chirruping
> just like robins! But the man had to fall down. The woman done
> it, sir—pushed me down; caught me off me guard. Couldn't keep
> his feet for all our sakes; fell, and ruined the whole caboosh.

All the passages I have chosen are seldom mentioned or recognised for
their special qualities, and they are only a fragmentary illustration of
O'Casey's unique ability to fabricate extravagant pictures with words. It
should also be evident that I have purposely avoided mentioning what might
be called the big bow-wow revelation scenes, like the surrealistic creation of
his own birth as the third and last Johnny to survive at the beginning of the
first volume; the spectacular transformation scene when dirty Dublin is
temporarily resurrected and redeemed on the banks of the Liffey in the
second volume; the tragicomic and gritty portrait of Mild Millie as his Cathleen Ni Houlihan of the Dublin slums in the third volume; the ultimate
epiphanisation of Lady Gregory in half-stained and half-wobbly glass in the
fourth volume; the crunchy epiphanisation of New York as the sacramental
city of Whitman's glorious masses in the fifth volume; the Blakean epiphany
for all suffering children, that they might escape "the mind forg'd manacles"
and be free, in the "Childermess" chapter of the sixth volume.

At one point in the last volume as he thinks about the story of his life
and how he first began to write it, O'Casey dreams his way back to his
beginning and wonders how he was able to recapture it: "His own beginning
would be the first word, the little logos born into the world to speak, sigh,
laugh, dance, work, and sing his way about a day, for tomorrow he would
die. . . . Only in sleep might he dream it back; never again, except in sleep."
Thus, the story of his life, as if seen through the magic of a Wildean veil or
a Yeatsian mask, unfolds with the freedom of a dream, a series of dream
pictures for those two spiritual senses, the eye and the ear, a vision that
moves beyond death in eternity. He dreams his way back through half a

million visual words and he is instinctively following in the Celtic tradition of the *aisling*, the genre of the dream-vision or poem of revelations; the intricately fabricated *aisling* which can only be perceived through a druidic or metaphoric image of wobbly glass, as in the *aisling* of MacConglinne, the *aisling* of Earwicker, the *aisling* of Casside.

Yeats was always a writer of revelations, visions, *aislings*, and sometimes the early Yeats dreamed his way back to the daimonic power of art more feelingly than the later Yeats. It was the later Yeats who urged O'Casey to create art in which "the whole history of the world must be reduced to wallpaper," which fortunately O'Casey refused to do. It was the early Yeats of 1905 in a moment of supreme insight who must have had a perfect vision of the kind of art O'Casey would go on to create in his autobiography when he wrote: "All good art is extravagant, vehement, impetuous, shaking the dust of time from its feet, as it were, and beating against the walls of the world. This is precisely what O'Casey does in the story of his life and why it is good art: he is extravagant, vehement, impetuous; he shakes the dust of time from his feet; he beats against the walls of the world; and as a result he fabricates his synesthetic book of revelations with a mighty wobble and crunch.

CAROL KLEIMAN

The Silver Tassie

SOLVING THE "TASSIE" CONTROVERSY

Two years after receiving the Hawthornden Prize for *Juno and the Paycock*—
an event which closely followed the riots over *The Plough* (1926)—Sean
O'Casey made literary history in a quite different fashion by quarrelling
with the Abbey directorate over the rejection of his first clearly experimental
play, *The Silver Tassie*. W. B. Yeats, as the most prominent director of the
Abbey Theatre, was largely responsible for the play's rejection, and though
he allowed *The Tassie* to be performed at the Abbey in 1935, he never really
changed his mind about the play. But it was O'Casey, himself, who chose
to turn the rejection, of what he obviously thought to be his masterpiece,
into a public scandal. Indeed, in later years, he seemed to recognize a certain
inevitability about what had occurred, for, as he commented in a letter to
his American agent, "I've never written anything that didn't cause a dispute,
a row, a difference, or something." O'Casey loved "mental fight," just as
surely as he hated "corporeal" war, and, in retrospect, the *Silver Tassie* controversy (as well as all the smaller controversies surrounding the later plays)
can be seen, in part, as a reflection of his own pugnacious spirit. Yet now,
since the celebration of the centenary of his birth, perhaps the time has come
for the caricatured figure of O'Casey the fighting Irishman—the one his
detractors still hasten to attack—to pass into history, so that it can be replaced
by the more complete portrait of the man that is reflected by the larger body
of his works.

From *Sean O'Casey's Bridge of Vision: Four Essays on Structure and Perspective*. © 1982
by the University of Toronto Press.

Though O'Casey was not, as he believed, the victim of an Abbey directorate conspiracy, he was, and still is, the victim of "Yeatsean arrogance," of what O'Casey himself mockingly called "the conceit of Zeusian infallibility." "Solving" the *Silver Tassie* controversy, then, means breaking free of this conceit altogether by appealing, not so much to external sources, as to the play itself. Let *The Tassie*—both the texts and the productions—resolve the only really serious charge brought against the play by Yeats: the charge that *The Tassie* is disunified both stylistically and in terms of character and action. Here we will find that, in keeping with the tradition of experimental theatre, a more innovative approach is needed: one that, startling as it may seem at first, would nevertheless allow for the possibility of *The Silver Tassie* being realized more successfully onstage.

In replying to Yeats's long letter which attempted to explain why the Abbey had rejected the play, O'Casey lampoons all Yeats's talk of unities, saying: "I have held these infants in my arms a thousand times and they are all the same—fat, lifeless, wrinkled things that give one a pain in his belly looking at them." The reply is vintage O'Casey: anger and pain transmuted magically by wit. But O'Casey does more than mock Yeats; he suggests a way of answering him:

> I'm afraid I can't make my mind mix with the sense of importance you give to "a dominating character." God forgive me, but it does sound as if you peeked and pined for a hero in the play. Now, is a dominating character more important than a play, or is a play more important than a dominating character? You say that "my power in the past has been the creation of a unique character that dominated all round him, and was a main impulse in some action that filled the play from beginning to end." In "The Silver Tassie" you have a unique work that dominated all the characters in the play.

At first, in his haste to contradict Yeats, O'Casey seems to be implying that there is no dominating character in *The Tassie*, a statement which is clearly not true. For Harry Heegan dominates three acts of the play and the Croucher dominates act 2. The final statement is clear enough, however, since it suggests that all the characters in the play are dominated, and therefore, in a sense unified, by the central theme—or "character"—of the play itself. And the central theme of *The Tassie* is war: war possesses all the characters in the play and dominates them. The relationship, then, between act 2 and the rest of the play, both symbolically and in terms of character and action, is bound up in the mystery of an individual identity—Harry

Heegan's—caught up, overshadowed, and possessed by the dark forces of war. The unravelling of this mystery involves our understanding of the complex sense in which Harry Heegan is, paradoxically, both a man crucified by war and, at the same time, an embodiment of the spirit of war: both a Christ and an anti-Christ. In the strange figure of the Croucher, as will be demonstrated, all these identities merge, so that, as both character and symbol—of a power much larger than himself—Harry Heegan becomes the dominating force *throughout* the play.

O'Casey must have been greatly distressed to find that Yeats was unable to realize anything of the magnitude of *The Tassie*'s vision. Worse still, Yeats had accused him of knowing nothing of his subject: "You are not interested in the Great War; you never stood on its battlefields or walked its hospitals, and so write out of your opinions." But it was the well-meant suggestion that the Abbey's rejection of *The Tassie* be kept secret that angered O'Casey to the point where he did himself the irrevocable disservice of making the rejection and Yeats's damning criticism of *The Tassie* public.

Thus, despite the fact that Raymond Massey's brilliant direction of *The Silver Tassie* at the Apollo Theatre in October 1929 went further towards unifying the play onstage than any subsequent production has yet done, reviewers and critics have never had the opportunity of seeing the play except in the context of Yeats's critical remarks, a context which has contributed immeasurably to the difficulty of viewing the play—so far ahead of its time in style and technique—as anything other than a disunified structure, though its inexplicably gripping power has come to be almost universally recognized. Not so surprisingly, then, even otherwise favourable reviews of the Apollo production echoed Yeats's criticism: "It lacks the homogeneity, the essential unity of a really good play," wrote the critic for *The New Statesman* in the October 19, 1929 edition.

Moreover, in calling the play "too abstract" Yeats had prepared the way for the more specific charge of "Expressionism," "that word, that method, that mistake!" levelled against the same production by Richard Jennings of *The Spectator*, and for the growing conviction that the play, with its strange mixture of Expressionism and realism, is also irrevocably disunified stylistically. The play ran for only twenty-six performances at the Apollo, though Massey tells us in his autobiography, *A Hundred Different Lives*, that C. B. Cochran, the producer, thought of *The Tassie* as his "proudest failure." To complete the paradox, the Expressionism of the play, in 1929, could not help but discredit it at the box office, whereas today—such are the vagaries even of literary fashion—it is frequently the Expressionism of the second act that helps to draw the audience. And with each relatively more successful revival, there has actually been an added incentive to increase the stylistic disunity of the play by exaggerating the Expressionism of act 2 out of all proportion in O'Casey's original intention.

There were other critics, too, who agreed with Jennings that "we must not be too hard upon the Abbey Theatre. It had a case." And their frequent use of the term "caricature" seems to confirm what had been Walter Starkie's opinion of the play: "In *The Silver Tassie* the characters seem to come from a shadow world; they are not beings of flesh and blood. . . . He was not able to create, as he did before, living men and women." Oddly, though he disliked *The Tassie*, Starkie was the one director who clearly asserted O'Casey's right to have the Abbey produce the play. But Lennox Robinson was adamant in his refusal. "It is a bad play," he told Lady Gregory categorically. His words are echoed, yet strangely qualified, some forty years later, by Hugh Leonard writing in *Plays and Players* of the Aldwych's revival: "It is [a] bad, a terrible play. Perversely, but not incompatibly, it is also a masterpiece."

"It's All Very Curious, Isn't It?"—the title of an article which appears in *The Flying Wasp*—is O'Casey's "reply" to criticism of this sort. How can *The Tassie* be "a terrible play" and also "a masterpiece"? O'Casey had ample time throughout his more than forty years as a creative artist to grow tired of the "flawed genius" label. And nowhere is it more in evidence than in the the *Silver Tassie* controversy, the place where it all began.

THE WINNING OF THE GRAIL

At present, however, the theatrical history of *The Silver Tassie*, beginning with the Apollo production, reflects not only this continuing controversy but also a fascination with certain aspects of the play, both structural and thematic. In fact, as reviewers and critics have so often noted, *The Tassie* may well be called a "passion play." For the element of ritual which the term suggests is readily confirmed, not just in the Expressionism of act 2, but in the play as a whole. As well as the protagonist, Harry Heegan, certain other characters—Sylvester Heegan and Simon Norton, for example—have, from the beginning of the play, a symbolic as well as a realistic role. These two characters, who bear a generic resemblance to Boyle and Joxer, are the comic, music-hall duo who appear at the opening curtain and slapstick their way mindlessly through what is undoubtedly O'Casey's most savage and bitter play. Yet, at moments, they also appear as stylized as figures in a Greek chorus.

The strongly ritualistic basis on which O'Casey builds—clearly underlined in the Apollo production by Massey's innovative use of elevations and doubling—was first articulated by Winifred Smith in her article "The Dying God in the Modern Theatre." She writes:

> The opening act, as Shaw observed, is far from realistic, though a first glance at the stage shows a recognizable Irish [tenement] room, whose homely life is centered around the hearth; a second glance is more revealing, for it falls on the object in the middle of the room, a table covered with a purple cloth, like an altar, on which are displayed various gold and silver medals won by Harry; behind it a window opens toward the sea, showing a mast in the form of a cross, with a starry light at its top. Susie, quoting Scripture—an Old Testament prophecy of doom—as she polishes Harry's arms, is obviously the priestess serving the altar; just as obviously the two old men by the fire, in their reminiscences of the young hero's prowess, are the chorus celebrating the divine superiority of the chosen youth. These three prepare [for] the entrance of Harry, who is at last borne into the room on the shoulders of a Bacchanalian crowd, the girls with "their skirts kilted above their knees" in true Maenad fashion; he and his sweetheart, Jessie, drink from the Silver Tassie, the Grail, the cup of communion, that will soon be full of his blood as it is now full of the wine of rejoicing.

O'Casey, himself, in a letter to Ronald G. Rollins, confirms that much of the play's symbolic design is a conscious one:

> Yes, *The Silver Tassie* is concerned with the futile sacrifice of a young hero in war, and the symbols, the chanted poetry and the ritual of sacrifice are embedded in the drama . . . I wanted a war play without noise, without the interruptions of gunfire, content to show its results, as in the chant of the wounded and in the maiming of Harry; to show it in *its main spiritual phases*, its inner impulses and its actual horror of destroying the golden bodies of the young, and of the Church's damned approval in the sardonic hymn to the gun in Act II.

O'Casey's letter shows, too, that his intent is satiric, that the ritual of human sacrifice as enacted in the war and approved by the Church is a barbaric thing. The play questions, not only the purpose of war, but also the purpose of those rituals, age-old and time-immemorial, which seek to give a meaning to the sacrifices of the golden bodies of the young that war demands. It is not that the ritual, in itself, is wrong, but that it has been used wrongly. Thus, in act 2, the ritual of the mass becomes a Black Mass, a way of condoning death, not when it is an inevitable part of a natural cycle, but when it is the conscious choice of a state and a church dedicated to war for reasons which, if not allowed to remain obscure, turn out, finally, to be perverse. O'Casey does not speak specifically of the Great War, however, for *The Silver Tassie*, as thesis play, probes the issues involved, not on any narrowly partisan level, but on a much more universal one.

Yet the play grew out of an intensely personal experience, as O'Casey tried to explain in his letter to Yeats. "And does war consist only of battle-fields?" he asks pointedly; then, after talking about the autobiographical element in *The Tassie*, he concludes by asking the question a second time:

> But I have walked some of the hospital wards. I have talked and walked and smoked and sung with the blue-suited wounded men fresh from the front. I've been with the armless, the legless, the blind, the gassed, and the shell-shocked; one with a head bored by shrapnel . . . with one whose head rocked like a frantic moving pendulum. Did you know "Pantosser," and did you ever speak to him? . . . Or did you know Barney Fay, who got field pun-ishment No. 1 for stealin' poultry (an Estaminay cock, maybe) behind the trenches, in the rest camps, out in France? And does war consist only of hospital wards and battlefields?

As this passage clearly shows, the painful awareness summed up in *The Tassie* by Harry's bitter words, "the Lord hath given and man hath taken away!," springs from an overwhelming sense of pity for, and sympathy with, the wounded soldiers O'Casey had actually known. Here is the antithesis of the oversimplified and basically callous attitude towards the victims of war— such as Harry—expressed in the words of the song:

> For he is a life on the ebb,
> We a full life on the flow!

In *The Tassie*, then, O'Casey shows that a society too willingly com-mitting itself to war is composed of individuals whose unthinking and selfish attitudes permit the sacrifice of sons, husbands, and lovers in warfare. The artificial flowers so carefully arranged in the symbolic setting of act 1 are a sure sign that there is no longer the reverence for life which we find in the women of the Dublin trilogy, and, later, in Ayamonn's mother in *Red Roses for Me*. It is not a pretty picture O'Casey is painting, and critics have been quick to point out the "gallery of predatory women," so unlike Juno and

Mary Boyle, and Nora Clitheroe. The fact is, to recognize at last the implications of O'Casey's deliberately rhetorical question, war "consists" of much more than hospital wards and battlefields. A warlike spirit resides in the attitudes of men and women who are habitually in a state of war with one another.

Thus, while the legend of Harry Heegan's exploits on the playing field and the "chronicle" of how he stretched the Bobby "hors dee combaa" on the ground make such mock wars seem laughable enough, comedy begins to modulate towards tragedy when Teddy Foran returns from the trenches without having learned anything about "the sacredness of life." Mrs. Foran's tearful description of her china being strewn about like "flotsum an' jetsum," a memorable colloquialism which she uses again the hospital scene to refer to the wounded soldiers, points to the parallel O'Casey is drawing. Similarly, Teddy's smashing of the wedding bowl prepares for Harry's crushing of the silver tassie later in the play, for both actions symbolize a broken communion. This use of quarrels and domestic turmoil (the repossessed or broken furniture, the broken delftware) to convey a more universal "state o' chassis" is, of course, a frequent device of the early plays, including *Cathleen Listens In*, where its use is more obviously allegoric and symbolic.

In *The Silver Tassie*, however, O'Casey organizes his symbols not simply into allegory, but into those rituals of communion and sacrifice which have always informed man's life, frequently on an unconscious level. For in "tr[ying] to go into the heart of war," O'Casey found himself exploring, through symbol and ritual, the often savage and merciless heart of man. The metaphor is one he uses in the autobiographies where, earlier, he had described "the odious figure of war astride the tumbled buildings, sniffing up the evil smell of the burning ashes." Together, these two images reveal the outline of a recognizably human figure: it is the Croucher of act 2, a gigantic image of Man possessed by War, and so torn by despair and suffering that he is sick at heart. In *The Tassie*, then, the dominant theme of War is embodied in the Croucher, as well as being variously personified in certain other characters, but especially in Harry Heegan.

Who is it, one might ask, that has so elaborately arranged, in the bed-sitting room of the Heegan family, the symbols of Harry's victories, both in war and on the playing field? Mrs Heegan shows too little interest in such accomplishments to have given these symbols of his victories such a prominent display. And Sylvester, though he loves to boast about Harry's extraordinary feats, seems too permanently settled by the fire to have ever busied himself about the house. Likely it is Harry himself, probably with Susie's help, who has arranged the setting in anticipation of his triumphant return from the football field, as, certainly, it is Harry who will later use this same setting as a ceremonial altar to celebrate his victory.

In the meantime, both the medals on the purple velvet shield and the photograph of Harry in "football dress" on the red-coloured stand symbolically represent, onstage, the eagerly awaited hero. For Harry's triumphant entrance, which does not occur until more than midway through act 1, has been carefully designed from the opening curtain. In this way, O'Casey has Harry's presence dominate the scene *even when he is absent*, a structure which is closely paralleled in act 2, so that—of all the characters—it is Harry who continues to dominate the play right through to the final exit.

The symbolic import of Harry's heroic stature becomes even more apparent when he is actually brought onstage carried upon the shoulders of his friends, though a closer look at the text reveals that O'Casey's original intention, at least before he saw Massey's Apollo production, which introduced this innovation, was simply to have the scene described by Susie:

> They're comin', they're comin': a crowd with a concertina;
>   some of them carrying Harry on their shoulders, an'
>   others are carrying that Jessie Taite too, holding a silver
>   cup in her hands . . .
> (. . . *Then steps are heard coming up the stairs, and first* Simon
>   Norton *enters, holding the door ceremoniously wide open to
>   allow* Harry *to enter, with his arm around* Jessie, *who is
>   carrying a silver cup joyously, rather than reverentially,
>   elevated, as a priest would elevate a chalice.*)

The origin of Harry's elevation onstage—an entry which is so right for the play it has since become a stage tradition (and one O'Casey must have agreed with)—is recorded by Stephen Gwynn, writing in the *Fortnightly Review* of the Apollo production: "Then in comes the hero, carried by admirers." Produced in this way, the scene is obviously much more dramatic, for, not only do we have Jessie's ritualized entrance carrying—"as a priest would elevate a chalice"—the silver tassie from which wine is later drunk, but we have also the elevated body of the intended sacrifice, Harry Heegan, whose youthful, almost godlike figure, like the host, will be broken in the latter part of the play. The parallel elevations here help to underline, right from the beginning, the symbolic identification of the silver tassie with Harry, who has won the cup three times. Significantly, it is Harry who tells Jessie: "Lift it up, lift it up, Jessie, sign of youth, sign of strength, sign of victory!," for it is Harry who creates the ritual that is about to be enacted: a glorification of the mock war he has just won on the playing field and of himself, its hero. This "war," like the homefront battle of Teddy Foran and his wife, ironically prefigures the real war, in which the mock hero or god becomes the sacrificial victim. The parallel elevations also prepare for the sacrilegious smashing of the tassie in the second half of the play, where the depths to which Harry has fallen, crouched despairingly in his wheelchair, provide a striking visual contrast to the height to which he had risen, both literally and figuratively, in act 1.

Of even more significance than these two elevations within the first act, however, is Massey's elevation of the Croucher in act 2 in the same area onstage in which Harry Heegan was elevated during the previous act. These parallelisms cannot help but work, perhaps subliminally at first, to provide some measure of unity between acts 1 and 2. Indeed, Massey's entire approach to the play, as described in his autobiography, reveals his imaginative and innovative response to the challenge of integrating, into the play as a whole, an act which "at first reading . . . appeared to be parenthetical," but which he felt instinctively to be "no interpolation but the core and substance of the play." Accordingly, Massey's innovative elevations, as we shall see, help to unify the play by clarifying the mysterious relationship between Harry, the Croucher, and the other soldiers.

For all the soldiers, as Susie makes plain, are participants in a diabolic ritual: "The men that are defending us have leave to bow themselves down in the House of Rimmon, for the men that go with the guns are going with God." Susie's reference to the House of Rimmon (2 Kings 5:18) ironically confirms the idolatrous context for the drinking of wine that Harry has just prepared, a mock communion that will be dramatically reenacted in the final half of the play. This ritual, together with Harry's impassioned language and the images of field and virgin and gun, prepares for the battle zone scene of act 2, a flat landscape "dotted with rayed and shattered shell-holes," and for the actual arrival of the soldiers in the ruined monastery with its black-robed Virgin—the place where the elevated figure of the Croucher is the main participant in a stranger and more frightening ritual, the place where all the soldiers finally worship the gun.

Harry's mood and his words are reckless, and they veil the despair he feels at leaving life and love behind: "Out with one of them wine-virgins we got in 'The Mill in the Field,' Barney, and we'll rape her in a last hot moment before we set out to kiss the guns! . . . Into the cup, be-God. A drink out of the cup, out of the Silver Tassie!" Here, the ritual drinking of wine from the tassie occurs twice: the first time Jessie participates in what is, in effect, a betrothal ceremony, a pledge to life and love; the second time—in anticipation of his future isolation—Harry drinks alone.

Ideally, the silver tassie, as we have seen, would be the Holy Grail. In this context it would symbolize the purity and innocence of the heroic young man who has won it, and the righteousness of his quest. But the tragedy lies in the fact that, if the quest is not a righteous one, these virtues which have existed in Harry will be torn from him. Then, ironically, this ritual communion, as surely as the Black Mass of act 2, will lead to destruction and sacrifice, for those who participate in the rituals of an unjust and godless war must be, in the final analysis, idolaters at the altar of life. And so, when Harry drinks from the cup alone, he unwittingly pledges his youth and strength, not to the service of life and love, but to the service of war.

As if in confirmation of this fact, and in preparation for Harry's departure, the lively and bright colours of the football hero, the play-warrior, the lover-of-life, are covered over by the drab khaki of the soldier's uniform. The transformation—the first of several to occur to Harry and the other soldiers—is startling as Susie hands Harry his steel helmet and carries his rifle, as Mrs Heegan hurries her son into his topcoat, as Sylvester gives Harry his haversack and trench tools and carries is kit-bag. Clearly, the participation in the idolatrous communion is wholesale as all help in the ritual dressing and arming of the warrior for battle. Here, the Expressionist choral chant, "You must go back," draws attention to the ritual even as it underlines the responsibility of its participants so that, as the words are picked up and elaborated on by the voices outside, "Carry on from the boat to the camp . . . From the camp up the line to the trenches," we have a sense of an entire nation having blindly and selfishly dedicated itself—and its life and youth—to the senseless destruction of war.

The intrusion of the choral voices from outside dramatizes the larger forces that are operative and symbolically represents the impinging of blind fate or destiny upon the individual. But what we should also hear is simply the voice of the people expressing the will of the majority: "They must go back." The pronouncement appears to carry the force and weight of a categorical imperative, and it must be reckoned with, though its validity, throughout the rest of the play, will be called more and more into question. Here, the culmination of act 1 of *The Silver Tassie* in an integrated Expressionist choral effect, clearly anticipates the progression that becomes evident in the play as a whole: from the implicitly symbolic, heightened realism of the Dublin trilogy to the more formally organized (stylized) symbolism of ritual, a ritual which is nevertheless firmly embedded in reality.

O'Casey obviously felt that the technique was successful, for he uses it again, in a similar way, in the fourth act of *Red Roses for Me*, where a chorus comprised of the poor working men and women of Dublin claim Ayamonn as their leader—"He comes with us!"—a claim that will result, finally, in his martyrdom. It is right that Ayamonn should answer the call, for there are some causes that must be fought and, if necessary, died for. But was the Great War one of these causes? Act 2 of *The Silver Tassie* makes clear that, in O'Casey's view, it was not.

As Harry and the other soldiers embark, the sacrifice which is about to be enacted is suggested by the slow moving away of the ship's masthead, which, throughout act 1, has formed a cross seen through the window above the altar at which the ritualized drinking of wine has taken place. And a life-size cross, whose Christ figure, like a wounded soldier, has an arm torn by an exploding shell, is one of the first images that demands our attention immediately following the curtain-rise of act 2.

THE CROUCHER

Among the ruins of a monastery, in the battle zone of the second act, the desecrated crucifix leans forward grotesquely, the Christ figure stretching out an arm as if in supplication to the Virgin. But the stained glass madonna, made "vividly apparent" by lights inside the ruined monastery, is "white-faced, wearing a black robe," apparently unresponsive and uncaring. Here, the very absence of colour—the black and the white—suggests the sterility of the Church and its remoteness from man's life. Ironically, in this scene of desecration, the two figures become a parody of the pietà, even as the suffering figure opposite them—the soldier undergoing field punishment and tied, spread-eagled, to the great wheel of the gun carriage—becomes a parody of the crucifixion. "Underneath the crucifix on a pedestal, in red letters, are the words: PRINCEPS PACIS." The inscription, in this context, is obviously intended to be ironic: the sacrifices being enacted are not to the greater glory of God, but, instead, make a mockery out of everything the Prince of Peace stands for.

Occupying a central position onstage, a big howitzer gun, with a long "sinister" barrel pointing towards the front, symbolizes the machinery of war and War itself. Both are made by man and venerated by him, and the result of this idolatry, which has "the Church's damned approval," is man's physical and spiritual desolation. The ruined monastery, now used as a Red Cross Station in which lie the dead and dying, suggests the Church's own desolate state. Unknowingly, the Church has become the House of Rimmon, a place of sacrilege.

The landscape stretching to the horizon is bleak and frightening: "Here and there heaps of rubbish mark where houses once stood. From some of these, lean, dead hands are protruding. Further on, spiky stumps of trees which were once a small wood. . . . Across the horizon in the red glare can be seen the criss-cross pattern of the barbed wire bordering the trenches." The visual impact, like that in a nightmarish landscape by Hieronymus Bosch, is staggering. Understandably, the scene evokes a litany of despair, intoned by the strange figure of the Croucher, whose own spiritual desolation is expressed physically in his worn and almost ghostlike appearance. Elevated on a ramp above the brazier, he seems larger than life, and, when the soldiers enter to huddle around the fire, his shadow hovers over them like the shadow of the Angel of Death.

A mass for the dying can be heard coming from a part of the ruined monastery, and the Kyrie Eleison provides a haunting response to the Croucher's ironic reversal of the words taken from the prophet Ezekiel:

> CROUCHER: And the hand of the Lord was upon me, and
>   carried me out in the spirit of the Lord, and set me down
>   in the midst of a valley.
>   And I looked and saw a great multitude that stood upon
>   their feet, an exceeding great army.
>   And he said unto me, Son of man, can this exceeding
>   great army become a valley of dry bones?
>   (*The music ceases, and a voice, in the part of the monastery left
>   standing, intones:* Kyr . . . ie . . . e . . . eleison. Kyr . . . ie
>   . . . e . . . eleison, *followed by the answer:* Christe . . .
>   eleison.
> CROUCHER (*resuming*): And I answered, O Lord God, thou
>   knowest. And he said, prophesy and say unto the wind,
>   come from the four winds a breath and breathe upon these
>   living that they may die.

As the Kyrie Eleison fades into silence, only to be replaced by the bitter responses of the disheartened soldiers, it becomes apparent that the ritual in which all now participate is a celebration, not of life, but of death.

This scene, with its stark visionary power rising so quickly from the opening curtain, is a tour de force of dramatic art, for the Croucher is O'Casey's strangest and most ingenious creation, deriving its inspiration initially from the Expressionist stage, yet going far beyond Expressionism in the complexity of its total achievement. Here, realism and symbolism mingle in a way that suggests affinities with Ibsen—with, for example, the Rat-Wife in *Little Eyolf*, whose entry betokens death. In the Croucher, then, we glimpse that most paradoxical of creations: a realistic figure of flesh and blood whose symbolic dimensions yet seem to take us into a realm beyond the natural world. Such a vision, in fact, can only be transfixed for a moment or two in time. Thus it is only during those moments, at the beginning of act 2, for instance, where the Croucher becomes the principal celebrant in an idolatrous communion, that we can sense a demonic spirit, at times a visible presence, hovering over all.

Of *The Silver Tassie* O'Casey wrote, "I wished to show the face and unveil the soul of war." And, in the Black Mass of act 2, we actually have unveiled to us, in the mysterious figure of the Croucher, both the face and the soul of war. For, clearly, it is the demonic God of War that has possessed this despairing soldier. Throughout the rest of the act, until just before the end, he sits as motionless as an idol except for the illusion of movement created by the play of light and shadow across his face and body. In the flickering light, though there are moments in which the crouching form still looks like that of a sick and sleeping soldier, there are other moments in which we glimpse again the death's head, the horrible skull-like face of War. These transformations, which take place in the twinkling of an eye, are strange, but powerful. And while the stage action below may seem to call attention away from the Croucher, it is impossible to forget that he is there.

For when the soldiers enter and huddle together in a close mass over the brazier just beneath the ramp, they are clearly linked both aurally (by the chanting) and visually (by their stooped postures) with the Croucher above. Though their unwitting participation in the diabolic ritual seems spontaneous, it is somehow evoked by that dark and shadowy presence until, together, they become an image of a larger humanity, in which for the moment all individuality is merged.

Here O'Casey's complex mingling of realism and Expressionism results once more in a number of strange and startling transformations as the individual soldiers of act 1 "dissolve," in act 2, into the group of soldiers who are, for the most part, anonymous. In order to create these effects, O'Casey attempts a very specialized kind of doubling, which, as we shall see, is not unlike the kind Ernst Toller so frequently used. The only soldier who clearly retains his identity is—not Harry as we might have expected—but Barney. Tied to a gunwheel for stealing an Estaminay cock, he occupies a position onstage that immediately rivets our attention. At the same time, there is a soldier in act 2 who more gradually draws attention to himself, for he looks "very like Teddy." This soldier, as O'Casey must have intended, should be played by the same actor who plays Teddy, though ever since the Apollo production this doubling has, as often as not, been neglected in casting.

Far from neglecting it, however, Massey apparently welcomed the sug-

gestion and even went on to cast the actor who played Harry Heegan, Charles
Laughton, as the 1st Soldier in act 2; though a statement in his autobiography
indicates that he did so, not so much to satisfy the audience's wish to see
Harry onstage again, as to realize what he understood of the play's Expressionist structure, and so integrate act 2 into the play on a symbolic, rather
than on a realistic, level. He writes: "Although the three soldiers from the
first act appear in this scene, all the characters are ciphers and have no
connection with the rest of the play." Massey's use of doubling, then, shows
that his rapport with *The Silver Tassie* was such that he understood the
thematic and symbolic relationship between act 2 and the rest of the play:
that war can strip man of his individual identity, and plunge him into a
nightmare world where he is a robot-like part of a vast machine. But he
remained unaware of the full potential of the doubling device to unify the
play in terms of character and action, a unity which is essential if the ritual
of war is to form an integral part of the play's vision.

In having a clearly recognizable character from act 1—Barney—appear
in act 2, O'Casey is obviously identifying the scene as that part of the war
zone to which the three soldiers have disembarked, as Mrs Foran says,
"safely." But if Barney is here, and someone who looks very like Teddy,
then where is their inseparable companion from act 1? where is Harry
Heegan? Indeed, might not O'Casey be inviting the audience to ask this
question? And do we not find ourselves searching for Harry, over and over
again in the features of the other soldiers, as each face in turn is lit up and
momentarily distorted by the eerie red glow from the fire? Thus we anticipate
Harry's arrival throughout act 2, much as we anticipated his triumphant
entry, which did not occur until more than midway through act 1. In fact,
Harry's absence from the beginning of both acts and the growing anticipation
of his appearance further increases the parallelism between acts 1 and 2, a
unifying device already strongly at work in the play.

Unfortunately, however, Massey's innovative doubling of the role of
Harry Heegan and the 1st Soldier—the same actor in the same uniform—
completed the needed recognition scene prematurely. The result, in the
Apollo production, was that the audience recognized Harry at the beginning
of the act and the unifying effect of parallelism was actually distorted. Certainly, of all Massey's innovations, this was the only one O'Casey did *not*
incorporate into the Stage Version of the text, nor has it, so far as I am
aware, ever been tried out again onstage.

And yet the idea of having Harry appear somewhere in act 2—preferably
after the midpoint of the act—is a fascinating one since, not only would it
fulfill the expectations of the audience, but it would also answer, in a very

concrete and practical way, Yeats's charge that, in *The Tassie*, "there is no dominating character, no dominating action, neither psychological unity nor unity of action." The problem Yeats raises here has been such a difficult one that most O'Casey critics have continued to comment on it. Robert Hogan, for example, finds that, without Harry, act 2 is undramatic; lyricism and "stage magic" replace drama: "the act is static, sheer mood. It depends for effectiveness less upon the dramatist than upon the set designer." His solution is drastic: omit act 2 (and possibly act 3) from *The Tassie* altogether. By contrast, David Krause, whose pioneering work on O'Casey will always stand as a touchstone for later critics, takes a more positive approach. In keeping with the precedent set by the Apollo production, Krause suggests: "Surely Harry is too important to be dropped completely. Perhaps there could have been a soldier "very like Harry," or possibly Harry, with his ukulele, could have been represented in distortion by a figure somewhat like the Croucher."

In fact, what holographs of *The Tassie* show is that Harry Heegan, at one point in the play's development, did appear quite recognizably in act 2, and disappeared from that act as a realistic character only some time after the image of the Croucher began to shape itself strongly in O'Casey's mind in conjunction with the image of an anonymous, legless soldier. In the holographs, as these two images fuse, what we can see in the Croucher—in that wounded crouching soldier who participates in a diabolic ritual—is a soldier "very like Harry," or, rather, very like what Harry is to become. But how to depict onstage the relationship between the symbolic Croucher and the realistic soldier, Harry Heegan, whose identity is now engulfed by war, remained an insuperable problem, one in which the decision of whether or not Harry should actually appear in act 2 as a recognizable figure, or when he should appear, was critical.

The difficulty O'Casey had in solving this problem is further reflected in his treatment of Teddy, who also appeared originally in this act, like Barney, as a clearly recognizable figure. Yet Teddy's name was deleted from act 2 in the very copy of the typescript that had been returned by the Abbey, as if this revision, in the face of Yeats's criticism, was somehow meant to validate Harry's continuing absence. Thus, when Teddy disappears he is replaced simply by an anonymous soldier. In a still later typescript, however, O'Casey, having had time to consider the problem further, returned Teddy to the battle zone scene by adding the notation "very like Teddy," beside the first speech of the 4th Soldier. As we have seen, it must have been this stage direction which prompted Massey (while engaged in the practical expedient of reducing a large cast) to have the actor who played Teddy double as one of the anonymous soldiers in the second act—and to have the actor who played Harry double as the 1st Soldier.

In agreeing to this additional doubling in the Apollo production, O'Casey showed his willingness to experiment further with the idea of returning Harry, as well as Teddy, to act 2 and so have all three soldiers there in some guise or other. But in failing to incorporate this particular doubling into the Stage Version of the text, O'Casey strongly indicated his recognition of the fact that this innovation was not working onstage. For what has happened to Harry and to the other soldiers can only be fully understood if the process of "looking for Harry" is not interrupted by a recognition scene which takes place much too soon.

In fact, with every entrance (and there is a lot of coming and going in this supposedly "static" act) we should be aware of looking for Harry. Though we do not find him, there are many things that remind us of him— the football game, for example, which suddenly erupts on mid-stage, occasioned by the brightly coloured ball that the frivolous Mollie has sent her soldier, "To play your way to the enemies' trenches when you all go over the top." The ball is red and yellow, the colours of life, the colours of Harry's football uniform. And so it seems, for an instant, in the midst of death, Harry springs to life, joyous, triumphant as we last saw him.

The effect of this scene, juxtaposed with the immediately preceding one, is electrifying. For, just moments earlier, comedy and pathos have modulated swiftly into terror as the soldier who has eagerly anticipated cigarettes or playing cards in the parcel from home receives instead:

3RD SOLDIER: A prayer-book!
4TH SOLDIER: In a green plush cover with a golden cross.
CROUCHER: Open it at the Psalms and sing that we may be
    saved from the life and death of the beasts that perish.
BARNEY: Per omnia saecula saeculorum.

At once, the solemn intoning of the Croucher's prayer and the Latin response chanted by Barney recall the way in which the act began. Again the Croucher assumes strange and inhuman dimensions, though, paradoxically, the crouching form continues, at the same time, to suggest man's mortal nature, humanity bowed beneath the shadow of a dark and menacing figure. It is in the shadow of death, then, that the gayly coloured ball bounces and the soldiers, who remind us of Harry and his joyous zest for life, begin to play— though not for long.

As the enemy's attack advances, and the soldiers prepare to defend themselves, the act moves swiftly to its conclusion in a further series of strange and frightening transformations, which, as in Harry's startling transformation towards the end of act 1 from triumphant football hero to soldier, again involves both costuming and the physical movement of the actors onstage. When the soldiers put on their gas masks, "their forms crouched in a huddled act of obeisance" to the gun—"We believe in God and we believe in thee"—they no longer look human. There is something bestial about their appearance which recalls, and mocks, the Croucher's prayer "that we may be saved from the life and death of the beasts that perish." In fact, once the Croucher himself joins the sacrilegious worshippers of the gun, he can no longer be distinguished from the other soldiers, whose crouching forms now fill the stage. All have lost their identity, all have become less than human—anonymous links in the impersonal, and soulless machinery of war.

For what has just occurred, marked by that moment when the soldier crouched on the ramp descends to the stage below, is the final terrifying incarnation of the God of War, not in one soldier only but in all who, in their prayer to the gun, have willingly invoked his demonic spirit.

Yet, frightening as all these transformations are, there is one which is more terrifying still, for, in that exact moment between the time when the Croucher rises to come down from the ramp and before he reappears amidst the crouching forms of the other soldiers—the Croucher vanishes! And in the skull-like features of the despairing soldier who stands before us now, we should glimpse, instead, the drawn, anguished face of Harry Heegan, the missing soldier whose arrival we have so long anticipated. Then, before we can be quite certain of what we have just seen, the soldier puts on his gas mask, and there once again is the ugly, monstrous, terrifying face of War: the staring, empty eyes, the body deformed by the crouched posture, the voice chanting lifelessly in response to the corporal's hymn of praise to the gun.

To realize act 2 onstage in this way, however, as part of an integrated narrative and symbolic structure, obviously requires one further innovation, one that the holographs and typescripts suggest, and that Raymond Massey's Apollo production was actually moving towards: that is, the doubling of the roles of Harry Heegan, and—not of the 1st Soldier—but of the Croucher, himself. As we have seen, Massey's parallel elevations of Harry and the Croucher in the almost identical area onstage have already underlined their spiritual kinship, a relationship which is also confirmed by the fact that both are the main celebrants in a sacrilegious communion in which all the soldiers finally participate. These two sets of parallels, then, mutually reinforce each other to create a strong sense of the diabolic pattern that is weaving its way into Harry's life, one that—once it is thrust upon him—he will accept.

Seen in this way, on the level of character and action, as an integral part of O'Casey's haunting portrait of man possessed by the spirit of war, act 2 of *The Tassie* is clearly meant to convey, not the physical, but the spiritual death of Harry Heegan. For it is important that we understand the nature of the terrible spiritual transformation that Harry undergoes in war, of which his crippled and impotent body, his permanently "crouched" form, is but the exterior sign.

Here O'Casey's use of the mysterious figure of the Croucher to reveal what has happened to Harry Heegan recalls Ernst Toller's practice of revealing the inner, spiritual state of his protagonists by casting them in different symbolic roles. In *Masses and Man*, for instance, when he wishes to show the anguished feelings of guilt that the Woman (Sonia) experiences after she betrays her pacifist principles and joins actively in the revolution of the workers, Toller portrays her as a figure crouched motionless in despair and anguish, undergoing, in a purgatorial setting, the torments of the damned. Similarly, in *Transfiguration*, Toller has his protagonist, a soldier like Harry, appear in a great variety of symbolic guises, such as The Wanderer and The Prisoner.

To what extent O'Casey was consciously aware of the exact nature of Toller's experiments is difficult to say, but it is impossible to read either of these two plays without noticing that many of the images, symbols, and characters which O'Casey uses so economically in act 2 of *The Tassie* seem to have come to him initially out of the plenitude of Toller's wild and extravagant imagination. For example, in the "troop-train" scene of *Transfiguration*, certain elements of the setting seem oddly familiar: "Badly burning oil-lamps shed a meagre, flickering light on the sleeping SOLDIERS huddled close together. With them one silent soldier (with FRIEDRICH's features) and another with a skull for a head: both shadowy figures." When he conceived his own symbolic Croucher, did O'Casey have in mind, either consciously or unconsciously, the silent "huddled" soldier and the one with "a skull for a head," as well as the anguished crouching figure in *Masses and Man*? Was it partly the imaginative kinship of all those huddled and despairing creatures that allowed O'Casey to come up with an expressionist creation which was yet uniquely his own?

If the process was, in fact, a largely unconscious one, then this helps to explain why O'Casey did not indicate in the stage directions, as Toller undoubtedly would have, that Harry and the Croucher should be played by the same actor. On the contrary, in a letter to Lennox Robinson in which O'Casey assumes the Abbey will be producing *The Tassie*, he suggests a doubling of the roles, not of the Croucher and Harry Heegan, but of the Croucher and Surgeon Maxwell, a doubling which is sometimes carried out onstage. Thus, we are forced to give some credence to that flat denial O'Casey made to Rollins in 1960: "I never consciously adopted 'expressionism,' which I don't understand and never did."

Intent on taking into account the specific resources of the Abbey Theatre (and, by an irony of fate which the *Silver Tassie* controversy clearly underlines), O'Casey had inadvertently suggested a practice in casting that actually forestalled the one doubling of roles which would have immediately clarified the dramatic outline of the play itself. Nor does such an innovation require the alteration of even a single word of O'Casey's text. All it requires is the continuation of a practice which has been commonplace enough, both on the contemporary stage and earlier, but which had sometimes been used in a rather special way in Expressionist theatre.

The difficulties which *The Silver Tassie* continually encounters in production would seem to support these conclusions, and to confirm that a more innovative approach to the organic design of the play as a whole is a necessity. For the decision of whether or not the role of the Croucher and the role of Harry Heegan can be doubled effectively in the theatre—whether or not the production will actually "work"—is one which can only be finally demonstrated onstage. Though it is clear that a decision to try out such an innovation should not hinge simply upon the conscious intent of the playwright, but rather upon the imaginative pattern which the play itself reveals.

What we notice in *The Silver Tassie*, then, is that, after act 1, when Harry is absent, the figure who dominates the stage in Harry's place is the Croucher, and, when the Croucher vanishes, Harry reappears. Both are figures larger than life; both have a symbolic as well as a realistic role, a role, moreover, which is identical: to show both the physical and the spiritual loss which man undergoes when he experiences war. And, in order to complete this overall design, what could be more natural than for Harry to reappear, not in the last half of the play only, but at that moment towards the end of act 2 when the Croucher first vanishes? Not only would this one final innovation provide the solution to the problem Raymond Massey was struggling with in the Apollo production, "the integration of this scene [act 2] into the play as a whole," but it would also prepare for the drastically altered role that Harry will play in acts 3 and 4. Most important of all, this recognition scene would satisfy the expectations of the audience, who have been looking everywhere for Harry since act 2 began, but who have, until now, been unable to understand the exact nature of the transformations that have been taking place.

In fact, from a practical viewpoint, it may be that the only way to show the kind of diabolic changes that have taken place, and so realize onstage the body of Harry Heegan possessed by the God of War, would be, as we have said, to have one actor play both roles. Then, throughout the act, there will, of necessity, be something about the Croucher—his build, the sound of his voice—which stirs memories of Harry almost imperceptibly within us until, when the recognition scene does occur, though we are initially startled, we feel, nevertheless, that it is right.

So far as the actor who plays this double role is concerned, he will no longer be left, during act 2, a mere passive backstage spectator of the very moods and passions which he will be called upon to embody so dynamically in acts 3 and 4. Instead, he will have already portrayed, in the Croucher, the spirit of despair which seizes Harry, and will already have felt the spiritual death which has just occurred. He will then be able to understand what has happened to Harry to change him from the triumphant, joyous, and godlike young man of act 1 to the despairing, inhuman, demon-possessed figure of acts 3 and 4. With this understanding the depth of the portrait grows, and no longer should performances occur in which a superficial viewing of Harry is allowed to predominate.

Moreover, as we go on to examine the last two acts, the structure of the play itself develops in a way which continues to suggest that this particular doubling—which both embodies and reveals the complex interrelationship of the two roles—would be a most effective way, not only of realizing in the theatre O'Casey's unique blend of realism and Expressionism, but also of discovering the essential unity of *The Silver Tassie*.

THE JUGGERNAUT IN THE GARDEN

Act 3 reverses the process begun at the opening of the second act by "dissolving out," as it were, from the anonymous masses, the individual soldiers whose lives have been irrevocably reshaped by the tragedy of war. Thus, as well as being unified by recurring colour imagery, ritual, and the symbols of sacrifice, the last two acts develop from the previous two in terms of character and action: with the reappearance of Barney, not as sacrificial victim, as we might have expected, but as hero; of Teddy, now blind, and of the grotesquely transformed Harry, whose shattered spine confines him to a wheelchair. At first Teddy appears as an absurd "stumblebum," who inadvertently wounds Harry with words at every turn. But, by act 4, he has come to terms with the dark world he now inhabits and, as a blind seer, helps Harry to that one moment of spiritual insight that marks the resolution of the play. As they leave, Susie tells us: "Teddy Foran and Harry Heegan have gone to live their own way in another world." Yet it is only with the exploration of the dimensions of that other world, and the tortuous route by which Harry reaches and finally comprehends it, that O'Casey's vision in *The Silver Tassie* is complete.

The last half of the play, therefore, shows us the harrowing of that hell which was revealed, in act 2, to be the destination of Harry and the other soldiers. As his name suggests, it is Harry upon whom the chief burden of guilt, expiation, and atonement falls, though whether he will be capable of the task remains in doubt to the very last moment. The role which he must continue to play in this "mass Passion" is developed within the context of the already established symbols, but is broadened now by the addition of the image of the garden.

As is so characteristic of O'Casey, symbols and images are made concrete, embodied in the stage setting, stage properties, make-up, lighting, and, of course, in the appearance and actions of the actors themselves. During the second half of the play, then, images of light and colour contrast the oppressive darkness of the war zone, a darkness which has been illuminated momentarily, however, by the red glow from the fire, and, by the "white glare" from the silently firing guns. It is this white glare that is packed up in the intense surgical whiteness of the hospital ward in act 3, even as the fiery red is dominant among the brilliant colours seen through the arched entrance to the dancehall in act 4. Both suggest the aftermath of war: the sterile, pain-filled existence of those who are crippled—and the apparently joyous and carefree life of those who seem to have come through war's holocaust unscathed. Though, in this way, the last two acts are diametrically opposed, each contains the symbols of sacrifice. For, in the hospital scene, the colours of war—black and red—are evident in the coverlets on the beds, while above, so that the wounded may pull themselves up, hang wooden cross-pieces. Similarly, in the Avondale club room to which the dancehall is adjacent, these same colours and shapes fuse in the overhead lanterns to form "an illuminated black cross with an inner one of gleaming red."

In the background of both scenes glass casements reveal a garden: at times a lost Eden, at times a Gethsemane where there is suffering and betrayal; and, finally, by the end of act 4, perhaps a garden of promise and renewal, ever so faintly suggested by the green of the two sycamore trees. As the recurring symbols suggest, the structure of both acts continues to centre on the sacrificial victims of war, especially on Harry, whose angry, volatile presence continues to dominate the play. Though at times he is sunk in despair or momentarily elated by hope, too often Harry is caught up in a warlike rage that makes of him more a figure to be feared than pitied.

His entrance in act 3—for, as usual, Harry is not onstage when the curtain rises—is a dramatic one, prepared for ironically by Sylvester's un-intentionally prophetic words, "how are the mighty fallen, and the weapons of war perished!" No longer elevated triumphantly on the shoulders of his friends, but instead—as O'Casey clearly specifies in the stage directions—"crouched in a self-propelled invalid chair," Harry is the embodiment of that other isolated and despairing figure, the Croucher of act 2, a transformation which will be dramatically reenacted in the Juggernaut scene, more than midway through act 3. The unexpected appearance of Harry trapped in the wheelchair should also recall, from the previous act, the equally unexpected appearance of Barney tied to the gunwheel, though, with the turning of the wheel of fortune, their destinies have been reversed. Here, the two images merge to form a composite one which is summed up now in the tortured person of Harry Heegan: man victimized by war and imprisoned by the machine becomes, finally, a symbol of all suffering and crucified mankind.

Harry's newly mechanized existence, marked by his incessant and pur-poseless movement onstage in the wheelchair—"Down and up, up and down. Up and down, down and up"—is a futile substitute for the movement of his own paralysed limbs and an expression of his rage and despair at what has happened. Significantly, the pain Harry suffers is mental, not physical, and is symptomatic of his spiritual desolation, a despair driven to an agonized pitch of intensity by the sense that no one understands what has happened to him, nor does he understand it himself.

In the visiting scene, the one person he so desperately wants near him is Jessie, but she is as terrified of what has happened as he is himself, and no one can make her come in from the garden, not even Harry, whose pathetic calling of her name is answered only by silence. The sense of Harry's tragic isolation is further underlined by Susie, who hurries in to clear the ward of visitors and order him to bed. The screen which Simon "places around Harry, hiding him from view," emphasizes even more the finality of Harry's separation both from Jessie and from everyone around him. The next moment, when the screen is taken away, we are startled by the trans-formation he has undergone, a transformation which denies Mrs Foran's empty words of comfort heard moments earlier—"The drawn look on his face isn't half as bad as when I seen him last"—and mocks Mrs Heegan's cheerful reply: "Look, the hollows under his eyes is fillin' up, too." For Harry's agony has etched a death-like pallor in his face and the black spread Susie has placed over him covers him like a shroud. As Susie turns off the lights in the hospital ward, leaving only the red light over the fireplace, the sudden oppressive darkness, in conjunction with the piteable image Harry now presents, as he struggles, with the help of the crossbar, into a sitting posture, once more abruptly realizes onstage the huddled, despairing form of the Croucher with his drawn, skull-like head.

The components of the two scenes are parallel in structure: the elevated hospital bed with its dark covering occupies the almost identical area of the stage as does the Croucher's ramp in act 2; the lighting—an eerie red glow permeating the ominous darkness—casts similarly grotesque shadows; and when, suddenly, the bell of the adjacent convent rings out for the last religious service of the day, we are reminded of the slow and stately notes of the organ in the ruined monastery which accompanied the Croucher's despairing prophesy of doom. In fact, the deep, brassy tone of the slowly tolling bell accentuates the ominous note in Harry's words so that, as he speaks, we hear once more a prophecy of death and destruction: "In a net I'll catch butterflies in bunches; twist and mangle them between my fingers and fix them wriggling on to mercy's banner. I'll make my chair a Juggernaut, and wheel it over the neck and spine of every daffodil that looks at me, and strew them dead to manifest the mercy of God and the justice of man!"

Implicit in the reference to the Juggernaut—a metaphor which connotes the overpowering, destructive force of war—and realized concretely onstage by the menacing form of Harry crouched in the wheelchair, is the image of an idol carried by a chariot, beneath whose wheels the living are ruthlessly sacrificed. By act 4, where Harry literally "make[s his] chair a Juggernaut" in which he runs into Barney and smashes through the glass doors of the clubhouse, we see in the misshapen, war-torn figure of Harry, not the ideal-ized form of this god, but an image which accurately portrays his awesome and savage nature. As Harry's savage actions continue to strip him of all humanity, what we see, too, is an image of mechanized man: the inhuman, soulless, murdering force behind the impersonal machinery of war.

No wonder, then, that Harry's words repel Susie, for they denounce both man and nature and deny the possibility of mercy or justice. His wish to destroy the beauty of nature, to break the spine of every daffodil, even as his own spine has been shattered, means that Harry has brought the desolate landscape of the war zone back with him, an accurate reflection of his own spiritual desolation. In the absurd universe which he now inhabits, a world as senseless as the one Beckett's Hamm in *Endgame* wishes to destroy, Harry appears grotesque and his words ridiculous as he curses Susie, together with all living things: "To hell with you, your country, trees, and things, you jibbering jay!" Susie has no answer except for the stunned calling of his "name"—"Twenty-eight!"

Appropriately enough, in a godless world, in a world given over to the machine, Christian names are replaced by numbers and categories. Susie

calls Sylvester and Simon, "Twenty-six" and "Twenty-seven," and she reminds them, "I am to be addressed as 'Nurse Monican,' and not as 'Susie.' "
Alternately, the patients are spoken of as "poor devils," a phrase which echoes ironically throughout act 3 to point to the sometimes foolish, sometimes tragic, incarnations of demon-possessed man. The poorest devil of all, of course, is Harry, as his despairing cry, "God of the miracles, give a poor devil a chance!," makes plain. In the context of this ironic prayer, the Sisters' "Salve Regina," sung offstage like that other plea for mercy, the "Kyrie Eleison," should recall, from act 2, the terrible Black Mass which still threatens to separate Harry from life, and from God, forever.

Yet, terrifying as Harry is in act 3, he is even more terrifying in act 4, which takes place at the Avondale Football Club, the place of his former triumphs. Everywhere he turns he is goaded into fury by the reminder of his bitter loss and vanished victories. His wrath, as he propels himself madly around the dancehall in pursuit of Jessie and Barney, is really a measure of his pain, though here Harry also appears as a figure of nemesis—one of the most familiar guises of War—seeking, in the absence of any other kind of justice, retribution and vengeance. And, in this guise, it is no wonder that Jessie cannot see the Harry she once loved. Certainly he can no longer be recognized in the crouched and frenzied figure who circles the dancehall again and again as if he and the machine are one entity, trapped in some senseless and destructive pattern of its own. What Jessie is fleeing from is not Harry, but the mechanized "thing" that hurtles after her: the spectre of War, the Juggernaut beneath whose wheels she refuses to be crushed. And, of course, she is right.

The choice that Jessie has had to make is not an easy one, as is signified by her reluctance, at the end of the play, to join in the dance. Her cry, "Poor Harry!," is the only heartfelt expression of sorrow and pity that rises heavenward on his behalf throughout the play. The cry, like the pathetic flowers that she sends to Harry in act 3, and which are flung so hopelessly on the black quilt at the foot of Harry's bed, as "on a grave," suggests, too, her own sense of loss and grief. Of all the women in the play, she is actually the most sympathetic, and, in retrospect, she appears "predatory" only if we believe the envious words of Susie and Mrs Heegan, or the vicious accusations of Harry, himself.

To Harry, Jessie is the sum of the life and love and joy that he has lost forever, a loss that becomes too great for him to bear when he sees Jessie in Barney's arms. In the grotesque quarrel with Barney which follows, Harry—exactly as he had promised—makes his chair a Juggernaut and bursts into the clubhouse from the garden to appear before Jessie and Barney like an avenging demon. Harry calls Jessie a "whore," and, as Barney bends over the wheelchair to seize him by the throat, these two crouching figures decorated with medals of honour become an image of all that is noble and godlike in man having been crippled and debased to the level of a beast.

Previously, during the ritual wine drinking which begins act 4, Harry has seen himself, ironically, as a "creeping thing" trying to praise the Lord, and demands: "But stretch me on the floor fair on my belly, and I will turn over on my back, then wriggle back again on to my belly; and that's more than a dead, dead man can do!" Implicit here is the image of a serpent, an image that suggests his own guilt. In this vivid context of a guilty and lost humanity, we should recall once more the bestial, crouching forms of the worshipping soldiers at the end of act 2, with whom, to some extent, Harry's identity is still merged. Deliberately, as he did in act 1, Harry calls for the silver tassie so that it may be filled with wine. This time, however, Harry is aware of the true nature of that earlier communion, even as he is aware of the symbolic colour of the wine: "red like the blood that was shed for you and for many for the commission of sin!"

The phrase "for the commission of sin" now clearly defines the earlier ritual as an idolatrous one. Yet Harry drinks again for, Christ-like, he has accepted the fact that this bitter cup will not pass away, but must be drunk to the full. Unlike Christ, however, he feels no bond of sympathy and love that would allow him to bridge the vast abyss separating him from man and from God.

The measure of the distance which separates Harry from others is shown in his frantic attempt to join in the revelry of the dancers, an attempt which fails partly because the dance itself, as the black streamers among the coloured ones suggest, is not a true celebration of life. Though often, especially in *Red Roses for Me*, O'Casey uses dance and song as a metaphor for that joyous celebration of life which is a truly sacred communion, the celebration here is clearly not of that nature. Instead, the scene is one of the most tortured in the entire play. As Harry, clad in a black suit and a red and black paper hat, tries desperately to take charge of the revelries—"Trumpets and drum begin! . . . Dance and dance and dance"—then madly whirls his wheelchair around to the tempo of the tune, there is a pathos surpassing anything achieved by the grotesque scenes of the Expressionists. At the same time, in its painful mingling of farce and tragedy, the scene also anticipates the metaphysical intensity so characteristic of the Theatre of the Absurd.

Yet the scene goes beyond the Absurd, for, out of the bleak, metaphysical dimensions of the tortured landscape that Harry inhabits, a still, small voice is heard: "Dear God, I can't." Ironically, the cry is both a denial

and an affirmation. It is the mark of a soul fallen by the wayside and desperately trying to struggle back to God. Teddy's hand on Harry's shoulder
is the first sign that there will be any help on the journey, as, spontaneously,
in balanced strophe and antistrophe, each carefully weighs the full measure
of the lot that has been meted out to him, trying to see that the scales balance,
that the measure is just:

> HARRY: I can see, but I cannot dance.
> TEDDY: I can dance, but I cannot see. . . .
> HARRY: I never felt the hand that made me helpless.
> TEDDY: I never saw the hand that made me blind.
> HARRY: Life came and took away the half of life.
> TEDDY: Life took from me the half he left with you.

Harry's crushing of the silver tassie, probably beneath the wheels of
the Juggernaut (a scene which occurs offstage, as did the parallel one in
which Harry was crippled), suggests his own role in the tragedy that has
been enacted. As the chanting soldiers of the second act have warned us,
God's children are "self-slaying," and now we have proof that the hand that
is raised in war to strike a brother falls inevitably on one's own head. With
this realization, despite the distorted form which now permanently veils his
own humanity, he can ask once more to be recognized by God and by man:

> Dear God, this crippled form is still your child . . . Dear Mother,
> this helpless thing is still your son. Harry Heegan, me, who, on
> the football field, could crash a twelve-stone flyer off his feet . . .
> And now, before I go, I give you all the Cup, the Silver Tassie,
> to have and to hold for ever, evermore . . . Mangled and bruised
> as I am bruised and mangled. Hammered free from all its comely
> shape.

The simplicity of his words speaks movingly of Harry's new-found humanity
and makes good his plea for recognition, though, even as he speaks, his words
become tinged with renewed bitterness at the thought of the terrible price
he has paid. Moreover, the angry suggestion that the tassie be opened out
again for Barney and Jessie indicates that, not only will there be other
idolatrous communicants at the altar of life, but also, despite Harry's sacrifice, there will be other wars.

But for all the residue of bitterness and self-mockery, Harry's agony
has lessened. He is no longer inconsolable, no longer totally isolated from
those around him. Now, at last, he is able to accept the bond of love and
comradeship that Teddy offers, and which is hallowed by their common

suffering: "Come, Harry, home to where the air is soft. No longer can you stand upon a hill-top; these empty eyes of mine can never see from one. Our best is all behind us—what's in front we'll face like men, dear comrade of the blood-fight and the battle-front!" Together, they move into the garden, a place which is evocative, not of Eden so much as of Gethsemane, a place which, as it is set peripherally in opposition to the stark wasteland of act 2, and the absurd foregrounds of acts 3 and 4, suggests the possibility, at least, of spiritual renewal.

For there is more than stoic endurance here: there is an understanding of the terrible suffering that man, in his blindness, brings upon himself, and in which he may unwittingly imitate the passion of Christ. Thus, as the dedication of the play makes plain—"To Eileen with the yellow daffodils in the green vase"—there is, as always with O'Casey, in the face of suffering and death, a positive affirmation of life. If this affirmation in *The Tassie* comes as a whisper, rather than as a shout, it is because of the terrible intensity of the suffering. And if there is something more than faintly ironic, perhaps even quite absurd, about a Christ figure—Harry—who, though risen from his harrowing of hell, is only half-risen, and, therefore, impotent and powerless, there is also something incredibly audacious about the quality of the artistic vision which can bring us face to face with such a creation without leading us into despair.

"Personally, I think the play is the best work I have yet done. I have certainly put my best into it, & have written the work solely because of love & a deep feeling that what I have written should have been written." Though *The Silver Tassie* was fated to become his own private Gethsemane, O'Casey's letter to Lady Gregory makes clear the spirit in which the play was conceived and written, and the optimism with which it was sent forth. That its reception—and the resultant controversy—was so disastrous both for its author and for the Abbey Theatre is one of the greatest ironies in the history of modern drama.

For what O'Casey needed—and what Yeats refused him and Massey once gave him—was an experimental theatre in which to reshape and revitalize his plays onstage. In such a theatre, what *The Silver Tassie* can demonstrate is that it does not deserve to be thought of as a flawed masterpiece, but as a play which can finally overcome all flaws to achieve that perfection of form which is, and has always been, its birthright.

HEINZ KOSOK

Juno and the Paycock

The historical events which form the background to *Juno and the Paycock* fill the time-span between the events of *The Shadow of a Gunman* and those of *Kathleen Listens In*. The play is set in September (acts 1 and 2) and November (act 3) of the year 1922, at a time when the first climax of the Civil War was over. The Republican troops, beaten in several battles, had returned to the type of guerilla-warfare that had proved successful in the War of Independence. Their conflict with the Free Staters over the 1921 Treaty with England is the darkest chapter in recent Irish history. The decision for or against the Treaty, the question whether an oath to the British crown was acceptable to Irish politicians or not, led to bitterness and hatred among the Irish troops who only recently had fought together against British dominion, and it has continued to influence political life in Ireland to the present day. Above all, however, the Civil War inflicted new suffering on the majority of the people, who had taken no part in the fighting and who found themselves at the mercy of fanatics on both extremes. This aspect of the conflict is the subject of O'Casey's play.

Juno and the Paycock was produced by the Abbey on March 3, 1924. Again only a short time had elapsed between the historical events treated in the play and the premiere. As in *The Shadow of a Gunman*, O'Casey makes use of a number of personal experiences; indeed he especially included several of his acquaintances with their peculiar idiosyncrasies of gesture, speech and habit, sometimes not even changing their names. A great deal of painstaking

From *O'Casey the Dramatist*, translated by Heinz Kosok and Joseph T. Swann. © 1985 by Colin Smythe Ltd.

labour has been spent on the reconstruction of the identity of these models for Jack Boyle, Joxer Daly and others. More important, however, than such biographical spade-work is the fact that Dublin audiences seem to have recognized immediately the traits that make these figures into typical representatives of the world of the Dublin slums. It was its twofold actuality, its temporal closeness to the historical events and its topographical immediacy to the slums of the Dublin city centre, which made for the play's spontaneous acceptance by the Abbey audience. Yet the favourable reception it found in London the following year, resulting in its publication and in the award to its unknown author of the Hawthornden Prize, cannot be explained merely by its immediate actuality. The London production made it clear that *Juno and the Paycock*, in spite of its Dublin roots, takes up a basic human situation in a way that affects audiences (and readers) from quite a different national and social background. This effect has not been lost over the years: *Juno and the Paycock* is the O'Casey play most frequently acted outside Ireland and has been accepted into the theatrical repertoire of many different countries.

Its appeal is partly due to the fact that from the point of view of technique *Juno and the Paycock* is O'Casey's most conventional play. Audiences and critics are not impeded in their understanding by those barriers of experiment in technique which O'Casey introduced in his later plays. The author here shows that he can handle traditional techniques to perfection; when he deviated from these in his later works (beginning with *The Plough and the Stars*), this cannot therefore be ascribed to lack of skill, but has to be seen as a consequence of his dissatisfaction with conventional forms. O'Casey's own derogatory remarks about *Juno and the Paycock*, with which he began to shock his most ardent admirers a few years after the first production, are probably due to this dissatisfaction with the play's lack of formal originality.

If in *The Shadow of a Gunman* the dominant structural element was the dramatic figures themselves, in *Juno and the Paycock* it is a logically developed plot, rich in events, which progresses from the expository opening scene through first hints of imminent danger to the false climax of act 2 with the subsequent unmasking of illusion, the possibility of a happy outcome and its frustration to the final catastrophe. In accordance with conventional techniques, three lines of action are interwoven, each of them triggered off and propelled by a motif familiar from the history of drama. There are, however, three deviations from a well-made play in the nineteenth-century tradition: (1) as in *The Shadow of a Gunman*, the action is not autonomous but takes place against an historical background by which it is influenced at decisive moments; (2) while two of the three lines of action are conceived progressively, the third is constructed analytically, i.e., it does not show a complete sequence of events but only their final outcome, reconstructing what has gone before in an exposition that extends across the whole play; (3) a series of static scenes, showing no development but contributing significantly to the meaning of the play, is intercalated between the three lines of the action.

It will be advisable to deal with these three lines of action and the sequence of static scenes separately, although they are so closely interwoven that the attempt to isolate individual threads constantly endangers the whole texture of the play. This becomes apparent right at the start. The first two sentences of dialogue introduce all four areas of the action: the first sentence, spoken by the central character of that part of the action concerned with Mary, introduces the action around Johnny, the second sentence, spoken by Juno, the central character of the third line of action, prepares for the scenes around "Captain" Boyle and Joxer Daly. The whole exposition scene, which extends to the first moment of dramatic impact, the entry of Jerry Devine, is a masterpiece of realistic theatre. In a few sentences, without violating the limits of probability, a wealth of important information is introduced. The situation of the family as a whole and of its individual members is presented; in alternately direct and indirect characterization the personality of all the central characters is sketched in and their relationship towards each other is introduced; the report of the shooting arouses the audience's expectations and turns them in the intended direction. From now on the lines of action can progress simultaneously rather than consecutively.

The action concerned with Johnny is the easiest to isolate from the context of the play, although it shows a misunderstanding of the play as a whole when a critic declares that it is unrelated to the other parts of the plot. Among the few documents which bear on the genesis of O'Casey's plays, none is as important as the following by Gabriel Fallon:

> He had been telling me for some time about a play he had mapped out, a play which would deal with the tragedy of a crippled IRA man, one Johnny Boyle. He mentioned this play many times and always it was the tragedy of Johnny. I cannot recall that he once spoke about Juno or Joxer or the Captain; always Johnny.

At the outset, therefore, it was not the figure of Juno or of the Paycock with which O'Casey was mainly concerned, but the fate of Johnny. The same critic explains that *Juno and the Paycock* initially contained an additional scene, "the shooting of Johnny Boyle which took place in darkness in a roadside setting." This scene was cut by the Abbey directors, because it would have weakened the peculiarly oppressive finality of this part of the action, achieved precisely by the technique of suggestion. After some hesitation, O'Casey accepted this cut for the printed version. It is also reported that O'Casey wrote down the opening lines of his new work, one of the most effective openings of any play in English literature, on the very evening he had been so deeply disappointed by the unfavourable reception of *Kathleen Listens In*.

All the important events of this line of the action, with the one exception of Johnny's arrest and death, lie before the beginning of the play. The disclosure of these events, which runs parallel to the two other, progressive plot lines, is brought on by the motif of guilt pursuing a murderer, torturing him with apparitions of his victim and driving him to the verge of betraying his crime itself—a motif frequently used, from *Macbeth* to nineteenth-century melodrama, in order to render a murderer's pangs of conscience dramatically effective and visible. In *Juno and the Paycock* it also serves to generate suspense; at first it is not clear why Johnny should react so hysterically to any question concerning death in general and the death of Robbie Tancred in particular. Only gradually is it revealed that he has betrayed his former IRA comrade to the Free Staters and thereby caused his death. It is even more difficult to understand his reason for the betrayal. The only hint of an explanation is contained in his words: "It's not because he was a Commandant of the Battalion that I was Quarther-Masther of, that we were friends." But it is left open whether military ambition, jealousy of his successful comrade or the hope of being promoted more quickly after Robbie's death could really be the motive for his deed.

Johnny's fate is connected with a stage property that gradually takes on the function of a symbol: the votive-light in front of the picture of the Virgin that Johnny continually fears to see extinguished becomes a symbol of his life. O'Casey's progress in dramatic technique after *The Shadow of a Gunman* can be observed in detail, when one compares the function of this symbol with the role of the omen in the earlier play. In *The Shadow of a Gunman*, the knocking on the wall remained a blind motif, misleading the audience without dramatic justification. In *Juno and the Paycock* the votive-light is closely associated with Johnny's life, and, consistently with this, it goes out the moment his executioners enter the house. The improbability of the oil being exhausted at this precise moment can easily be overcome by the producer if he arranges for the votive-light to be upset during the symbolic removal of the furniture. In this way, Johnny's fate would be associated even more closely with that of his family, and the demands of realism would be maintained.

The figure of Johnny is a successful psychological study of fear grown out of guilt. The qualification is necessary, for Johnny has previously shown that he is by no means simply a coward. He has therefore more reason than, for instance, Tommy Owens in *The Shadow of a Gunman* to speak of his principles and to insist somewhat pompously: "Ireland only half free'll never be at peace while she has a son left to pull a trigger." It is, of course, possible to condemn such a ruthless attitude, but Johnny has at least proved that he is prepared to risk his health and his life for his convictions. O'Casey gives him more credit, potentially, than some critics are prepared to recognise, and it would be erroneous to take Juno's words, "Ah, you lost your best principle, me boy, when you lost your arm" as the author's own opinion. Whatever his personal preferences may be, the critic is confronted here with two radically opposing attitudes: that of the mother who cares for her family but does not look beyond it, and that of the patriot who is inclined to undervalue the existence of the individual. If Johnny is liable to censure, it is because of his betrayal of Robbie Tancred; his insistence on principles and patriotism, which Juno does not understand, is criticized only when he no longer behaves according to them. Johnny's later behaviour cannot be measured by ordinary standards. When he reproaches his mother, of all people, with "Not one o' yous, not one o' yous, have any thought for me!," or when he wants to cast Mary out, he must be understood as acting in a state of hysteria, arising from the consciousness of his guilt as well as from the fact that his betrayal has been discovered; he flees both from his conscience and from his pursuers. In the person of Johnny, O'Casey has depicted the fate of someone who through a single rash deed has jeopardized all the principles of his life, who has made his past worthless and his future hopeless, a Lord Jim situation without a second chance. Even if the family had in fact inherited the money, Johnny would not have been saved, because the apparition of his dead comrade would have followed him beyond any possible escape from his real pursuers.

The "Johnny" action has three main functions for the play. First, Johnny's injury, his persecution mania and his final kidnapping are part of the catastrophe that besets the Boyles, particularly affecting his mother; his death contributes to the ruin of the family. Secondly, it is in this line of action that the historical background events enter the play. Like other boys, Johnny (perhaps as a member of Fianna Eireann) has taken part in the Easter Rising, where he was wounded. After the Free State Treaty he has fought on the side of the Republicans and has lost an arm during the battle in O'Connell Street (July 1–5, 1922). Robbie Tancred was an officer of the Republican troops who after their defeat continued fighting as guerillas and who were known as diehards. The effect of these conflicts on the life of the ordinary individual can be deduced from Juno's words:

> look at the way they're after leavin' the people in this very house. Hasn't the whole house, nearly, been massacreed? There's young

Dougherty's husband with his leg off; Mrs. Travers that had her
son blew up be a mine in Inchegeela, in Co. Cork; Mrs. Mannin'
that lost wan of her sons in ambush a few weeks ago, an' now,
poor Mrs. Tancred's only child gone west with his body made a
collandher of.

Here it becomes apparent that the background events do not concern Johnny
alone. If they are less decisive in their impact than in *The Shadow of a Gunman*
and *The Plough and the Stars*, yet they still overshadow the stage actions,
dominating the characters' imagination and even entering their way of expression. Boyle asserts: "If th' worst comes . . . to th' worse . . . I can join a
. . . flyin' . . . column" and explains his newly won self-confidence with the
(characteristically incorrect) image: "Today, Joxer, there's goin' to be issued
a proclamation be me, establishin' an independent Republic, an' Juno'll have
to take an oath of allegiance."

The third function of this line of action is closely related to the historical
events. It serves to elevate the play beyond the limits of a mere family drama
and to underline its representative character. Johnny is shot because he has
betrayed the son of a neighbour, who again was responsible for another's
death: "I'm told he was the leadher of the ambush where me nex' door
neighbour, Mrs. Mannin', lost her Free State soldier son." While the Boyles'
suffering is presented in detail, the suffering of the Tancred family appears
in one scene only, and that of the Mannings is only alluded to a few times.
Thus in precise gradations from the extended stage events to the merest hint,
a chain of suffering is revealed, reaching far beyond the family and the
community of neighbours. Suffering, personified in Mrs. Tancred's stage
appearance in act 2, is not limited to the Boyles, it concerns the whole
country and points even beyond those national limits. Mrs. Tancred's and
Juno's sufferings for the death of their sons is simply a mother's suffering
for a loss which in her eyes must always appear meaningless.

In this respect, the "Johnny" action goes beyond the function of the
action concerned with Mary. In other respects, however, there are close
analogies between the two. They correspond with each other in four points:
they both depend on a single traditional motif, they provide the audience
with the same opportunities to judge the central characters, they show how
an individual life can be determined through a single irreversible decision,
and they contribute in a similar way to the fate of the family. The action
around Mary is governed by the motif of seduction, the girl being deserted
by her faithless lover. This is certainly one of the most traditional of all
literary motifs; in twentieth-century English drama, from Houghton's *Hindle*

Wakes to Wesker's *Roots*, it has been employed repeatedly. O'Casey's specific contribution to the literary tradition may be seen in the unobtrusiveness with which he has depicted Mary's seduction. He is less interested in her relationship to Bentham and her specific disaster than in its effect on the whole family, especially on Juno. The central function of this line of action, in analogy to that concerned with Johnny, is its contribution to the final catastrophe.

If Johnny is best judged by his attitude to the patriotic movement, Mary can be judged through her attitude to the strike in which she participates. Again, one should not see her only with her mother's eyes: Juno in her maternal egotism rejects any responsibility for others, but this is neither the author's opinion nor the quintessence of the play. Even though Mary transfers part of the sacrifice demanded of her to her mother, one should not under-value her willingness to come out on strike for a colleague who was not even well liked. Mary is neither entirely egotistical, nor is her insistence on prin-ciples and human solidarity so much windy rhetoric. Her behaviour towards Bentham and Jerry Devine is equally ambivalent. Her superficial vanity and her disdain for the milieu in which she has been brought up certainly con-tribute to her decision for Bentham and against Devine, but this is not the only reason. Even when she knows that Bentham has left her, she still insists on her love for him and refrains from condemning him. If she had merely considered him as a means of social advancement, her reaction at this stage would have been different. Mary's character shows the tension between the repressive conditions of her surroundings and her own weak attempts at intellectual and social emancipation. She tries to keep all traces of dialect out of her pronunciation and vocabulary, she reads Ibsen and learns Gaelic, but she does not succeed in liberating herself from the world of the slums. Her weaknesses, her delusion by Bentham and her continuous irritation in her relationship with her family, can be explained as arising from this conflict. Ironically it is Bentham, to whom she looks for release from her surround-ings, who is responsible for her irrevocable commitment to them. As with Johnny, a single false step leads inescapably to her downfall, and it would be hard to decide whether Johnny's death or Mary's future life might be reckoned the graver fate.

Closely associated with the "Mary" action is the figure of Jerry Devine. Dramaturgically, his entrance in act 2 opens up the possibility of a brief countermovement when he declares his continued love for Mary, permitting, it seems, a half-way "happy" solution. Over and above this, Devine (who in ironic contrast to his name poses as an atheist) is also interesting as a character; indeed he has certain traits in common with Mary. Like her, he endeavours to achieve emancipation from his social surroundings and is foiled in the attempt. In his failure he almost reaches tragic stature. He is convinced that he has freed himself from petty bourgeois and religious prejudices, and therefore promises Mary: "No matther what happens, you'll always be the same to me." This promise is repeated after her affair with Bentham: "What does it matter what has happened? . . . With Labour, Mary, humanity is above everying; we are the Leaders in the fight for a new life." But when he realizes that she is pregnant, he finds himself caught precisely in those moral conventions which he has struggled to transcend, and he reacts—to his own dismay—with the cliché that perfectly expresses them: "My God, Mary, have you fallen as low as that?" A "fallen woman" is for him as shocking an idea as it is for his less intellectual neighbours whom, as a socialist, he wants to lead to a new humanity based on mutual tolerance. If one considers Jerry's origins and his social background, it is hardly possible lightly to condemn such a reaction. Regret rather than criticism is called for, inasmuch as Jerry is intellectually capable of recognizing his own situation without having the strength to free himself from it.

A third line of action that might be called the "family" action, is based like the others on a traditional motif, an inheritance that, depending on the type of play in question, can either lead through a sudden turn to a happy conclusion or through its non-arrival to a final catastrophe. In *Juno and the Paycock* the motif is used for both purposes. At first the unexpected news of the death of a distant relative and his surprising legacy promises to bring a turning point in the fate of this family that is already on the way to disintegration. Not only would the inherited money have improved their hopeless financial situation, it would also, through the family's removal to another town, have mitigated the subsequent blows of fate: Johnny could have escaped from the revenge of his former comrades, Mary from the neighbours' hostile talk. The news that there has been a mistake in the drawing-up of the will hits the Boyles all the harder. This counter-turn is the end of the mock-release in tension, and it precludes any prospect of help from outside. From now on, it is left solely to the family members to cope with the multiple catastrophe and to rescue from the wreckage what they can. Only Juno succeeds, and she, therefore, deserves special attention. Before turning to her, however, a few remarks on the figure of Bentham and on the sequence of static scenes around Boyle and Joxer are in order.

Bentham, bourgeois and intellectual, who triggers off both turning-points in the family action, is cast more obviously as a type than any other character in the play. If in earlier plays the villain was frequently the nobleman bent on seducing the innocent, unprotected girl, here a representative of the middle-class forcibly enters the world of ordinary people and destroys it. One reason for O'Casey's characterization of Bentham as a stage bourgeois may be that he wanted to illustrate the impression made by such a figure on the tenement people. He had in that case to remain shadow-like, for they have no access to his mental world. They are, then, unable to realise that he follows aims as egotistical as most of theirs (whereas Juno, for instance, can always see through Joxer). There is no way of knowing whether Bentham is at first seriously interested in Mary and is repelled, as she thinks, only by the stupidity and tastelessness of her surroundings, or whether his intentions are from the start directed towards the inheritance of which he has heard by accident and which he tries to secure for himself through his marriage to Mary. Ironically he is foiled in his attempt to secure the money not, as would have been the case in nineteenth-century melodrama, through the virtuous girl's resistance but through his own trivial error in the drawing-up of the will: his idea of his own infallibility is thus reduced to absurdity.

If Bentham is capable of recognizing the reprehensibility of his actions, such moral standards can hardly be applied to "Captain" Boyle, the "Paycock" of the title. He is the most remarkable representative of a long series of characterless good-for-nothings in O'Casey's plays who nevertheless appear attractive in a strange way and who can certainly number Falstaff among their ancestors. Boyle, in his companionship with Joxer Daly, is also related to Sir Toby Belch and Sir Andrew Aguecheek. Yet such models should not be valued too highly; literary influences are less important than O'Casey's personal acquaintance with the people of the Dublin tenements. There he found sufficient examples of the type of the stupid and arrogant blatherer who is allergic to work, boasts of imagined heroic deeds and acts purposefully only when his way leads to the pub. It is one of O'Casey's remarkable achievements that he establishes a certain amount of sympathy for such a character although, in reality, repugnance would be more probable; and he does so despite the fact that Boyle neglects his family in a most irresponsible way, leaves the burden of care solely to his wife and at a decisive moment rejects his daughter in an outburst of moral indignation that in him is entirely unjustified.

The reason for Boyle's attraction lies mainly in the irresistible comedy of his appearances, this being based on the continuous confrontation of talking and doing, of pretension and fulfilment, of appearance and reality. While the audience quickly recognizes this discrepancy, Boyle is incapable of such an insight. It is with full conviction that he can boast of his experiences sailing the world although he has only travelled once, and that only to Liverpool; he can brag of his willingness to accept any work and nevertheless

feel pains in his leg whenever a job is offered to him; he can order a coat on
credit and announce in the same breath that he has known for some time of
the will's invalidity. He does not, however, lie on purpose, but permits
himself to be drawn again and again into the web of his fantasy, deceiving
himself with his image of an industrious, patriotic, calamity-stricken father
and husband. Unlike O'Casey's later plays, these scenes are dominated by
character-comedy rather than situation-comedy.

   Their impact is intensified by the introduction of Joxer, who supple-
ments Boyle (in spite of their character differences) in an ideal way. Both of
them contradict themselves continually, but if with Boyle this is due to lack
of judgement, with Joxer it is due to calculation. Joxer is more than a match
for Boyle because he knows the effects of his words and actions. He is by
no means only a submissive hanger-on who turns his admiration for his
master into the occasional triumph of a petty revenge. He is much more
closely related to the type of the parasite, personified in Ben Jonson's Mosca,
who is intellectually superior to his opposite number, can manipulate him
at will, and betrays his contempt for him only when there is nothing to be
gained. Actors have varied in their portrayal of Joxer between a fearful,
harmless, comic and a sinister, threatening, demonic figure; O'Casey's intention seems to lie somewhere between these extremes.

   The characters of Boyle and Joxer, who are unable to make decisions
and incapable of development, render the sequence of their scenes static
rather than dynamic. It is impressive evidence of O'Casey's dramatic power
that he is able to incorporate two central characters into his play who contribute nothing to the progress of the action. Even more remarkable is it
that their roles are not limited to comic relief, but that they contribute
significantly to the meaning of the play. Several times Boyle, without stepping outside his role, provides the audience with important insights which
one would hardly expect in burlesque drunkard scenes. Occasionally this
happens in a purely comic manner, when Boyle, for instance, without realizing the ambiguity of his words, assures his partner: "The two of us was
ofen in a tight corner." The most complex example of such an unconscious
contribution to the meaning of the play, exceeding by far the intellectual
horizon of the characters themselves, is the final scene. If one considers
Boyle's and Joxer's last appearance after the triple catastrophe to be no more
than the senseless babbling of two drunkards in whose dimmed consciousness
a few memories rise up like bubbles of marsh gas and burst without effect,
it is possible to argue that this scene is superfluous. Yet its relevance for the
meaning of the play as a whole makes it, in fact, indispensable.

   The setting of the final scene, the room emptied by the removal men, is, it has been suggested, itself "a physical symbol of a disintegrating family and a disintegrating country." This sense of calamity is underlined in Boyle's first words, "I'm able to go no farther," for this expresses not only his drunken exhaustion, but the end of his existence as "Paycock" after Juno has finally turned away from him. When he continues to brag that "Captain Boyle's Captain Boyle," he epitomizes his chronic incapacity for self-knowledge and the blind inadaptability which, contrary to his heroic understanding of himself, has contributed to the disintegration of his family. His slogan "Irelan' sober . . . is Irelan' . . . free," coming from the mouth of a drunkard, is, then, another instance of O'Casey's irony: already passing beyond Boyle's unconscious self-interpretation, it contributes to the meaning of the play as a whole. This movement is continued in a sequence of sentences in which Boyle in three stages, albeit unconsciously, sums up the play. Entering his flat, he shouts "The blinds is down, Joxer, the blinds is down!," then "The counthry'll have to steady itself . . . it's goin' . . . to hell," and finally "I'm, telling you . . . Joxer . . . th' whole worl's . . . in a terr . . . ible state o' . . . chassis!" The blinds have really been pulled down since the furniture has been taken away, but the lights over this family have gone out in a much more comprehensive sense. The whole country will approach destruction if the mutual extermination of its people, as the play has shown it, is continued, and the whole world is destined for chaos if people do not begin at last to turn it into a better place. The final sentence of the play thus directs the audience's attention once more to the only attempt that has been made at warding off chaos: Juno's acceptance of her own suffering and her sacrifice for Mary and her child.

Juno in several ways is the central character of the play. Dramaturgically she is the most important link between the different lines of action, participating equally in all of them. Moreover, she has to bear the weight of all three catastrophes, the effects of which are made manifest in her person. Formally, therefore, she is the dramatist's most important device in preserving the unity of his play. As a character, Juno from the start demands more attention than the others. She also stands out because she is the only one to undergo a development; and towards the end she takes on symbolic significance. If one wants to do justice to this play one should note that Juno is not portrayed from the start as the author's ideal. It is true that, from the beginning, she is superior to others. This becomes evident when she is the only one to accept human weaknesses in others and to understand them without merely criticizing them: she gets her husband's breakfast in spite of his parasitical life-style, she reassures Johnny, accepts the company of Mrs. Madigan and Joxer and looks after her sickly daughter. Yet Juno, like all the

other characters, is not without weaknesses herself. She, too, is egoistic, but
with the difference that her egotism is not limited to her own person but
includes her family. Whatever exceeds the bounds of her family finds her
uncomprehending and even offensive. She sees no point in Mary's strike and
shows no compassion for the girl who has been unjustly dismissed. Similarly,
she has no understanding for the Republican aims and criticizes Johnny's
participation in the War of Independence: this for reasons of family egotism
rather than political conviction. One may be inclined momentarily to compare her attitude to that of Countess Rosmarin in Fry's *The Dark Is Light
Enough*:

> Only
> Tell me what is in this war you fight
> Worth all your dead and suffering men.

Yet Rosmarin is quite willing to weigh the arguments for and against war,
and she retains her humanitarian convictions in spite of her understanding
for the fighters' justification, while Juno remains inaccessible to any such
understanding and does not even make an effort in this direction. Later her
egotism becomes even plainer when she forgets the funeral of Robbie Tancred, holds her family celebration precisely at the time of the funeral procession and even remarks rather nastily: "In wan way, she [Mrs. Madigan]
deserves all she got; for lately, she let th' Die-hards make an open house of
th' place." Mary is not entirely unjustified when she explains to her mother
why she could not have discussed with her the reasons for Bentham's dis-
appearance: "It would have been useless to tell you—you wouldn't understand." Even after Johnny's abduction, Juno's concern contains a certain
degree of egotism: "if anything ud happen to poor Johnny, I think I'd lose
me mind."

Juno's triumph in this crucial test lies precisely in the fact that her own
prediction does not come true. The news of Johnny's death call for her ability
to offer—at the moment of most intense grief—the kind of consolation to
others which she so badly needs herself. The loss of her own son enables
her to answer to Mary's lament for the child that will grow up without a
father: "It'll have what's far betther—it'll have two mothers." And even more
decisive is Juno's spontaneous willingness to go on her own to identify her
dead son: "I forgot, Mary, I forgot; your poor oul' selfish mother was only
thinkin' of herself. No, no, you mustn't come—it wouldn't be good for you.
You go on to me sisther's an' I'll face th' ordeal meself." Then she speaks
those decisive words which show that she has overcome her family egotism
and has won a new insight into the equality of all human beings in the face

of death: "Maybe I didn't feel sorry enough for Mrs. Tancred when her poor son was found as Johnny's been found now—because he was a Diehard! Ah, why didn't I remember that then he wasn't a Diehard or a Stater, but only a poor dead son!"

If Juno at this moment takes up the prayer spoken before by Mrs. Tancred, it becomes obvious that she has taken on symbolic traits: Juno "becomes by extension Mrs. Tancred and all bereaved mothers, including the Blessed Mother." Such a repetition would not have been justified if the prayer had merely contained a humanitarian message, repeated by the dramatist so that the audience would take more notice of it. It is inaccurate to think of Juno, although this frequently happens, as a personification of O'Casey's philosophy of life, simply because humanly speaking she is so appealing, and thus to designate O'Casey as a pacifist and fatalist. Taken to an extreme, this would mean that human beings ought patiently to suffer poverty, misery, disease and death without striving for an improvement in their lot. In reality each of the characters in this play incorporates an element of what then constitutes a whole. O'Casey "s'interdit scrupuleusement de prêter à ses personnages ses propres idées. Il ne permet pas à ses préférences individuelles d'obscurcir sa vue claire et courageuse des données de l'expérience. Ami des déshérités, il ne les a point idéalisés" [Raymond Brugère, "Sean O'Casey et la théâtre irlandais," *Revue Anglo-Americaine* 3 (1925/26)]. Juno, too, is an autonomous character: O'Casey does not isolate her from his other figures by turning her into an ideal that everybody ought to follow but by conferring on her the symbolic features of the suffering mother who, in spite of all her limitations, with an optimism bordering on obstinacy and against all hope, again and again takes up the battle for the people entrusted to her care.

In such a symbolic context Juno's name takes on new meaning. Her husband's explanation is striking for its banality: "You see, Juno was born an' christened in June; I met her in June; we were married in June, an' Johnny was born in June, so wan day I says to her, 'You should ha' been called Juno,' an' the name stuck to her ever since." Yet this serves mainly to typify his superficiality and lack of understanding, for Juno—even if the Boyles do not realize this—bears the name of that Roman goddess who, with her train of peacocks, functioned as the guardian of the hearth and the protectress of matrimony. The mythological context has an entirely different function here from that which it performs in *The Shadow of a Gunman*, where Davoren's comparison of himself to Prometheus leads to an ironic reduction of unjustified pretensions, while here the authorial comparison, of which Juno is not at all aware, discovers a hidden but universal analogy.

A further level of meaning in the character of Juno is more specifically national in import. The small world of the tenement house incorporates— as it does in *Kathleen Listens in*—all the basic attitudes relevant to the Ireland of the twenties: socialism and ultra-patriotism, sympathy for Republicans and for Free Staters, grandiloquent passivity and silent activity, criticism of the clergy and justification of their conduct, betrayal and human solidarity, and finally oppression arising from the miserable conditions of daily life. The house becomes in this way symbolic of the Ireland of those years, and Juno becomes a Cathleen ni Houlihan of the slums for whom, in the cir- cumstances of her life, the liberation from poverty, dirt and disease ranks above all political independence.

Juno's prayer, combining echoes of Shelley's *Adonais* with reminiscences of the prophet Ezekiel (11:19), requires a brief discussion of the element of religion in *Juno and the Paycock*. Critics have usually taken up Juno's sentence "Ah, what can God do agen the stupidity o' men!" as a confirmation of her religiosity and sometimes even as an instance of the whole play's Christian tendency. Yet this sentence suggests, in fact, the opposite interpretation inasmuch as it refers to the impotence of a God who can do nothing against human stupidity—and this, surely, implies that prayers to such a God must remain without effect. The scepticism of this view can be observed in various ways throughout the play. It lies behind Boyle's changing attitude to the clergy, whom he condemns at one moment, but whom in the next, when he has been treated respectfully by a priest, he admires. Boyle, in his de- scription of Devine, also provides the comic definition of a Christian: "I never heard him usin' a curse; I don't believe he was ever dhrunk in his life—sure he's not like a Christian at all!" Devine is the atheist of the play, and his opinions rub off on Mary: "Oh, it's thrue, it's thrue what Jerry Devine says—there isn't a God, there isn't a God; if there was He wouldn't let these things happen!" Even if this attitude is not implemented by the context, for Devine does not live up to his views and even thoughtlessly calls upon God when he rejects Mary, it is not, however, opposed by any effective and convincing belief. At the opposite extreme to Devine is Bentham: "One that says all is God an' no man; an' th' other that says all is man an' no God!"; but Bentham's confused theosophic ideas are not an acceptable al- ternative to atheism and do not find expression in human actions either.

It is, of course, possible to see these various attitudes to religion simply as part of the dramatist's technique of characterization. But even Juno's attitude to Christianity, which is usually accepted as the play's central stan- dard (and not only as an individual character trait), is not consistent at all. Not only does she refer to the impotence of God, she also insists: "With all timism leads her into a new battle against fate for the existence of the ople entrusted to her.

If in *Juno and the Paycock* transcendental references are limited to a few ics of traditional religion, all the more emphasis is placed on man's proving mself in this world. This, in fact, is the central theme of the play: human tegrity is put to the test in numerous different situations where several aracters, confronted with the same task, succeed or fail, and where success failure, determining moral rank, provides the coordinates for the evalu- ory system of the play. It is possible for the reader or spectator to verify s own spontaneous evaluations of individual characters by referring to these st-situations. It soon becomes clear that Juno succeeds in most of them, hile Joxer and Boyle fail in all the tasks put to them and the other characters ange somewhere between these two extremes. A few examples may illustrate nis.

At the beginning of the play, the irritable Johnny asks for a glass of ater. Mary's and Juno's different reactions enable the audience to recognize n initial difference between the two women:

> MARY: Isn't he big an' able enough to come out an' get it
> himself?
> MRS. BOYLE: If you weren't well yourself you'd like somebody to
> bring you in a dhrink o'wather.
> *She brings in drink and returns.*

The offer of a job for Boyle has a similar effect. While Juno has taken on an additional job without hesitation in order to keep her family, Boyle reacts indignantly to the chance of giving up his existence as a loafer. He charac- teristically takes refuge in his world of fantasy from which he suddenly produces the vision of a job at the other end of the town and soon believes in it himself. Joxer characteristically follows him in every detail. The family celebrations in act 2 provide two particularly revealing test-situations. All the participants are asked to sing a song. Juno and Mary succeed honourably if not brilliantly. The naive but kind Mrs. Madigan sings "*in a quavering voice,*" but at least she manages to finish her song, while Joxer on his own is not able to accomplish anything. Bentham who moves outside the circle of these people is not even confronted with such a task. The "Captain" takes up a special position, because he does not content himself by singing a song like the others, but recites a poem of his own, i.e., a product of his fantasy. If one recognizes the function of this scene as a test-situation, it is not possible to say that it "n' ajoute rien à la signification de l'oeuvre" [Robert de Smet, "Sean O'Casey et la tragédie des 'tenements,'" *Revue des Vivants* 8 (1934)].

our churches an' religions, the worl's not a bit the be
however, there are several moments when the dramatist
Christian standards into doubt, using other means th
particular character. The hymn, resounding from the fu
contrasted, for instance, with the superficial curiosity o
text of the hymn contains the words

> Blest be with loudest song
> The Sacred Heart of Jesus
> By every heart and tongue.

The Boyles (including Juno) and their guests react to th
worship with banal commentaries on the funeral as a spec
in Joxer's "Oh, it's a darlin' funeral, a daarlin' funeral!"
concludes act 2 has a similar effect:

> Hail, Mary, full of grace, the Lord is with Th
> Blessed art Thou amongst women, and blessed

In the context of the play these words function as a bitter
the fate of the living Mary who likewise expects a child
without grace and does not feel the presence of God. Mary
poem which depicts most plainly of all a world abandoned
the story of a demon, / That an angel had to tell."

Juno's prayer therefore is not the highest expression of
trust in God that might counterbalance the miserable situat
Even in itself it contains a reproach: "Blessed Virgin, where
me darlin' son was riddled with bullets?" The whole "pra
secularized, and its central sentence, "Sacred Heart o' Jesus,
hearts o' stone, and give us hearts o' flesh!," pleads for an atti
equally well be taken by the atheist Devine: the predominan
understanding and forgiving love. It is Juno alone, however,
principle into practice and thereby arouses the element of hor
of all reasons for pessimism, pervades the play. In this respec
anything else Juno's prayer can be distinguished from the oth
of Anglo-Irish literature, Maurya's last sentence from *Riders to*
Maurya says "They're all gone now, and there isn't anything
can do to me," this is the expression of a final resignation. A
long heroic battle, Maurya succumbs to an inexorable fate and
without murmur. For Juno, her prayer is not an ending but
of a new development: her (possibly irrational, but neverthele

This scene is preceded by a more serious test. When Johnny believes himself to have seen the apparition of the dead Tancred, somebody has to go into the bedroom to make sure that in reality the votive-light is still burning. Everybody under some pretext or other passes on the request to his neighbour. Not only do the terrified Johnny and the fearful Boyle refuse to enter the room, but also Mary, and even Juno hesitates, until Bentham voluntarily offers to go. This is one of the occasions that prevent Juno from being stylized into an implausible, ideal figure, while at the same time Bentham is given some positive traits. Another instance when Juno, like all the others, fails, is her attempt to cope with the unexpected prosperity. The room filled with useless junk "*of a vulgar nature*" and the gramophone that she carries in, show that she has not succeeded in handling the borrowed money in a useful way. On the other hand, she succeeds entirely in misfortune. When Mary's pregnancy becomes known, Johnny insists "She should be dhriven out o' th' house she's brought disgrace on!" and Boyle (as the frequency of the personal pronoun shows) thinks only of himself: "Oh, isn't this a nice thing to come on top o' me, an' the state I'm in! A pretty show I'll be to Joxer an' to that oul' wan, Madigan! Amn't I afther goin' through enough without havin' to go through this!," while Juno is able to forget her own person and to appreciate Mary's situation:

> What you an' I'll have to go through'll be nothin' to what poor Mary'll have to go through; for you an' me is middlin' old, an' most of our years is spent; but Mary'll have maybe forty years to face an' handle, an' every wan of them'll be tainted with a bitther memory.

In a similar way she triumphantly passes all serious tests and thus attains the moral rank that she occupies towards the end of the play.

Finally, the question of literary genre must be raised. O'Casey himself subtitled *Juno and the Paycock*, *A Tragedy in Three Acts*, but critics who usually consider such authorial designations with some scepticism, should be sceptical in this case, too. The play can be considered as a tragedy only if one applies the term in a very general sense to terrible, passion-evoking events which raise the spectator to a "higher" level beyond the limits of his own personal problems. If, however, one expects a tragedy, more specifically, to show the downfall of a human being of some intrinsic greatness, someone who has consciously experienced the conflict between two near-equal values, *Juno and the Paycock* remains outside the definition. Juno, who alone could qualify for a tragic role, is never in a situation where every decision must lead to failure. This would, perhaps, be the case if Boyle were an honourable husband with rigid principles whom Juno loved; this might force upon her the (conceivably tragic) option for either her rejected daughter or her husband. As the play stands, however, no hesitation is called for. It is Juno's specific quality that she takes up every challenge of fate and proves herself equal to it. It is true that there is a rudimentary tragic conflict in Devine, who fails in the decision between his love for Mary and his inherited moral conventions, but this remains an isolated episode and does not influence the play as a whole. If *Juno and the Paycock* is to be placed in any category at all, it belongs to tragicomedy, but only if tragicomedy is considered as an autonomous genre and not simply as a combination of comic and tragic scenes.

Juno and the Paycock can be seen in a twofold literary tradition. On the one hand it belongs to those literary works which, in realistic or symbolic form, centre on a dominant mother figure. Such works seem to have become more frequent in recent years; at a time when religious, ethical and moral standards have become ever more doubtful, a mother's care and willingness to sacrifice herself for her family has remained as one of the few unquestioned values. These works, of course, are not limited to drama; they have appeared both before and after *Juno and the Paycock* without immediately suggesting an influence on or by O'Casey. One might think of Steinbeck's Ma Joad (*The Grapes of Wrath*), Hauptmann's Mutter Wolffen (*Der Biberpelz*), Odets's Bessie Berger (*Awake and Sing!*), Wesker's Sarah Kahn (*Chicken Soup with Barley* and *I'm Talking about Jerusalem*), Gorky's Wassa Schelesnowa in the play of the same title and—in an entirely different social sphere—Waugh's Lady Marchmain (*Brideshead Revisited*). Even Wilder's Mrs. Antrobus (*The Skin of Our Teeth*) possesses, in allegorical foreshortening, the essential traits of the character in question, inimical to progress and without any understanding for political ideas, but indomitable and invaluable as a refuge for the people entrusted to her.

Other, slightly different works also have a central mother figure. The comparison with three of them may help to pinpoint Juno's peculiar position. One of them is *Riders to the Sea*, where Maurya's lifelong battle with fate ends in resignation because her struggle to preserve her family remains futile. Entirely different to this is another play, strongly influenced by Synge and using the same basic situation, but drawing from it opposite conclusions: Brecht's *Die Gewehre der Frau Carrar*. Here the miseries of the family have political causes; it is, therefore, possible to combat them through political or military action, as the mother figure realizes towards the end of the play, after prior insistence on a Juno-like attitude. The third variation is represented in Brecht's *Mutter Courage* where the title character is an example of obstinacy, uncritical adaptability to existing conditions and the refusal to listen to reason. These three plays form a system of coordinates in which Juno assumes the central position. With the obstinacy of Mother Courage she struggles not only for herself, but for her family, and, under similar circumstances to those of the other figures, she neither succumbs to Maurya's resignation, nor does she turn to Teresa Carrar's political activity.

A second literary tradition that is of importance for *Juno and the Paycock* is that of bourgeois tragedy. This statement demands two qualifications. On the one hand, the term "tragedy," as has been shown above, cannot properly be applied to O'Casey's play. On the other hand, the bourgeois milieu has here been exchanged for the proletarian, just as in the eighteenth century the bourgeois tragedy introduced a new social class to a form that up to then had been dominated by the nobility. Notwithstanding these changes, however, the basic pattern, transmitted from Lillo through Lessing, Schiller and Hebbel to the twentieth century, has remained largely unchanged. This becomes evident if one compares *Juno and the Paycock* to two typical plays of this tradition, Hebbel's *Maria Magdalena* (1846) and Hauptmann's *Vor Sonnenaufgang* (1889).

Considering O'Casey's reading, it is hardly possible that he was directly influenced by these two plays, which makes it all the more remarkable that *Juno* should exhibit the common features of a comprehensive literary tradition. In *Maria Magdalena*, Clara is caught, like O'Casey's Mary, in a network of lower-middle-class prejudices and inhuman moral standards. Like Devine, the Secretary does not succeed in overcoming these; his sentence: "Darüber kann kein Mann weg!" corresponds exactly to Devine's "My God, Mary, have you fallen as low as that?" One should add that Meister Anton, if with greater justification, insists on similarly narrow-minded ideas of virtue and morality as the "Captain." Also, the motif of the loss of a large sum of money as well as the subplot concerning the arrest of Clara's brother both contribute to the final catastrophe, which enhances the similarity to *Juno and the Paycock*. The most decisive difference is in the character of Juno, who protects Mary from the hopelessness of Clara's situation and from her tragic death. Such a redeeming character is lacking, too, in *Vor Sonnenaufgang*. In all other respects, however, there are remarkable similarities between Hauptmann's and O'Casey's plays, and, from a historical perspective, they can be seen in the context of the literary tradition which, at the time of their first productions, was obscured by the novelty of the plays' subject matter. The most remarkable parallel is in the characters of Loth and Devine. Both are idealists and want to better the situation of mankind, but fail when put to the test in a concrete situation, because they cannot overcome their prejudices. They withdraw their help precisely from that person who needs it most and who could be "redeemed" most easily. Hauptmann's Helene is, like Mary, half-educated, and therefore open to Loth's ideas. In both cases, moreover, the father is a drunkard and good-for-nothing who affords no refuge to his daughter. The motif of sudden wealth erupting into a milieu of poverty, bringing results with which the characters cannot cope intellectually, underlines this relationship. It is a striking fact that O'Casey and Hauptmann in their different personal spheres should have taken up such similar human problems and should have given them so similar a dramatic form.

Emphasizing O'Casey's adherence to a literary tradition, however, in no way diminishes the originality of *Juno and the Paycock*. This originality is most obvious in three respects: O'Casey opened up the social sphere of the slums for modern drama, he projected his play onto the background of historical events, and he created the redeeming character of Juno. These elements ensure a high degree of individuality even in this, his most traditional play.

Chronology

1880   Sean O'Casey born John Casey on March 30 in Dublin.

1885   Begins school at St. Mary's Infant School.

1886   O'Casey's father dies at age 49.

1888   Attends St. Mary's National School for one year.

1890   Attends St. Barnabas National School for a short time.

1894   Begins work as a stock boy at a wholesale chandlers in Dublin; remains there for eighteen months.

1895   O'Casey plays the role of Father Dolan in Dion Boucicault's *The Shaughraun* at the Mechanics Theatre (later called the Abbey Theatre).

1898   Confirmed in the Church of Ireland at the Clontarf Parish Church.

1900   Teaches Sunday School at St. Barnabas Church until 1903.

1902   Works as a laborer on the Great Northern Railway of Ireland; stays at this job nine years.

1906   O'Casey learns the Irish language and changes his name to its Gaelic form, Seán Ó Cathasaigh. He becomes the secretary of the Druncondra branch of the Gaelic League.

1907   Joins and writes for the St. Laurence O'Toole Club. In May, publishes his first article, "Sound the Loud Trumpet," in *The Peasant and Irish Ireland*.

1911   Joins the Irish Transport and General Worker's Union; dismissed from his job at the Northern Railway because he refuses to resign from the union.

1913   Becomes the secretary of the Wolfe Tone Memorial Committee. Becomes secretary of the Women and Children's Relief Fund, which is begun in support of the six-month Dublin Lockout. Joins the Irish Citizen Army.

1914   Becomes secretary of the Army Council of the Irish Citizen Army; begins writing their constitution and recruiting pamphlets, as well as a regular column—"By the Camp Fire"—for the *Irish Worker*. In June, he helps organize a march to Bodenstown, in memory of Wolfe Tone. In October, he resigns from the Irish Citizen Army after a dispute concerning Constance Markiewicz.

1915   Hospitalized for an operation on tubercular glands that have affected his health since childhood.

1916   Publishes an anti-war ballad, "The Grand Oul' Dame Britannia."

1917   Publishes *Lament for Thomas Ashe*, a tribute to a patriot and friend.

1918   Publishes *The Story of Thomas Ashe*, *The Sacrifice of Thomas Ashe*, *Songs of the Wren No. 1*, *Songs of the Wren No. 2*, and *More Songs of the Wren*. Mother dies.

1919   *The Story of the Irish Citizen Army* published.

1920   The Abbey Theatre rejects O'Casey's first two plays, *The Harvest Festival* and *The Frost in the Flower*. He begins work as a janitor.

1921   Becomes secretary of the Release Jim Larkin Committee.

1922   In April, the Abbey Theatre rejects *The Seamless Coat of Cathleen*; in September, it rejects *The Crimson in the Tri-Colour*. In November, however, the Theatre accepts *The Shadow of a Gunman*, which is performed in 1923.

1923   Abbey Theatre production of *Kathleen Listens In*.

1924   *Juno and the Paycock* and *Nannie's Night Out* produced at Abbey Theatre. O'Casey visits Lady Gregory at her home in Galway; joins the Society of Authors and Playwrights.

1925   O'Casey declines a position as registrar of the National Gallery of Ireland. *Juno* and *Gunman* published as *Two Plays*. *Juno and the Paycock* produced in Britain.

1926   *The Plough and the Stars* produced at the Abbey; two days after it opens, the play provokes nationalist riots inside the theater. After several days of disturbance, O'Casey debates with the nationalists. *Juno and the Paycock* opens in New York. O'Casey receives his first award, the Hawthornden Literary Prize, for *Juno*. *The Plough and the Stars* published.

1926   British premiere of *The Plough and the Stars*.

1927   In September, O'Casey marries actress Eileen Reynolds Carey in London.

1928   The Abbey Theatre rejects *The Silver Tassie* on April 20; this begins the estrangement between O'Casey and selection-board-member W. B. Yeats. O'Casey's son Breon born. *The Silver Tassie* published in June.

1929   *The Silver Tassie* opens on October 11 at the Apollo Theatre in London, directed by Raymond Massey with a Great War set by Augustus John. On October 24 it also opens in New York.

1930   Alfred Hitchcock releases a film version of *Juno*; in November, a copy of the film is burned in the streets of Limerick by Irish nationalists.

1931   First autobiographical sketch, "A Child Is Born."

1932   *A Pound on Demand*, a one-act play, written.

1933   *Within the Gates* published.

1934   *Within the Gates* premieres in London on February 7. In September, O'Casey travels to New York for the American premiere of this play. A collection of early short stories, poems, and one-act plays published under the title *Windfalls*.

1935   Son Niall born. *Within the Gates* banned in Boston. *The Silver Tassie* produced at the Abbey Theatre, seven years after its rejection there. In September, O'Casey returns for the last time to Dublin, where he meets with Yeats on friendly terms again. Publishes *Five Irish Plays*.

1937   *The End of the Beginning* premieres at the Abbey. *The Flying Wasp*, a collection of essays, articles, and reviews, published. John Ford's film of *The Plough and the Stars* released.

1938   The O'Caseys move to Devon, where they settle.

1939   *I Knock at the Door*, O'Casey's first volume of autobiography, pub-
        lished; banned by the Irish Censorship of Publications Board.

1940   *The Star Turns Red* opens in London. O'Casey joins the Advisory
        Board of the *Daily Worker* in London. *Purple Dust* published.

1942   Second volume of autobiography, *Pictures in the Hallway*, pub-
        lished. *Red Roses for Me* published.

1943   *Red Roses for Me* opens in Dublin at the Olympia Theatre; *Purple
        Dust* opens in Newcastle-upon-Tyne.

1945   O'Casey refuses an offer of $100,000 to write a screenplay for
        Thomas Wolfe's *Look Homeward Angel*. Volume three of autobiog-
        raphy, *Drums under the Windows*, published.

1946   *Oak Leaves and Lavender* published; opens in Sweden.

1947   The ban against *I Knock at the Door* and *Pictures in the Hallway* lifted
        by the Irish Censorship of Publications Board.

1949   *Inishfallen, Fare Thee Well*, the fourth volume of autobiography,
        published; awarded the "Page One Award" by the Newspaper
        Guild of New York. *Cock-a-Doodle Dandy* and first two volumes of
        Collected Plays published.

1951   Volumes three and four of *Collected Plays* published.

1952   Fifth volume of autobiography, *Rose and Crown*, appears.

1954   Last volume of autobiography, *Sunset and Evening Star*, appears.

1955   *The Bishop's Bonfire* premieres at the Gaiety Theatre; published in
        June.

1956   O'Casey hospitalized for two operations. *The Green Crow*, a col-
        lection of essays, published. A two-volume edition of his autobio-
        graphies published under the title *Mirror in My House*. Son Niall
        dies of leukemia.

1957   On February 15, *The Green Crow* is banned for a year by the Irish
        Customs office. *The Drums of Father Ned* accepted for the Inter-
        national Theatre Festival of 1958.

1958   In January, the Archbishop of Dublin disapproves of *The Drums
        of Father Ned*, scheduled for the Festival; this leads to the expulsion
        from the Festival of works by O'Casey, Joyce, and Beckett. In

response, O'Casey refuses to allow any production of his plays in Ireland; this ban maintained until 1964.

1959   *The Drums of Father Ned* finally opens in Lafayette, Indiana.

1961   O'Casey turns down an honorary degree from Trinity College, Dublin. Publishes *Figuro in the Night*, *The Moon Shines on Kylenamoe*, and *Behind the Green Curtains*.

1962   *Figuro in the Night* opens at Hofstra University, New York; *Behind the Green Curtains* premieres at the University of Rochester; *The Moon Shines on Kylenamoe* opens off-Broadway. O'Casey publishes *Feathers from a Green Crow*, a collection of early political writings.

1963   *Under a Colored Cap* published. On March 27, International Theatre Day, the Union of Soviet Writers in Moscow celebrates O'Casey. In July, a performance of *Figuro in the Night* is banned at a festival of Irish comedy in London.

1964   In January, O'Casey permits the professional production of his plays in Ireland. The Abbey Theatre presents several at the World Theatre Festival in London honoring Shakespeare's 400th birthday. In August, O'Casey suffers a heart attack; dies at Tor Bay Clinic on September 18, after suffering a second heart attack. His body cremated and the ashes scattered at Golders Green Crematorium in London.

Contributors

HAROLD BLOOM, Sterling Professor of the Humanities at Yale University, is the author of *The Anxiety of Influence, Poetry and Repression*, and many other volumes of literary criticism. His forthcoming study, *Freud: Transference and Authority*, attempts a full-scale reading of all of Freud's major writings. A MacArthur Prize Fellow, he is general editor of five series of literary criticism published by Chelsea House.

RAYMOND WILLIAMS is Judith E. Wilson Professor of Drama at Cambridge University. The most influential of British Marxist critics of literature, his books include *Culture and Society, The Long Revolution*, and *The Country and the City*.

RONALD G. ROLLINS teaches at Ohio Wesleyan University. His articles on Shaw, Synge, and O'Casey have appeared in the *James Joyce Quarterly, Irish University Review, Shaw Review*, and *Modern Drama*. His book on O'Casey, *Verisimilitude and Vision in Selected Plays of Sean O'Casey*, appeared in 1975.

DAVID KRAUSE, Professor of English at Brown University, is an editorial consultant for the *Sean O'Casey Review* and has written many articles on O'Casey and other Irish dramatists for various publications. He edited O'Casey's letters and is the author of several books on the playwright.

RONALD AYLING teaches at the University of Alberta. He acted as literary executor to the O'Casey Estate and catalogued the dramatist's papers in the New York Public Library's Berg Collection. His publications include *Blasts and Benedictions*, a posthumous selection of O'Casey's writings, an anthology of criticism, and a full-length critical work, *Continuity and Innovation in Sean O'Casey's Drama*.

KATHARINE WORTH teaches drama and theater studies at Royal Holloway College, University of London.

BERNICE SCHRANK is Professor of English at Memorial University of Newfoundland. She has done extensive work on Irish writers.

ROBERT G. LOWERY is the editor and publisher of the *Sean O'Casey Review* and editor of the *O'Casey Annual*.

CAROL KLEIMAN has taught at several Canadian universities. She is author of *Sean O'Casey's Bridge of Vision*.

HEINZ KOSOK is Professor of English at the University of Wuppertal, Germany. He has written several articles on O'Casey.

Bibliography

Achilles, Jochen. "Sean O'Casey's and Denis Johnston's National Plays: Two Dramatic Approaches to Irish Society." In *Studies in Anglo-Irish Literature*, edited by Heinz Kosok. Bonn: Herbert Grundmann, 1982.

Armstrong, William A. *Sean O'Casey*. London: Longmans, Green, 1967.

Atkinson, Brooks, ed. *The Sean O'Casey Reader: Plays, Autobiographies, Opinions*. New York: St. Martin's, 1968.

Ayling, Ronald. "History and Artistry in Sean O'Casey's Dublin Trilogy." *Theoria* 37 (1972): 2–13.

———. "Sean O'Casey and the Abbey Theatre, Dublin." *Dalhousie Review* 52 (1972): 21–33.

———, ed. *Sean O'Casey: Modern Judgements*. London: Macmillan, 1969.

Ayling, Ronald, and Michael J. Durkan. *Sean O'Casey: A Bibliography*. London: Macmillan, 1978.

Benstock, Bernard. "Chronology and Narratology in Sean O'Casey's Beginnings." *Genre* 12, no. 4 (1979): 551–64.

———. "The Mother-Madonna-Matriarch in Sean O'Casey." *The Southern Review* 6 (1970): 603–23.

———. *Paycocks and Others: Sean O'Casey's World*. Dublin: Gill & Macmillan, 1975.

———. *Sean O'Casey*. Lewisburg, Pa.: Bucknell University Press, 1970.

Bentley, Eric. "The Case of O'Casey." In *What Is Theatre? Incorporating the Dramatic Event and Other Reviews 1944–1967*, 25–28. New York: Atheneum, 1968.

———. *The Playwright as Thinker: A Study of Drama in Modern Times*. New York: Harcourt, Brace & World, 1967.

Blitch, Alice Fox. "O'Casey's Shakespeare." *Modern Drama* 15 (1972): 283–90.

Brandt, G. W. "Realism and Parables: From Brecht to Arden." In *Contemporary Theatre*, edited by John Russell Brown and Bernard Harris, 33–55. London: Edward Arnold, 1962.

Coakley, James, and Marvin Felheim. "Thalia in Dublin: Some Suggestions about the Relationships between O'Casey and Classical Comedy." *Comparative Drama* 4 (1970): 265–71.

Coston, Herbert. "Sean O'Casey: Prelude to Playwriting." In *Essays in the Modern Drama*, edited by Morris Freedman, 125–36. Boston: D. C. Heath, 1964.

Cowasjee, Saros. "The Juxtaposition of Tragedy and Comedy in the Plays of Sean O'Casey." *Wascana Review* 2 (Spring–Summer 1967): 75–89.

———. *O'Casey*. New York: Barnes & Noble, 1966.

DeBaun, Vincent C. "Sean O'Casey and the Road to Expressionism." *Modern Drama* 4 (1961): 254–59.

Donoghue, Denis. *We Irish: Essays in Irish Literature and Society*. New York: Knopf, 1986.

Durbach, Errol. "Peacocks and Mothers: Theme and Dramatic Metaphor in O'Casey's *Juno and the Paycock*." *Modern Drama* 15 (1972): 15–25.

Ellis-Fermor, Una Mary. *The Irish Dramatic Movement*. London: Methuen, 1939.

Esslin, Martin. *The Theatre of the Absurd*. Rev. ed. Garden City, N.Y.: Doubleday Anchor Books, 1969.

Esslinger, Pat M. "Sean O'Casey and the Lockout of 1913: 'Materia Poetica' of the Two Red Plays." *Modern Drama* 6 (1963): 53–63.

Fallis, Richard. *The Irish Renaissance*. Syracuse, N.Y.: Syracuse University Press, 1977.

Frayne, John P. *Sean O'Casey*. New York: Columbia University Press, 1976.

Gallagher, S. F., ed. *Woman in Irish Legend, Life, and Literature*. Totowa, N.J.: Barnes & Noble, 1983.

Gassner, John. "The Prodigality of Sean O'Casey." In *The Theatre in Our Times*, 240–48. New York: Crown, 1966.

Goldstone, Herbert. *In Search of Community: The Achievement of Sean O'Casey*. Dublin: Mercier, 1972.

Gregory, Augusta. *Lady Gregory's Journals, 1916–30*. Edited by Lennox Robinson. London: Putnam, 1946.

Hogan, Robert. *After the Irish Renaissance: A Critical History of the Irish Drama since* The Plough and the Stars. Minneapolis: University of Minnesota Press, 1967.

———. *The Experiments of Sean O'Casey*. New York: St. Martin's, 1960.

———, ed. *"Since O'Casey" and Other Essays on Irish Drama*. Totowa, N.J.: Barnes & Noble, 1983.

Irish University Review 10, no. 1 (Spring 1980). Special O'Casey issue.

James Joyce Quarterly 8 (1971). Special O'Casey issue.

Jeffares, A. Norman. *Anglo-Irish Literature*. Dublin: Gill & Macmillan, 1982.

Kavanaugh, Peter. *The Story of the Abbey Theatre*. New York: Devin-Adair, 1950.

Kenner, Hugh. *A Colder Eye: The Modern Irish Writers*. New York: Knopf, 1983.

Kilroy, Thomas, ed. *Sean O'Casey: A Collection of Critical Essays*. Englewood Cliffs, N.J.: Prentice-Hall, 1975.

Koslow, Jules. *The Green and the Red: Sean O'Casey . . . The Man and His Plays*. New York: Golden Griffin Books, 1950.

Krause, David. "O'Casey and Yeats and the Druid." *Modern Drama* 11 (1968): 252–62.

———. "Sean O'Casey and the Higher Nationalism: The Desecration of Ireland's Household Gods." In *Theatre and Nationalism in Twentieth-Century Ireland*, edited by Robert O'Driscoll, 114–33. Toronto: University of Toronto Press, 1971.

———. *A Self-Portrait of the Artist as a Man: Sean O'Casey's Letters*. Dublin: Dolmen, 1968.

Krause, David, and Robert G. Lowery, eds. *Sean O'Casey Centenary Essays*. Gerrards Cross, Eng.: Colin Smythe, 1980.

Krutch, Joseph Wood. *"Modernism" in Modern Drama*. Ithaca: Cornell University Press, 1953.

Lowery, Robert G. *Sean O'Casey's Autobiographies: An Annotated Index*. Westport, Conn.: Greenwood, 1983.

———, ed. *Essays on Sean O'Casey's Autobiographies*. Totowa, N.J.: Barnes & Noble, 1981.

———, ed. *A Whirlwind in Dublin:* The Plough and the Stars *Riots*. Westport, Conn.: Greenwood, 1984.

Malone, Maureen. *The Plays of Sean O'Casey*. Carbondale: Southern Illinois University Press, 1969.

———. "*Red Roses for Me:* Fact and Symbol." *Modern Drama* 9 (1966): 147–52.

Margulies, Martin B. *The Early Life of Sean O'Casey*. Dublin: Dolmen, 1970.

Maxwell, D. E. S. *A Critical History of Modern Irish Drama 1891–1980*. Cambridge: Cambridge University Press, 1984.

McHugh, Roger. "Counterparts: Sean O'Casey and Samuel Beckett." *Moderna Sprak* 67 (1973): 217–22.

McLaughlin, John J. "Political Allegory in O'Casey's *Purple Dust*." *Modern Drama* 13 (1970): 47–53.

Mikhail, E. H. *Sean O'Casey: A Bibliography of Criticism*. Seattle: University of Washington Press, 1972.

Mikhail, E. H., and John O'Riordan. *The Sting and the Twinkle: Conversations with Sean O'Casey*. London: Macmillan, 1974.

Mitchell, Jack. *The Essential O'Casey: A Study of the Twelve Major Plays of Sean O'Casey*. New York: International Publishers, 1980.

Murphy, R[obert] Patrick. "Sean O'Casey and the Avant-Garde." *Colby Library Quarterly* 11 (December 1975): 235–48.

The O'Casey Annual, 1982–.

O'Casey, Eileen. *Sean*. London: Macmillan, 1971.

O'Riordan, John. *A Guide to O'Casey's Plays from the Plough to the Stars*. London: Macmillan, 1984.

Orr, John. *Tragic Drama and Modern Society: Studies in the Social and Literary Theory of Drama from 1870 to the Present*. London: Macmillan, 1981.

Partridge, A. C. *Language and Society in Anglo-Irish Literature*. Totowa, N.J.: Barnes & Noble, 1984.

Pasachoff, Naomi S. "Unity of Theme, Image, and Diction in *The Silver Tassie*." *Modern Drama* 23 (1980): 58–64.

Pixley, Edward E. "*The Plough and the Stars*—The Destructive Consequences of Human Folly." *Educational Theatre Journal* 23 (1971): 75–82.

Price, Alan. *Synge and Anglo-Irish Drama*. New York: Russell & Russell, 1972.

Rogoff, Gordon. "Sean O'Casey's Legacy." *Commonweal* 81, no. 5 (23 October 1964): 128–29.

Rollins, Ronald G. "O'Casey, O'Neill, and Expressionism in *The Silver Tassie*." *Bucknell Review* 10 (May 1962): 364–69.

———. "Pervasive Patterns in *The Silver Tassie*." *Eire* 6, no. 4 (1971): 29–37.

———. *Sean O'Casey's Drama: Verisimilitude and Vision*. University: University of Alabama Press, 1979.

———. "*The Silver Tassie:* The Post-World-War-I Legacy." *Modern Drama* 22 (1979): 125–34.

Sahal, N. *Sixty Years of Realistic Irish Drama (1900–1960)*. Calcutta: Macmillan, 1971.

Schrank, Bernice. "Poets, Poltroons, and Platitudes: A Study of Sean O'Casey's *The Shadow of A Gunman*." *Mosaic* 11, no. 1 (1977): 53–60.

———. " 'There's Nothin' Derogatory in th' Use o' th' Word': A Study in the Use of Language in *The Plough and the Stars*." *Irish University Review* 15, no. 2 (1985): 169–86.

Scrimgeour, James R. *Sean O'Casey*. Boston: Twayne, 1978.

The Sean O'Casey Review, 1974–82.

Simmons, James. *Sean O'Casey*. London: Macmillan, 1983.

Smith, B. L. "From Athlete to Statue: Satire in Sean O'Casey's *The Silver Tassie*." *Arizona Quarterly* 27 (1971): 347–61.

Snowden, J. A. "Sean O'Casey and Naturalism." In *Essays and Studies 1971*, collected by Bernard Harris. London: John Murray, 1971.

Stein, Rita, and Friedhelm Richert, eds. *Major Modern Dramatists*, vol 1. New York: Frederick Ungar, 1984.

Templeton, Joan. "Sean O'Casey and Expressionism." *Modern Drama* 14 (1971): 47–62.

Thompson, William Irwin. "The Naturalistic Image: O'Casey." In *The Imagination of an Insurrection: Dublin, Easter, 1916: A Study of an Ideological Movement*. New York: Oxford University Press, 1967.

Williams, Raymond. *Drama from Ibsen to Eliot*. London: Chatto & Windus, 1952.

Zeiss, Cecilia. "Seán O'Casey's Final Tragicomedies: A Comment on the Dramatic Modes Employed in *Cock-a-Doodle-Dandy* and *The Bishop's Bonfire*." In *Studies in Anglo-Irish Literature*, edited by Heinz Kosok, 278–86. Bonn: Herbert Grundmann, 1982.

Acknowledgments

"The Endless Fantasy of Irish Talk" (originally entitled "Sean O'Casey") by Raymond Williams from *Drama from Ibsen to Brecht* by Raymond Williams, © 1952, 1968 by Raymond Williams. Reprinted by permission of the author and Oxford University Press.

"From Ritual to Romance in *Within the Gates* and *Cock-a-Doodle Dandy*" by Ronald G. Rollins from *Modern Drama* 17, no. 1 (March 1974), © 1974 by the University of Toronto, Graduate Centre for the Study of Drama. Reprinted by permission of *Modern Drama*.

"Master of Knockabout" (originally entitled "A Final Knock at O'Casey's Door") by David Krause from *Sean O'Casey: The Man and His Work: An Enlarged Edition* by David Krause, © 1960, 1975 by David Krause. Reprinted by permission of the author and Macmillan Publishing Company.

"Early Dramatic Experiments: 'Alienation' and *The Plough and the Stars*" by Ronald Ayling from *Continuity and Innovation in Sean O'Casey's Drama: A Critical Monograph* by Ronald Ayling, © 1976 by the Institut für Englische Sprache und Literatur, Universität Salzburg, Austria. Reprinted by permission.

"Music and Dance and the Shaping of O'Casey's Later Plays" (originally entitled "O'Casey") by Katharine Worth from *The Irish Drama of Europe from Yeats to Beckett* by Katharine Worth, © 1978 by Katharine Worth. Reprinted by permission of the Athlone Press.

" 'You Needn't Say No More': Language and the Problems of Communication in *The Shadow of a Gunman*" (originally entitled " 'You Needn't Say No More': Language and the Problems of Communication in Sean O'Casey's *The Shadow of a Gunman*" by Bernice Schrank from *Irish University Review* 8, no. 1 (Spring 1978), © 1978 by *Irish University Review*. Reprinted by permission of *Irish University Review, A Journal of Irish Studies*.

"Sean O'Casey and Socialist Realism" (originally entitled "Sean O'Casey: Art and Politics") by Robert G. Lowery from *Sean O'Casey Centenary Essays* (Irish Literary Studies 7), edited by David Krause and Robert G. Lowery, © 1980 by Robert G. Lowery. Reprinted by permission of the author and Macmillan Publishers Ltd.

"On Fabrications and Epiphanies in O'Casey's Autobiography" by David Krause from *Essays on Sean O'Casey's Autobiographies*, edited by Robert G. Lowery, © 1981 by David Krause. Reprinted by permission of the author, Barnes & Noble Books, Totowa, New Jersey, and Colin Smythe Ltd.

"The Silver Tassie" by Carol Kleiman from *Sean O'Casey's Bridge of Vision: Four Essays on Structure and Perspective* by Carol Kleiman, © 1982 by the University of Toronto Press. Reprinted by permission.

"Juno and the Paycock" by Heinz Kosok from *O'Casey the Dramatist*, translated by Heinz Kosok and Joseph T. Swann, © 1985 by Colin Smythe Ltd. Reprinted by permission of Barnes & Noble Books, Totowa, New Jersey, and Colin Smythe Ltd.

Index

189